X-MEN POWER PACK

The POWER of X

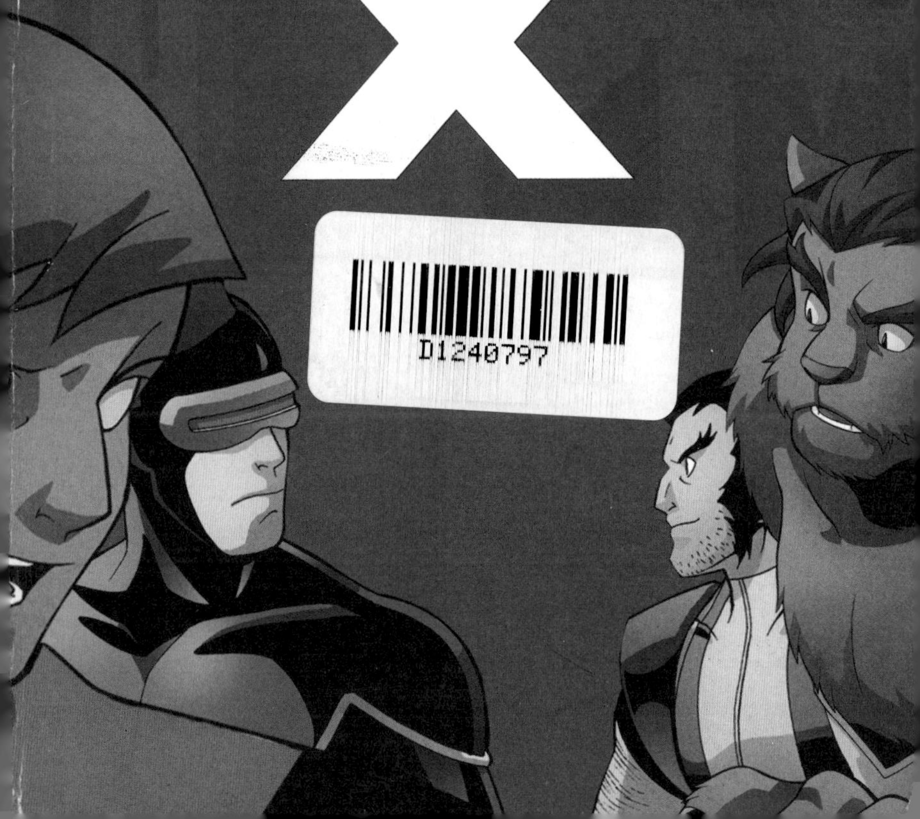

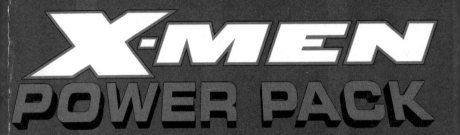

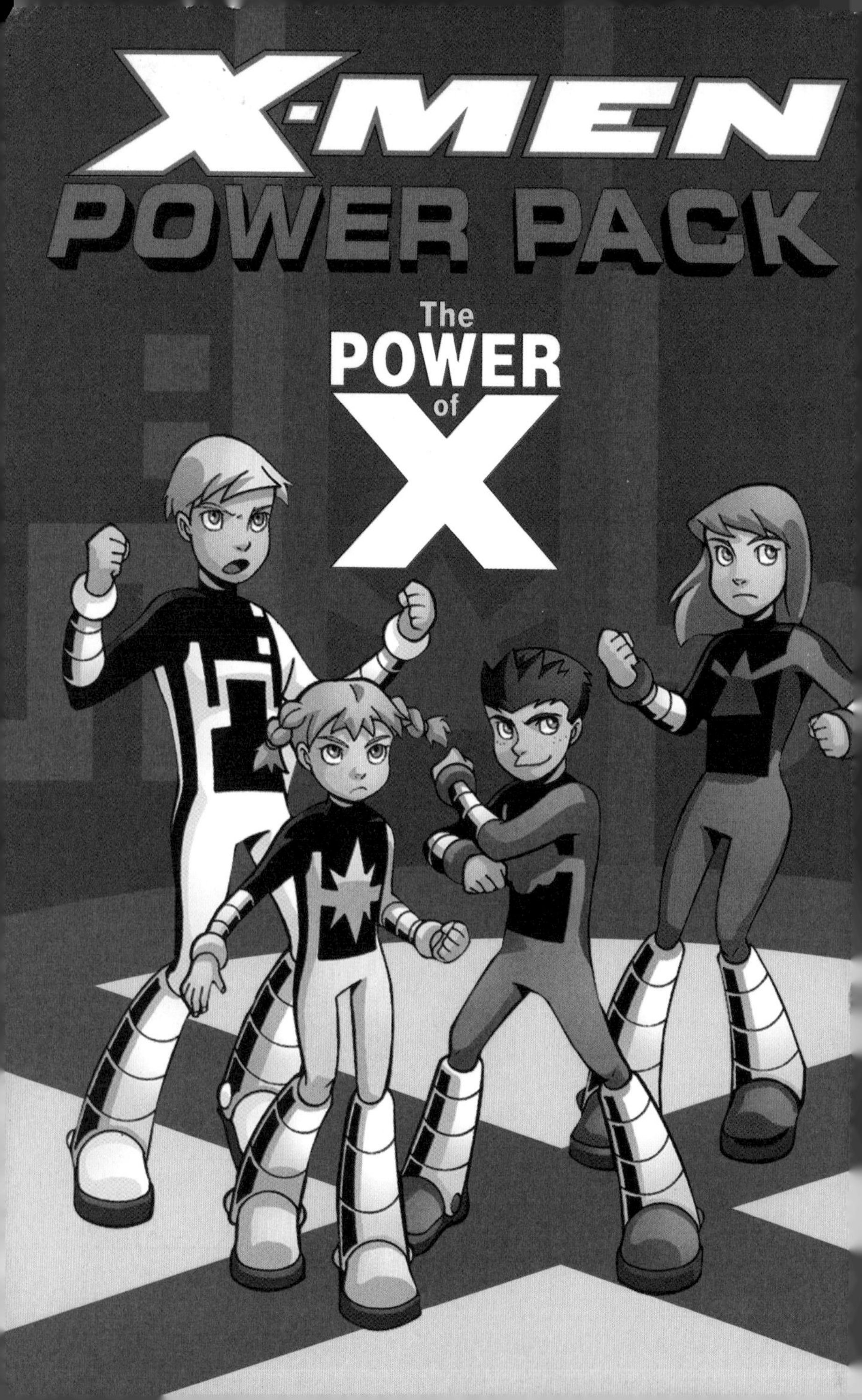
X-MEN
POWER PACK
The POWER of X

Writer: MARC SUMERAK
Art: GURIHIRU
Letterer: DAVE SHARPE
Assistant Editor: NATHAN COSBY
Editor: MACKENZIE CADENHEAD
Consulting Editor: MARK PANICCIA
Special Thanks to AKI YANAGI

Collection Editor: JENNIFER GRÜNWALD
Senior Editor, Special Projects: JEFF YOUNGQUIST
Vice President of Sales: DAVID GABRIEL
Book Designer: JHONSON ETENG
Vice President of Creative: TOM MARVELLI

Editor in Chief: JOE QUESADA
Publisher: DAN BUCKLEY

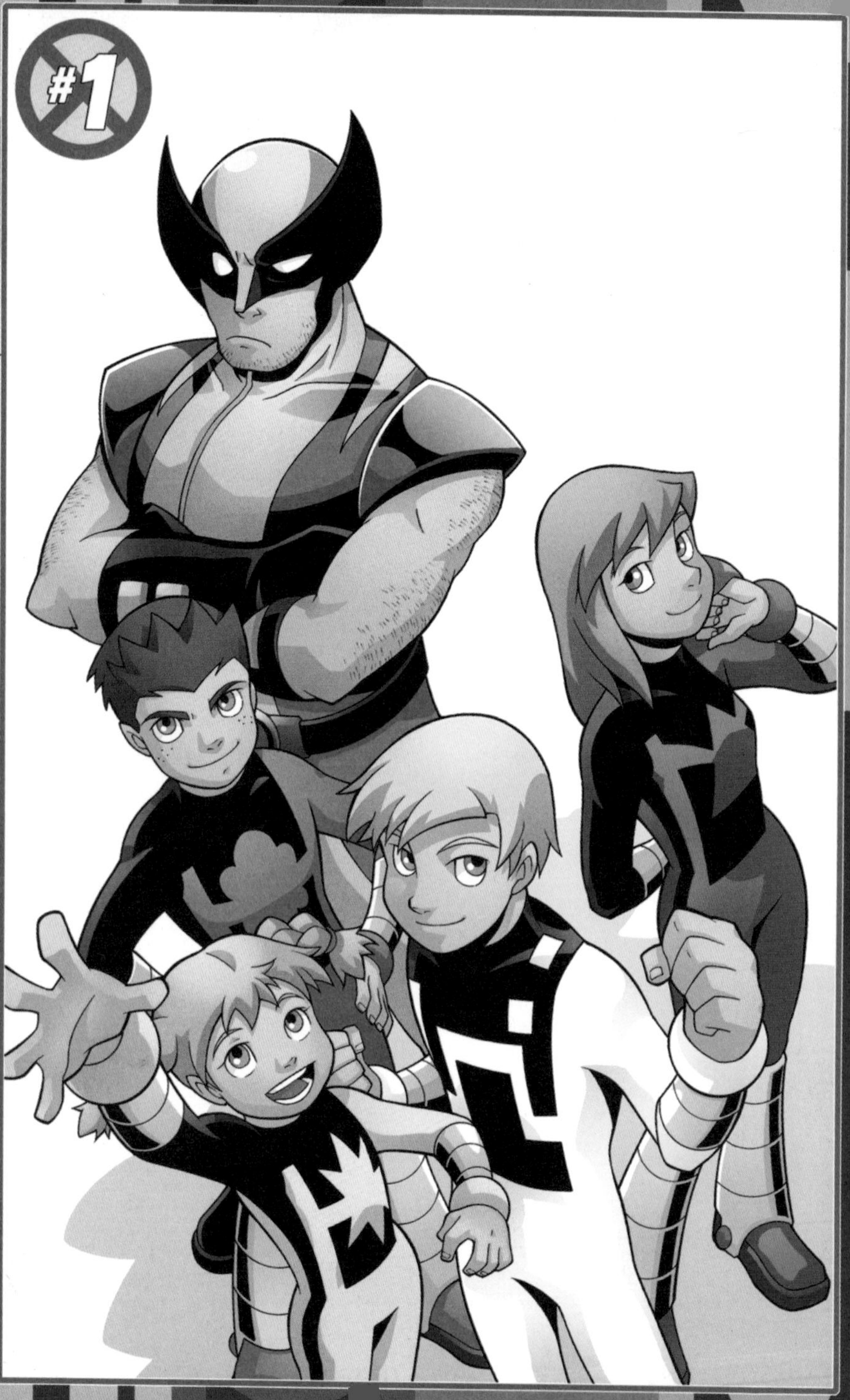
#1

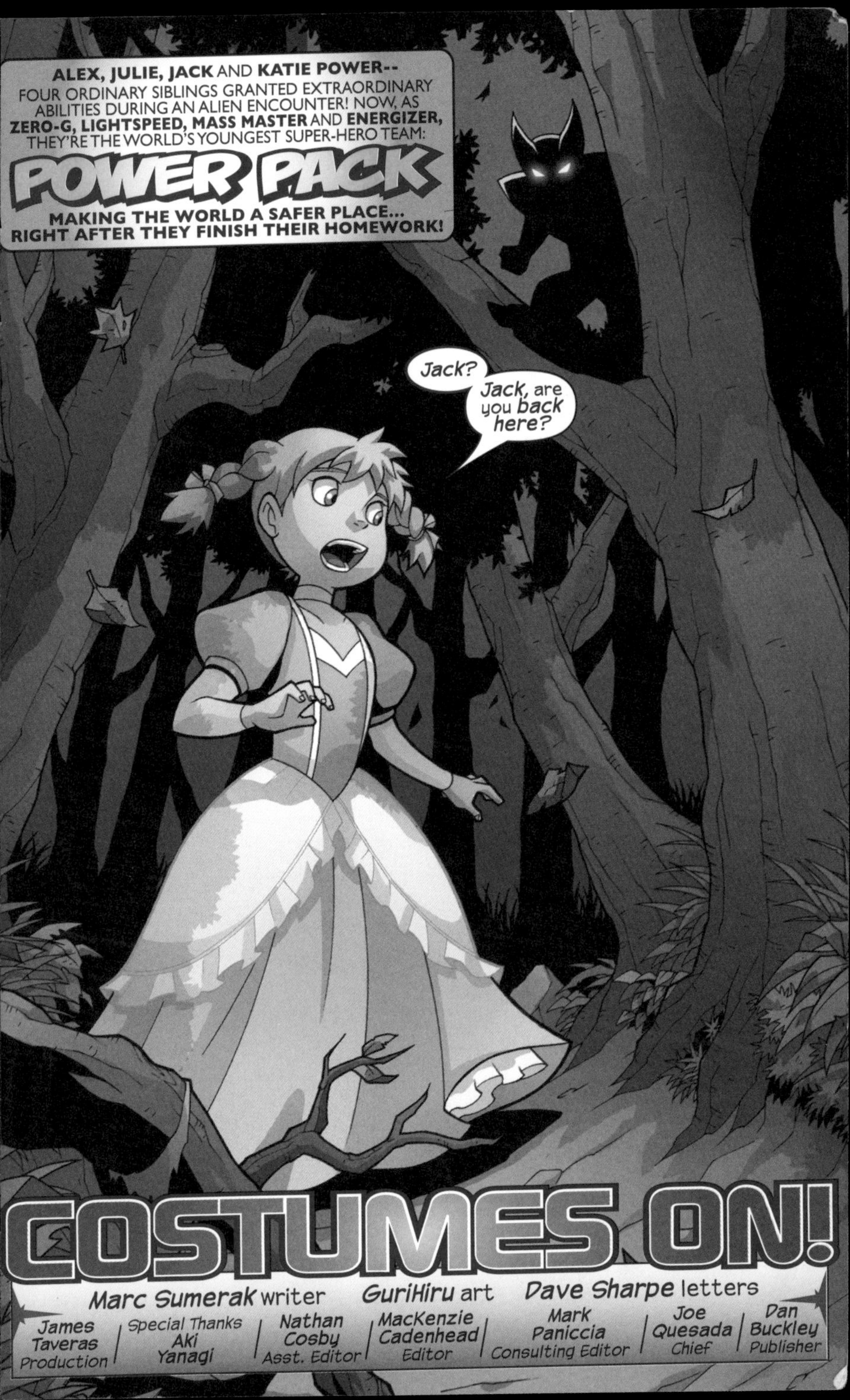
ALEX, JULIE, JACK AND KATIE POWER--
FOUR ORDINARY SIBLINGS GRANTED EXTRAORDINARY ABILITIES DURING AN ALIEN ENCOUNTER! NOW, AS ZERO-G, LIGHTSPEED, MASS MASTER AND ENERGIZER, THEY'RE THE WORLD'S YOUNGEST SUPER-HERO TEAM:
POWER PACK
MAKING THE WORLD A SAFER PLACE... RIGHT AFTER THEY FINISH THEIR HOMEWORK!
Jack?
Jack, are you back here?
COSTUMES ON!
Marc Sumerak writer GuriHiru art Dave Sharpe letters
James Taveras Production
Special Thanks Aki Yanagi
Nathan Cosby Asst. Editor
MacKenzie Cadenhead Editor
Mark Paniccia Consulting Editor
Joe Quesada Chief
Dan Buckley Publisher

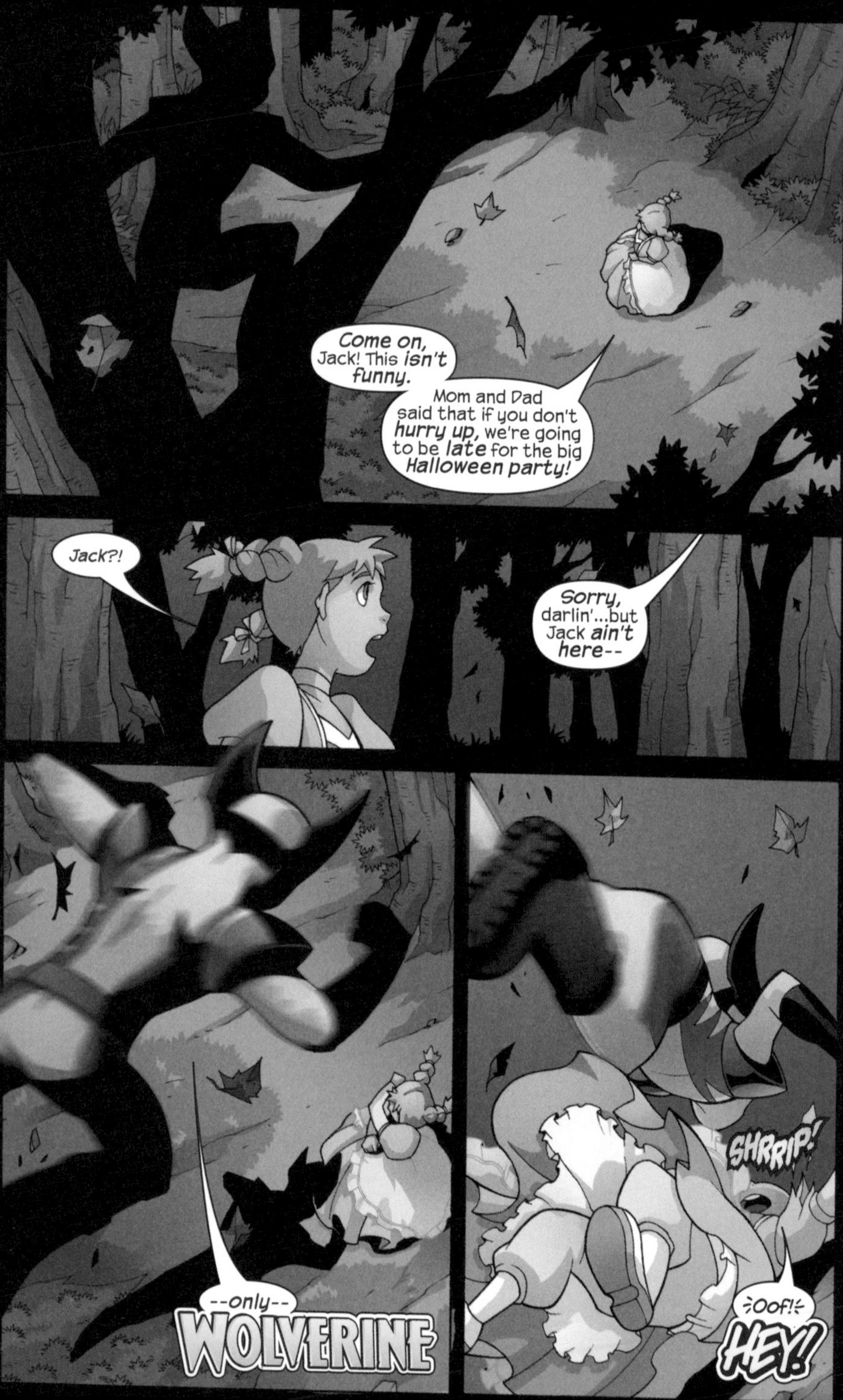
Come on, Jack! This isn't funny.
Mom and Dad said that if you don't hurry up, we're going to be late for the big Halloween party!
Jack?!
Sorry, darlin'...but Jack ain't here--
--only--
WOLVERINE
SHRRIP!
Oof!
HEY!

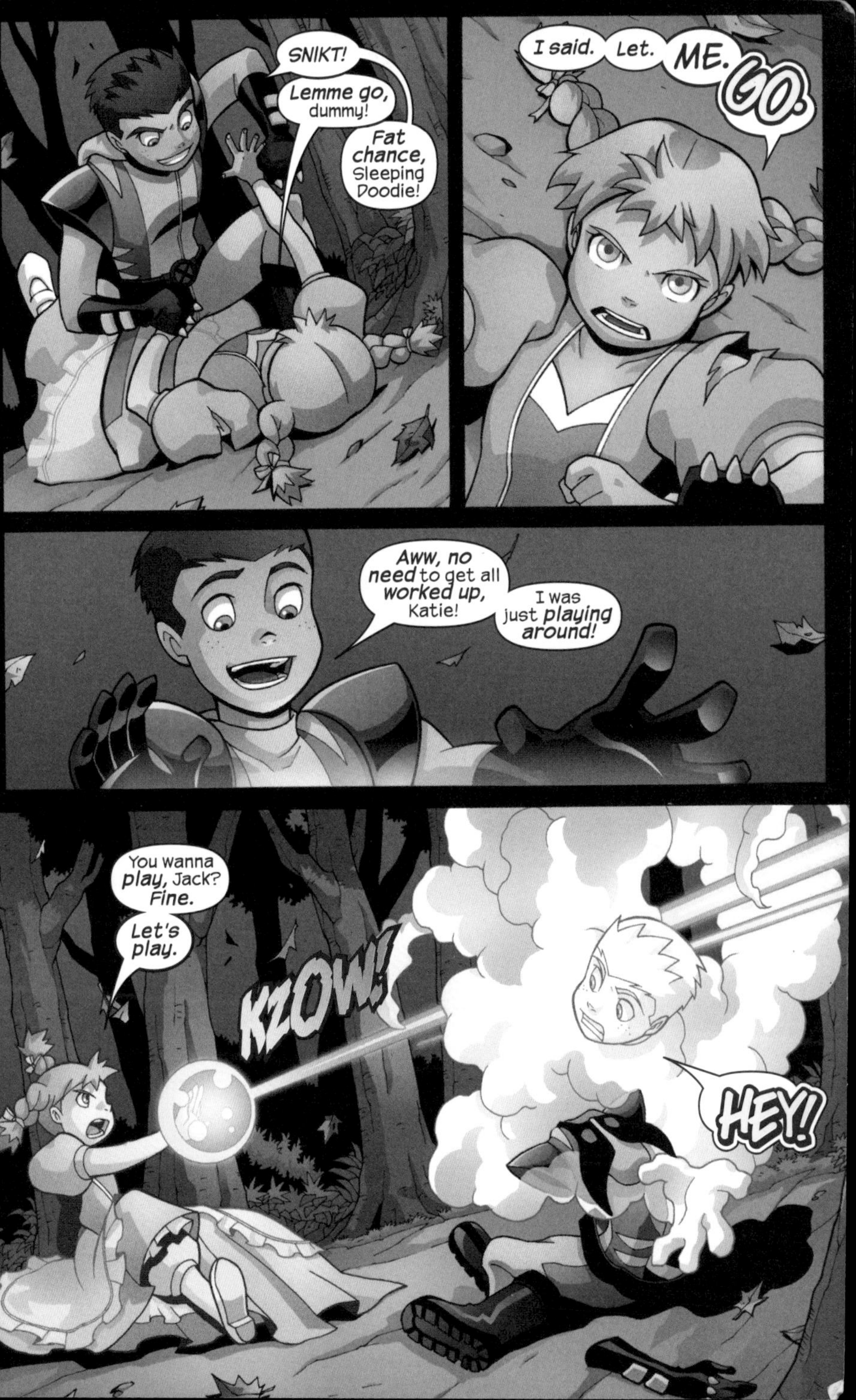
SNIKT!
Lemme go, dummy!
Fat chance, Sleeping Doodie!
I said.
Let.
ME.
GO.
Aww, no need to get all worked up, Katie!
I was just playing around!
You wanna play, Jack? Fine.
Let's play.
KZOW!
HEY!

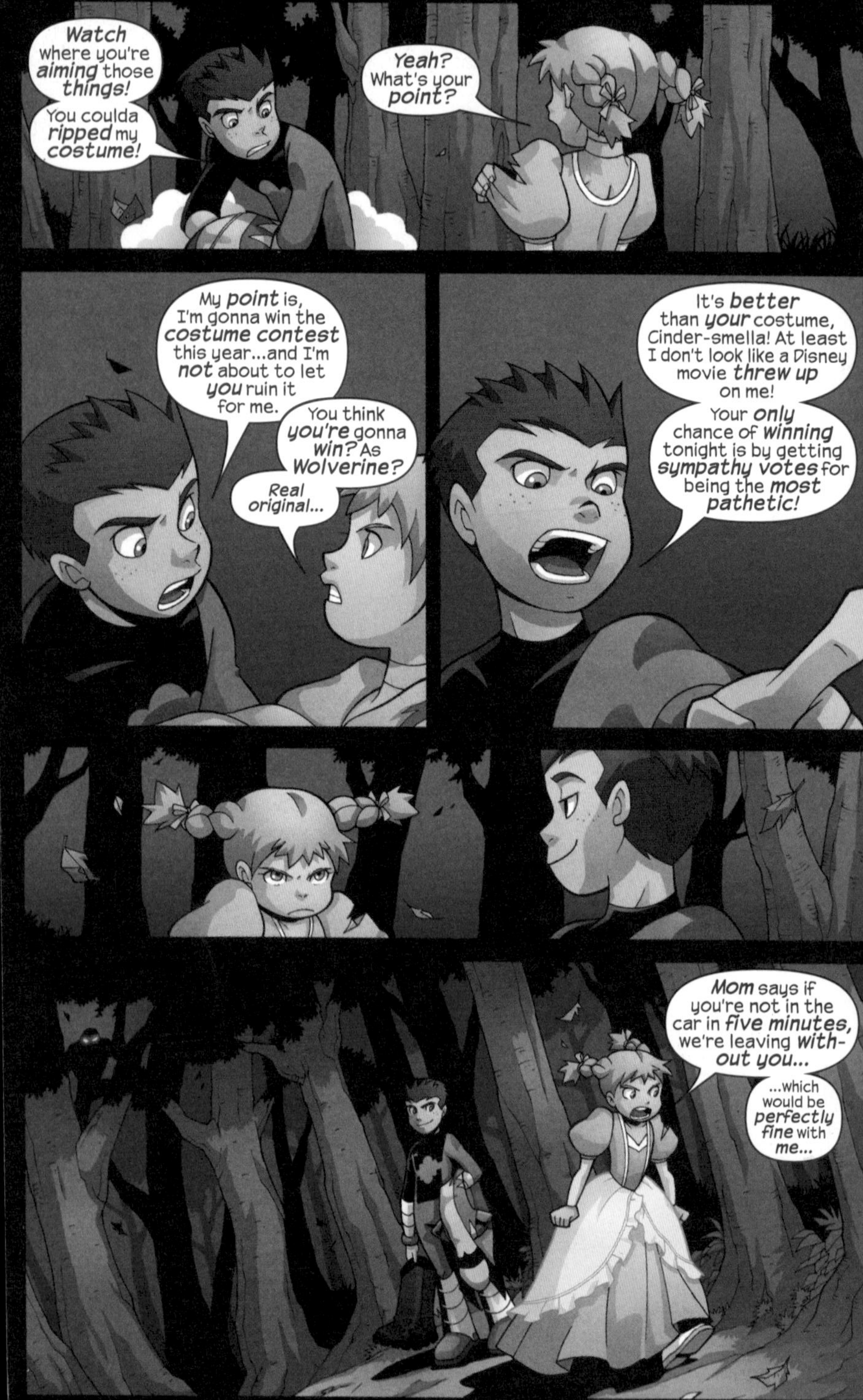
Watch where you're aiming those things!
You coulda ripped my costume!
Yeah? What's your point?
My point is, I'm gonna win the costume contest this year...and I'm not about to let you ruin it for me.
You think you're gonna win? As Wolverine?
Real original...
It's better than your costume, Cinder-smella! At least I don't look like a Disney movie threw up on me!
Your only chance of winning tonight is by getting sympathy votes for being the most pathetic!
Mom says if you're not in the car in five minutes, we're leaving with-out you...
...which would be perfectly fine with me...

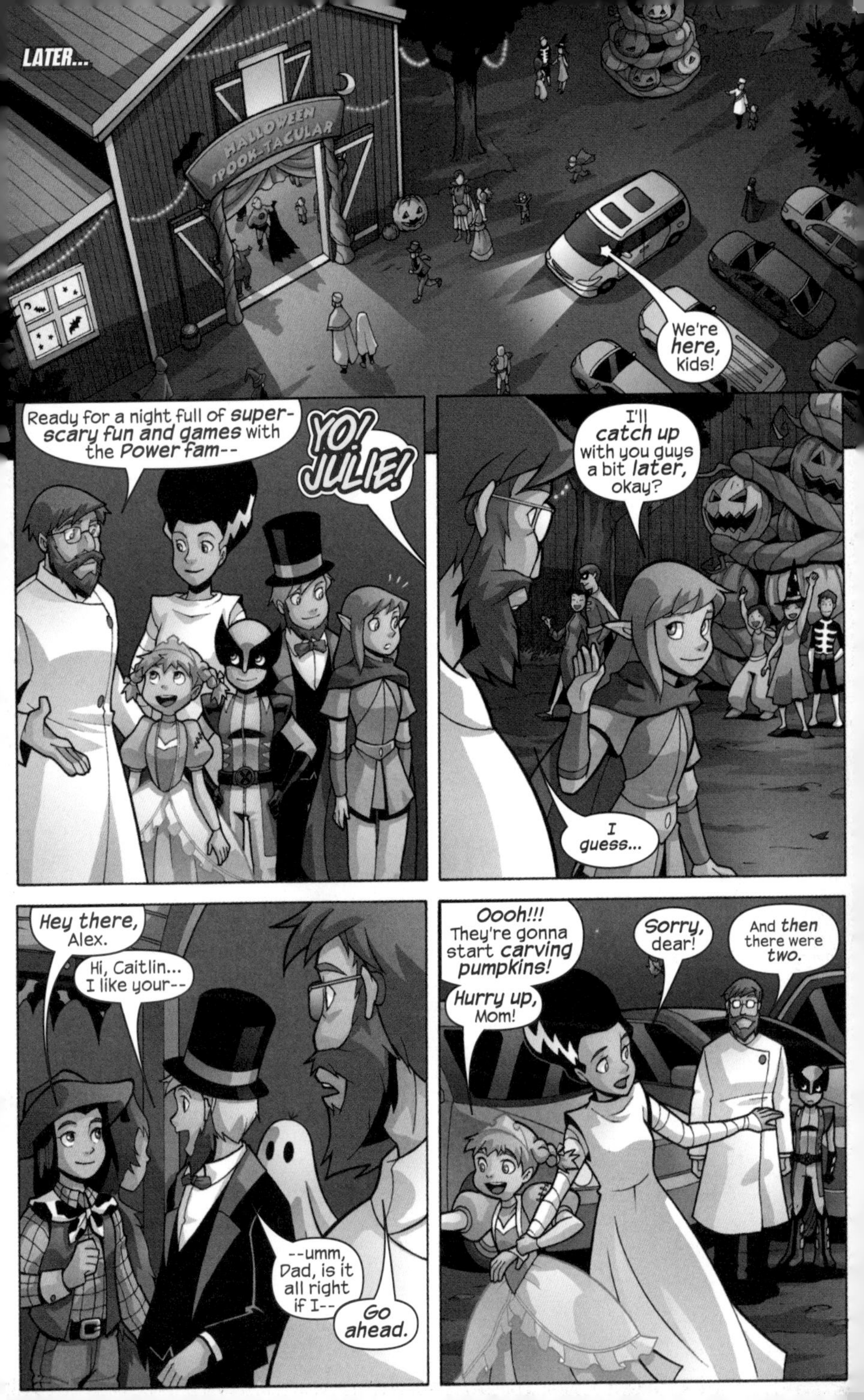
LATER...
HALLOWEEN SPOOK-TACULAR
We're here, kids!
Ready for a night full of super-scary fun and games with the Power fam--
YO! JULIE!
I'll catch up with you guys a bit later, okay?
I guess...
Hey there, Alex.
Hi, Caitlin... I like your--
--umm, Dad, is it all right if I--
Go ahead.
Oooh!!! They're gonna start carving pumpkins!
Hurry up, Mom!
Sorry, dear!
And then there were two.

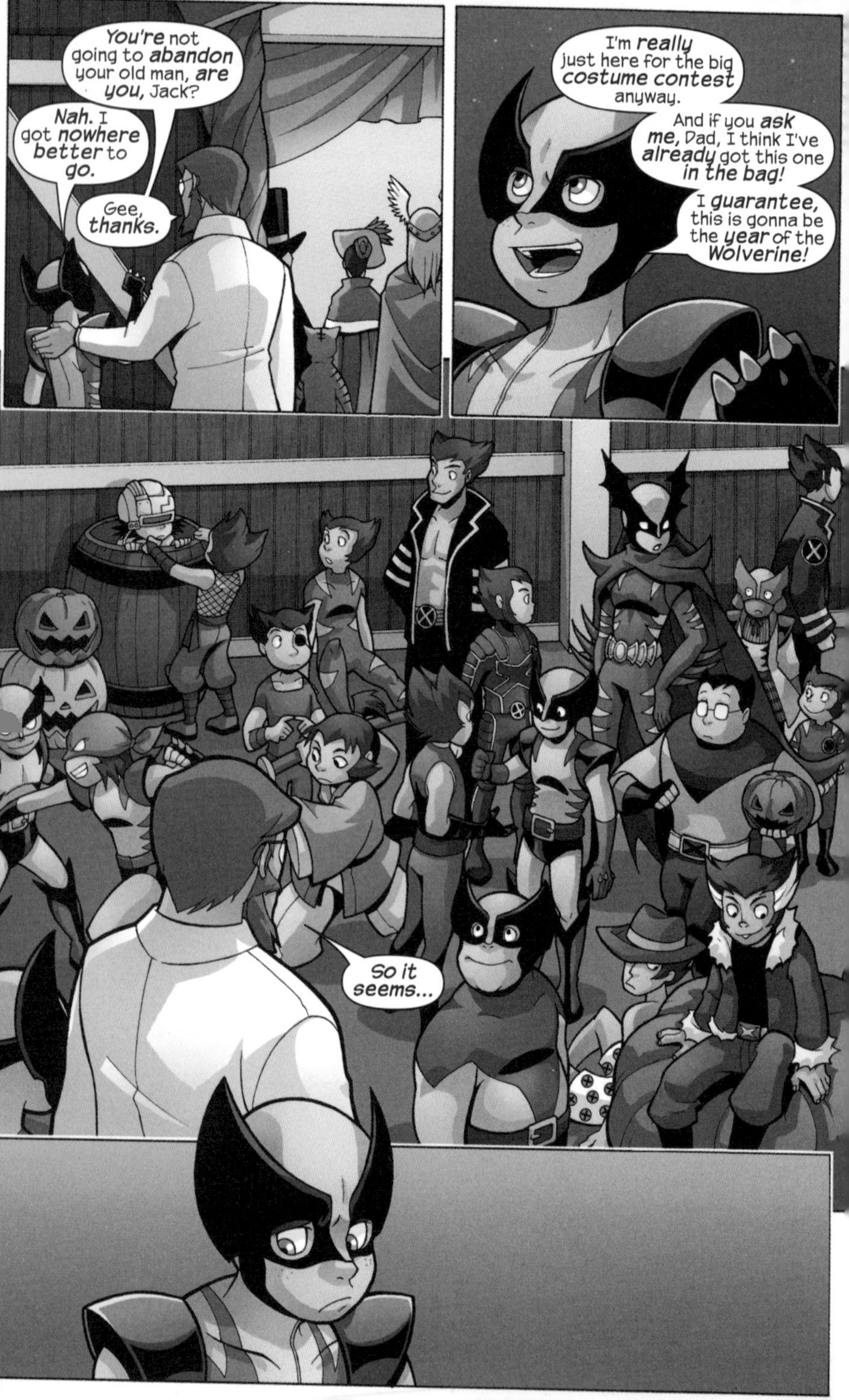
You're not going to abandon your old man, are you, Jack?
Nah. I got nowhere better to go.
Gee, thanks.
I'm really just here for the big costume contest anyway.
And if you ask me, Dad, I think I've already got this one in the bag!
I guarantee, this is gonna be the year of the Wolverine!
So it seems...

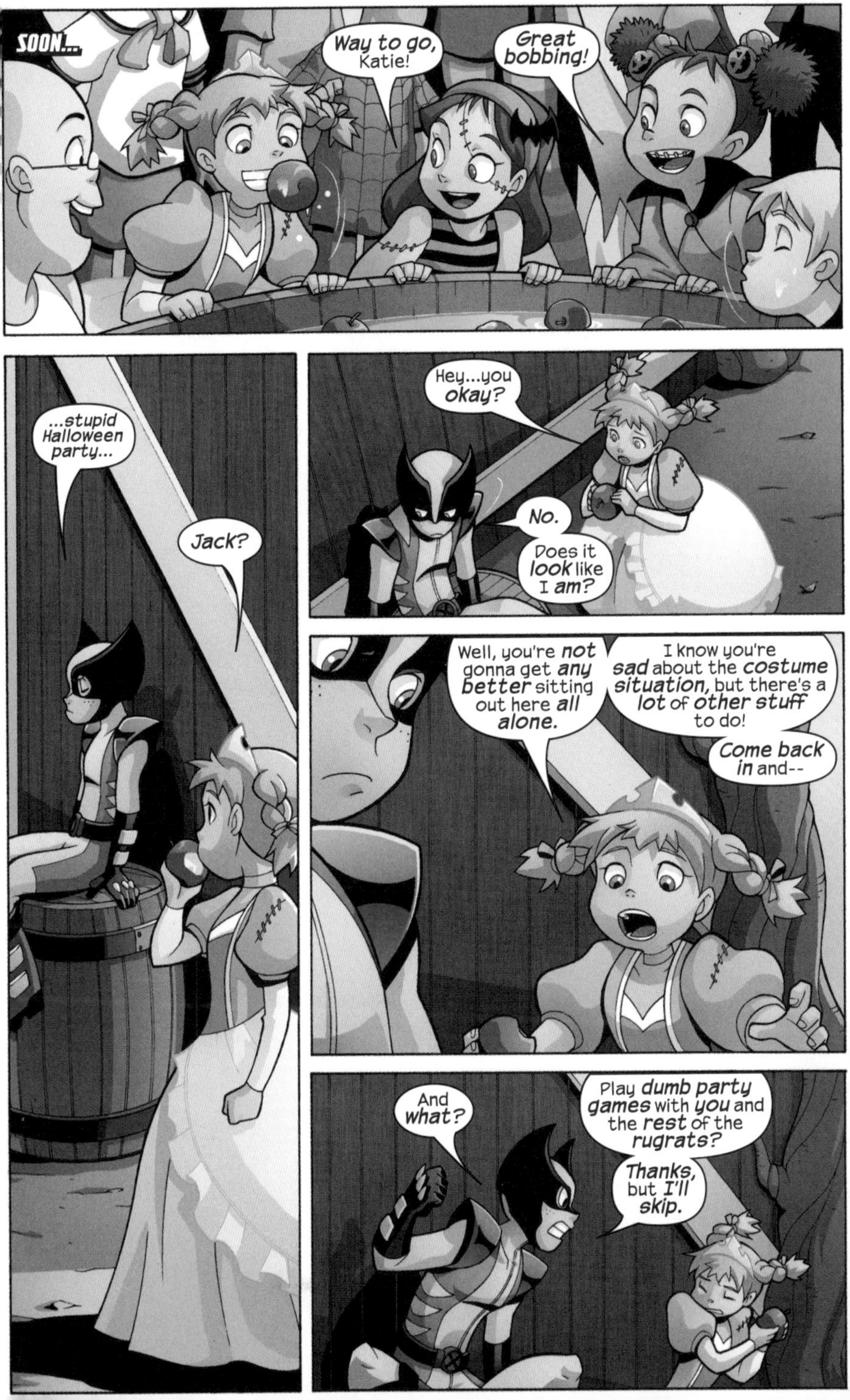

SOON...
Way to go, Katie!
Great bobbing!
...stupid Halloween party...
Jack?
Hey...you okay?
No.
Does it look like I am?
Well, you're not gonna get any better sitting out here all alone.
I know you're sad about the costume situation, but there's a lot of other stuff to do!
Come back in and--
And what?
Play dumb party games with you and the rest of the rugrats?
Thanks, but I'll skip.

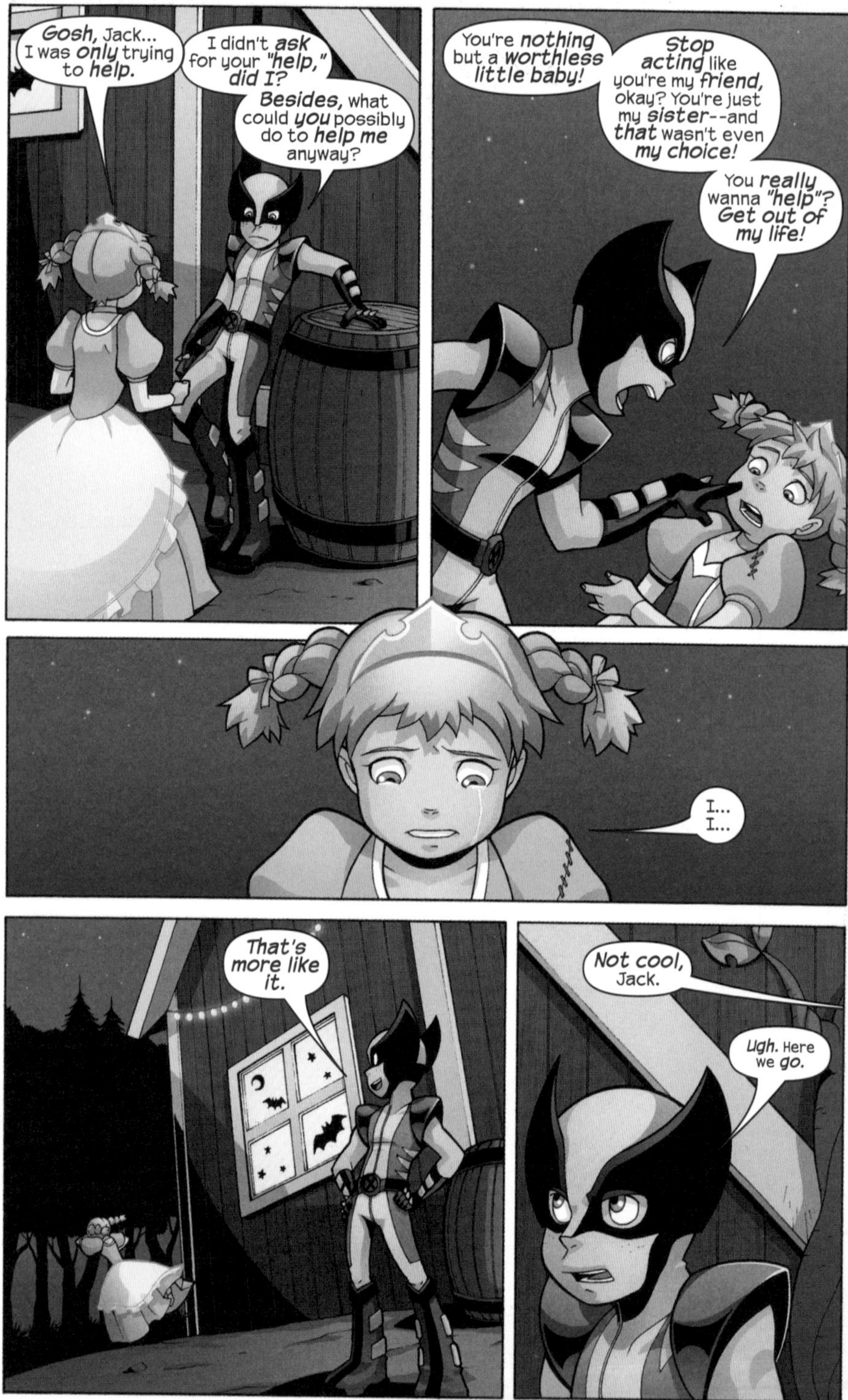

Gosh, Jack... I was only trying to help.
I didn't ask for your "help," did I?
Besides, what could you possibly do to help me anyway?
You're nothing but a worthless little baby!
Stop acting like you're my friend, okay? You're just my sister--and that wasn't even my choice!
You really wanna "help"? Get out of my life!
I... I...
That's more like it.
Not cool, Jack.
Ugh. Here we go.

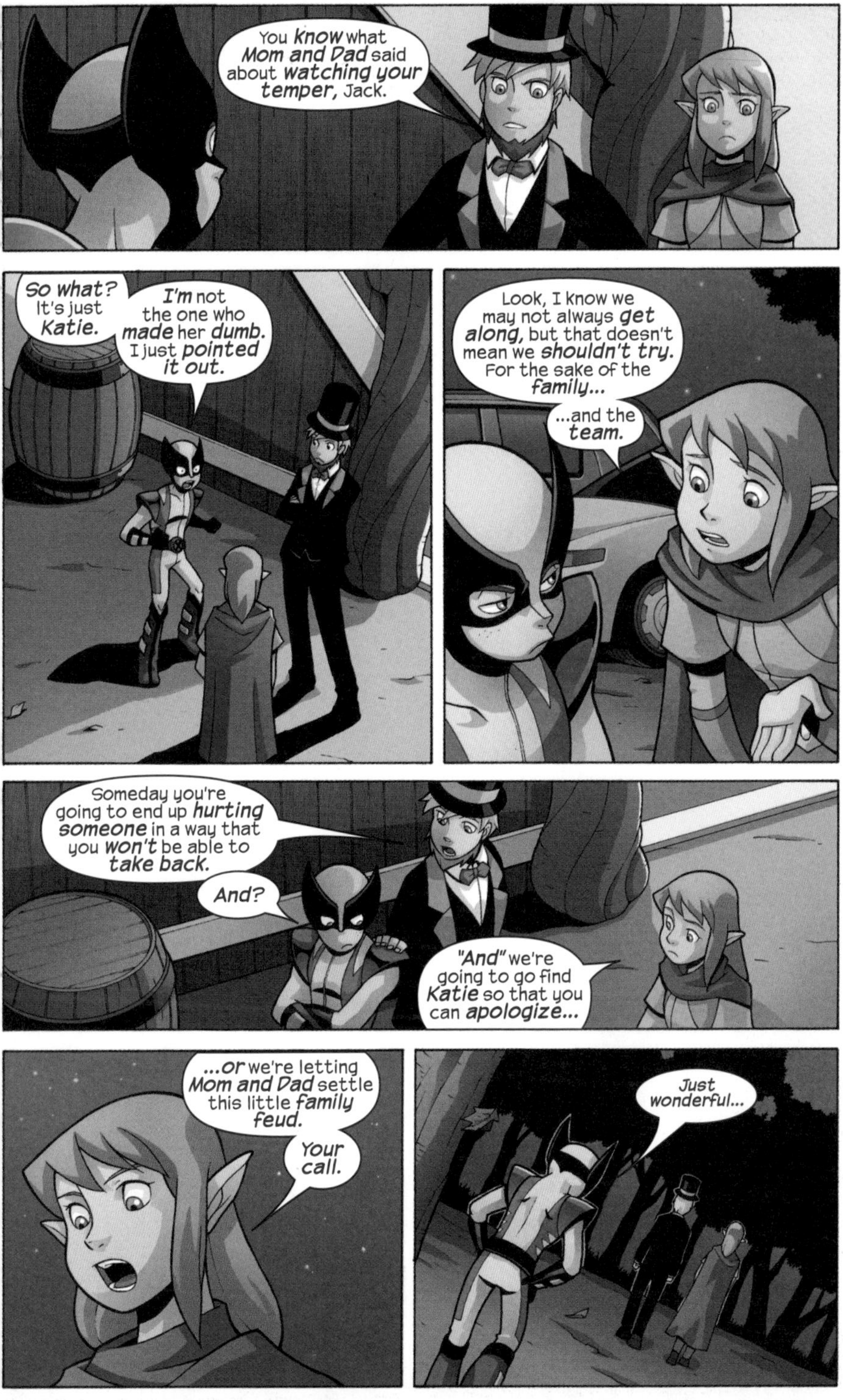
You know what Mom and Dad said about watching your temper, Jack.
So what? It's just Katie.
I'm not the one who made her dumb. I just pointed it out.
Look, I know we may not always get along, but that doesn't mean we shouldn't try. For the sake of the family...
...and the team.
Someday you're going to end up hurting someone in a way that you won't be able to take back.
And?
"And" we're going to go find Katie so that you can apologize...
...or we're letting Mom and Dad settle this little family feud.
Your call.
Just wonderful...

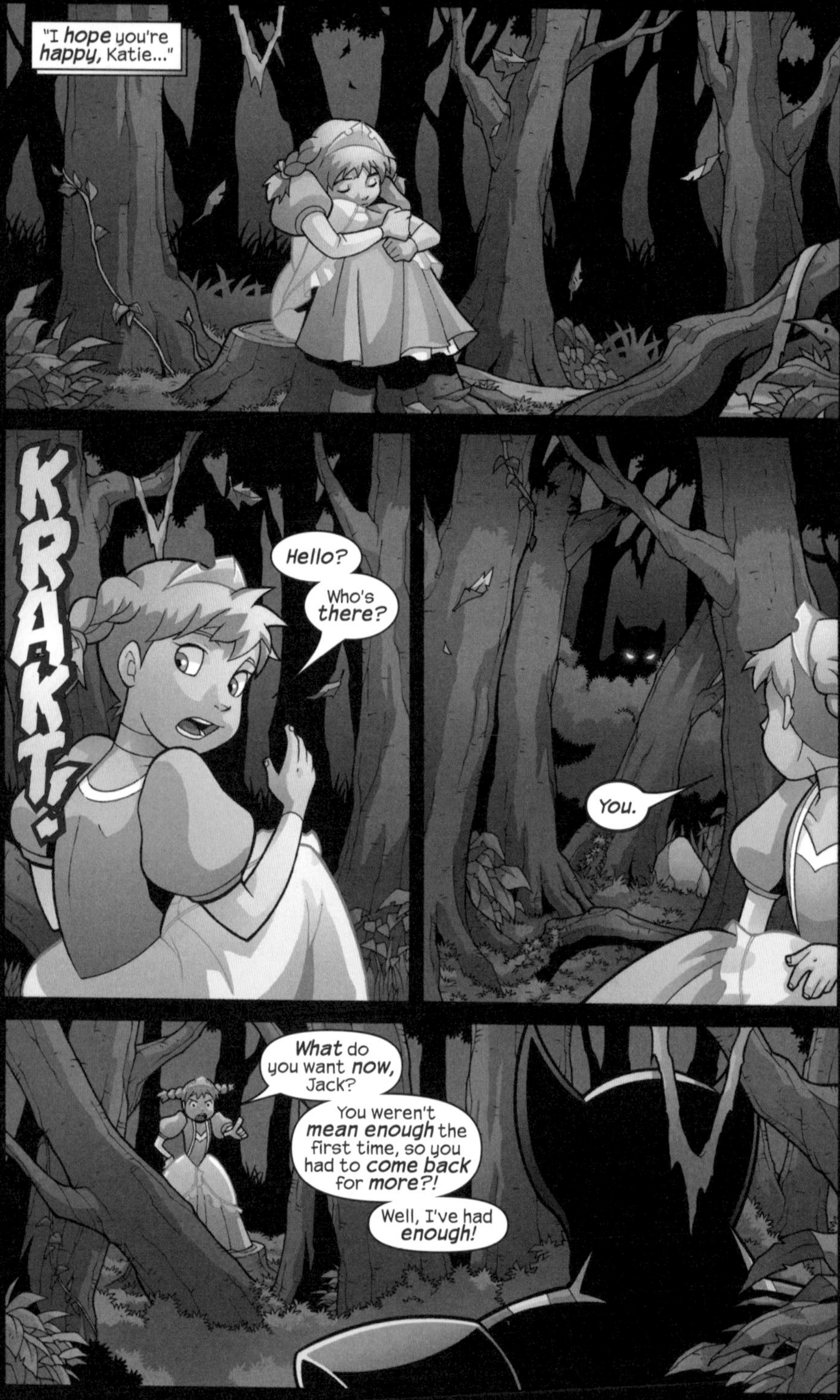
"I hope you're happy, Katie..."
KRAKT!
Hello?
Who's there?
You.
What do you want now, Jack?
You weren't mean enough the first time, so you had to come back for more?!
Well, I've had enough!

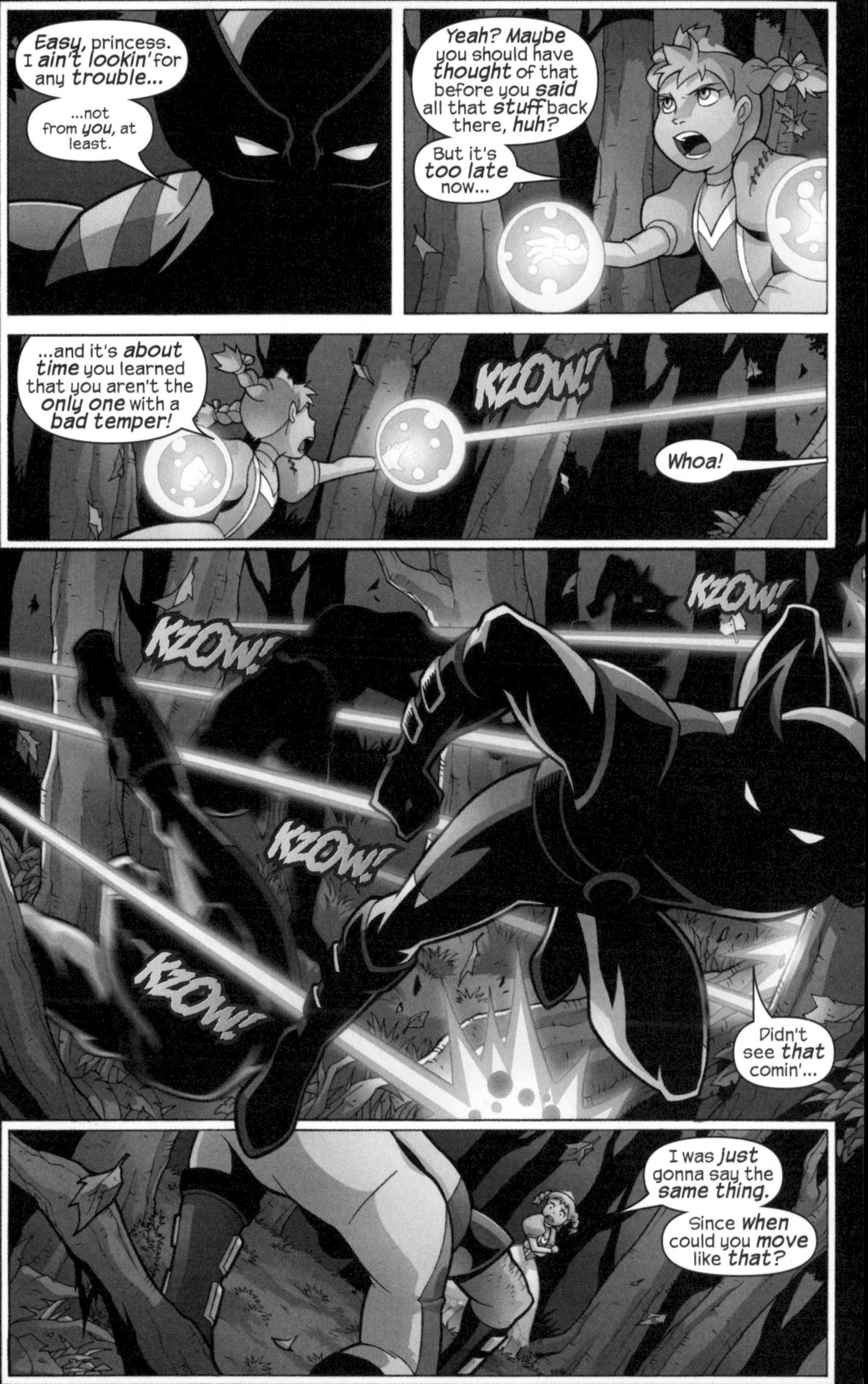
Easy, princess. I ain't lookin' for any trouble...
...not from you, at least.
Yeah? Maybe you should have thought of that before you said all that stuff back there, huh?
But it's too late now...
...and it's about time you learned that you aren't the only one with a bad temper!
KZOW!
Whoa!
KZOW!
KZOW!
KZOW!
KZOW!
Didn't see that comin'...
I was just gonna say the same thing.
Since when could you move like that?

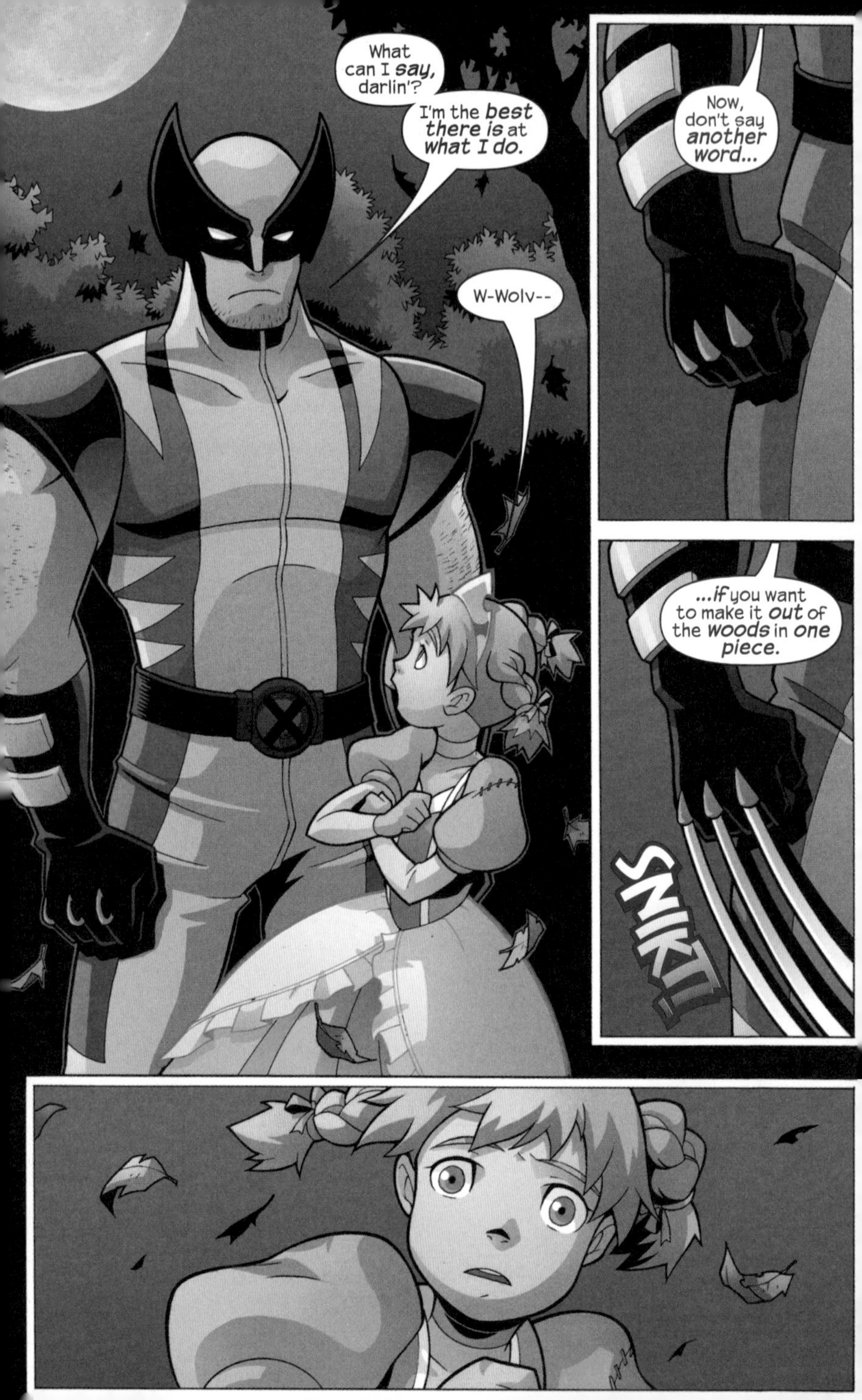

What can I say, darlin'?
I'm the best there is at what I do.
W-Wolv--
Now, don't say another word...
...if you want to make it out of the woods in one piece.
SNIKT!

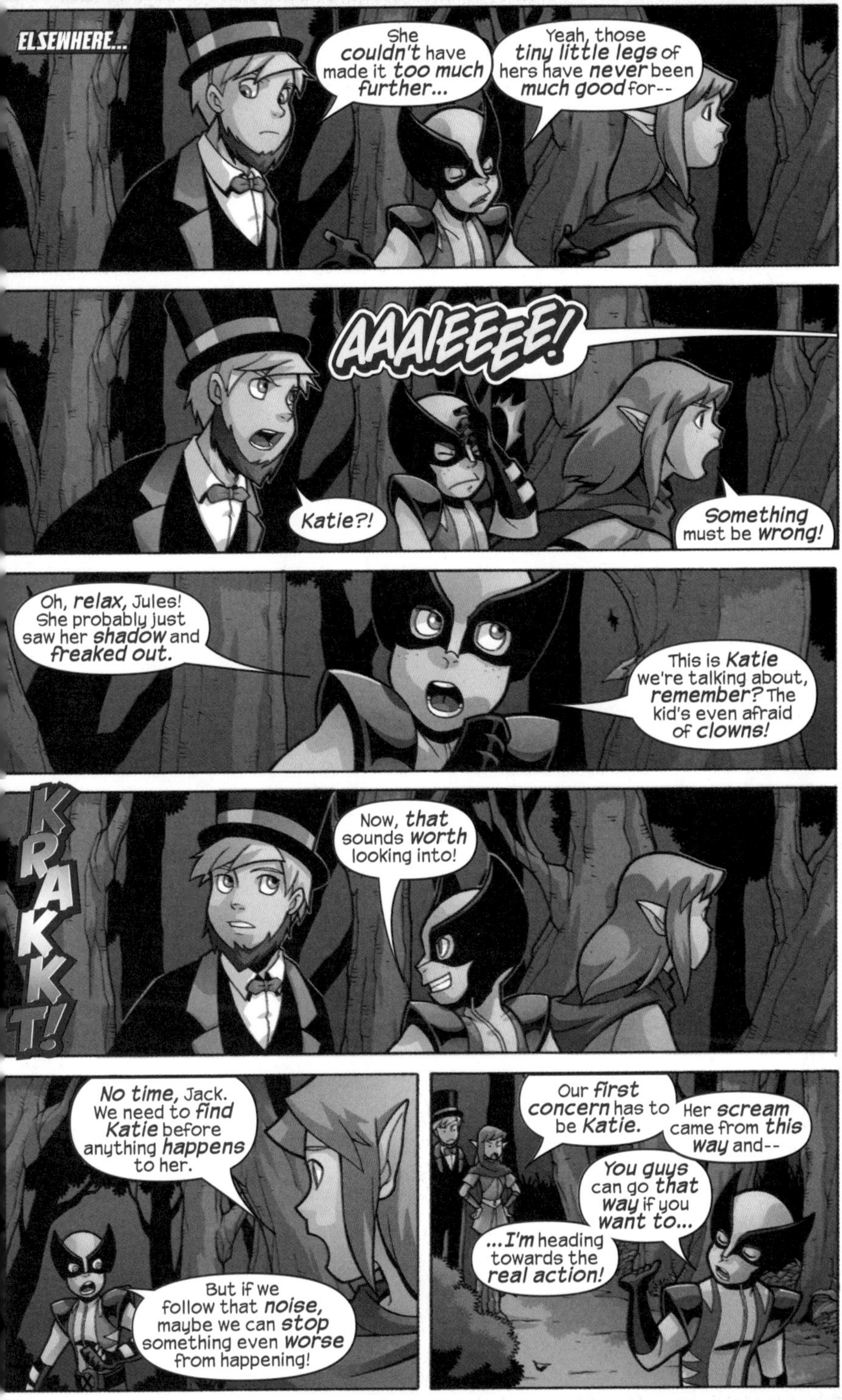
ELSEWHERE...
She couldn't have made it too much further...
Yeah, those tiny little legs of hers have never been much good for--
AAAIEEEEE!
Katie?!
Something must be wrong!
Oh, relax, Jules! She probably just saw her shadow and freaked out.
This is Katie we're talking about, remember? The kid's even afraid of clowns!
KRAKKT!
Now, that sounds worth looking into!
No time, Jack. We need to find Katie before anything happens to her.
But if we follow that noise, maybe we can stop something even worse from happening!
Our first concern has to be Katie.
Her scream came from this way and--
You guys can go that way if you want to...
...I'm heading towards the real action!

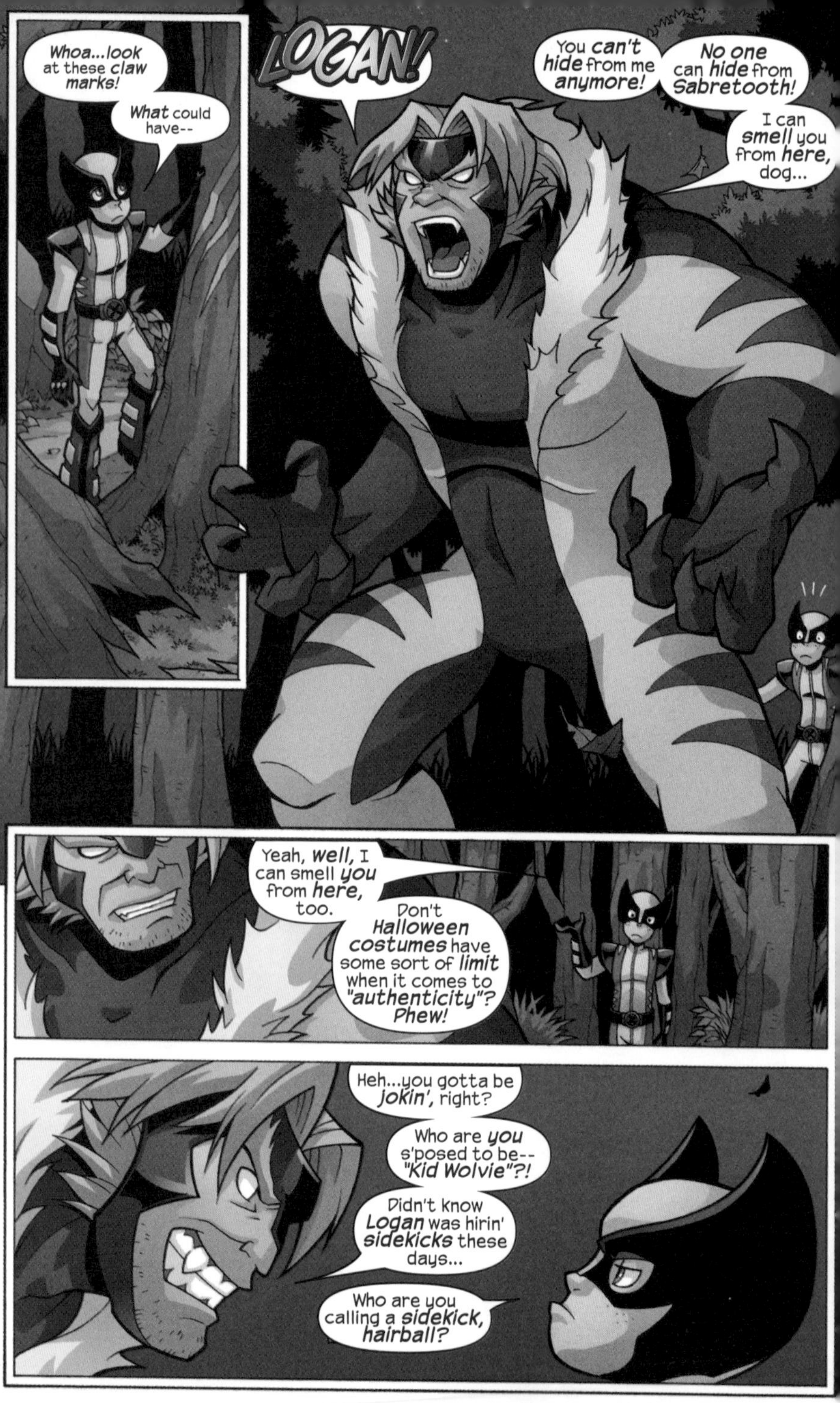
Whoa...look at these claw marks!
What could have--
LOGAN!
You can't hide from me anymore!
No one can hide from Sabretooth!
I can smell you from here, dog...
Yeah, well, I can smell you from here, too.
Don't Halloween costumes have some sort of limit when it comes to "authenticity"? Phew!
Heh...you gotta be jokin', right?
Who are you s'posed to be-- "Kid Wolvie"?!
Didn't know Logan was hirin' sidekicks these days...
Who are you calling a sidekick, hairball?

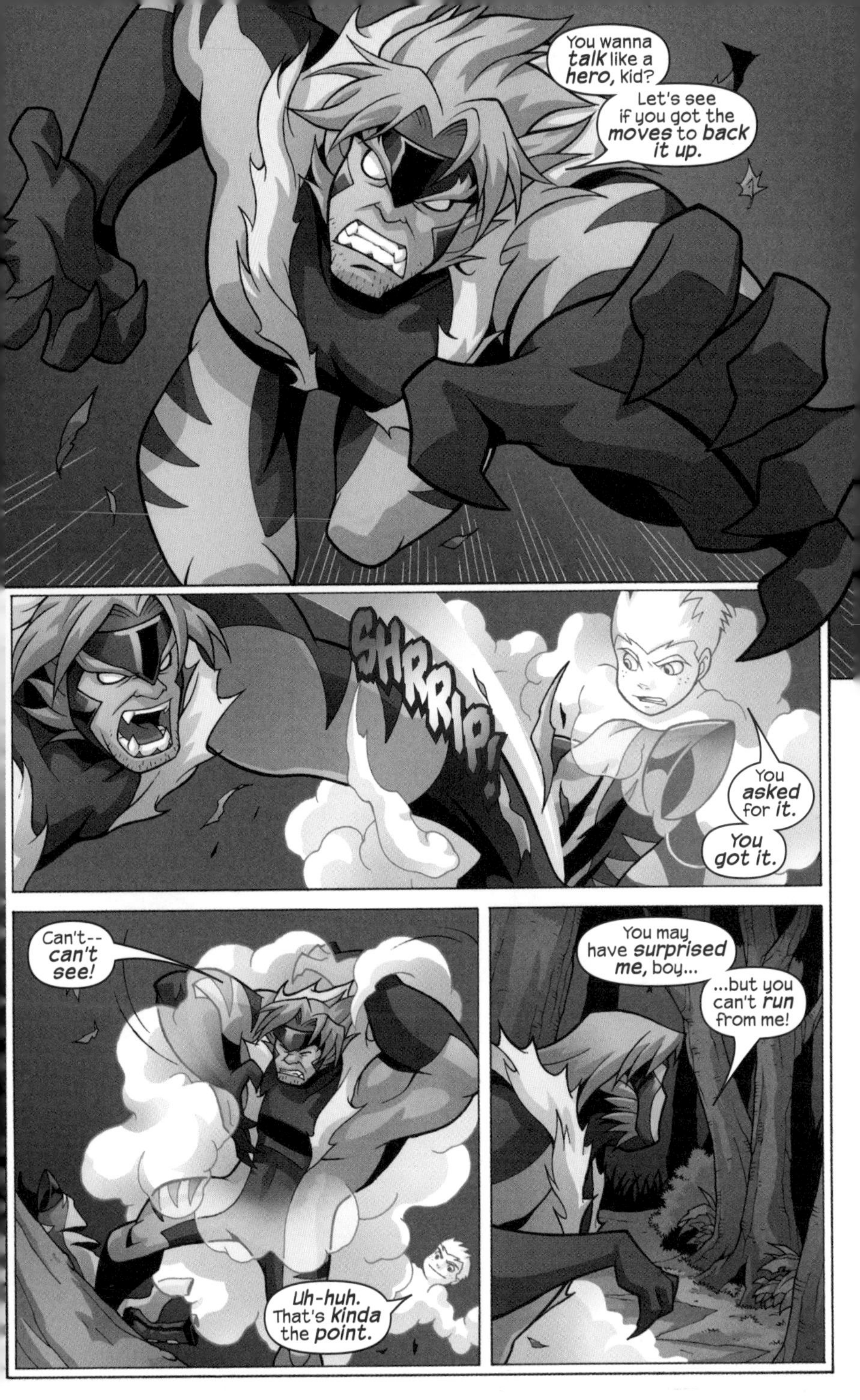
You wanna talk like a hero, kid?
Let's see if you got the moves to back it up.
SHRRIP!
You asked for it.
You got it.
Can't-- can't see!
Uh-huh. That's kinda the point.
You may have surprised me, boy...
...but you can't run from me!

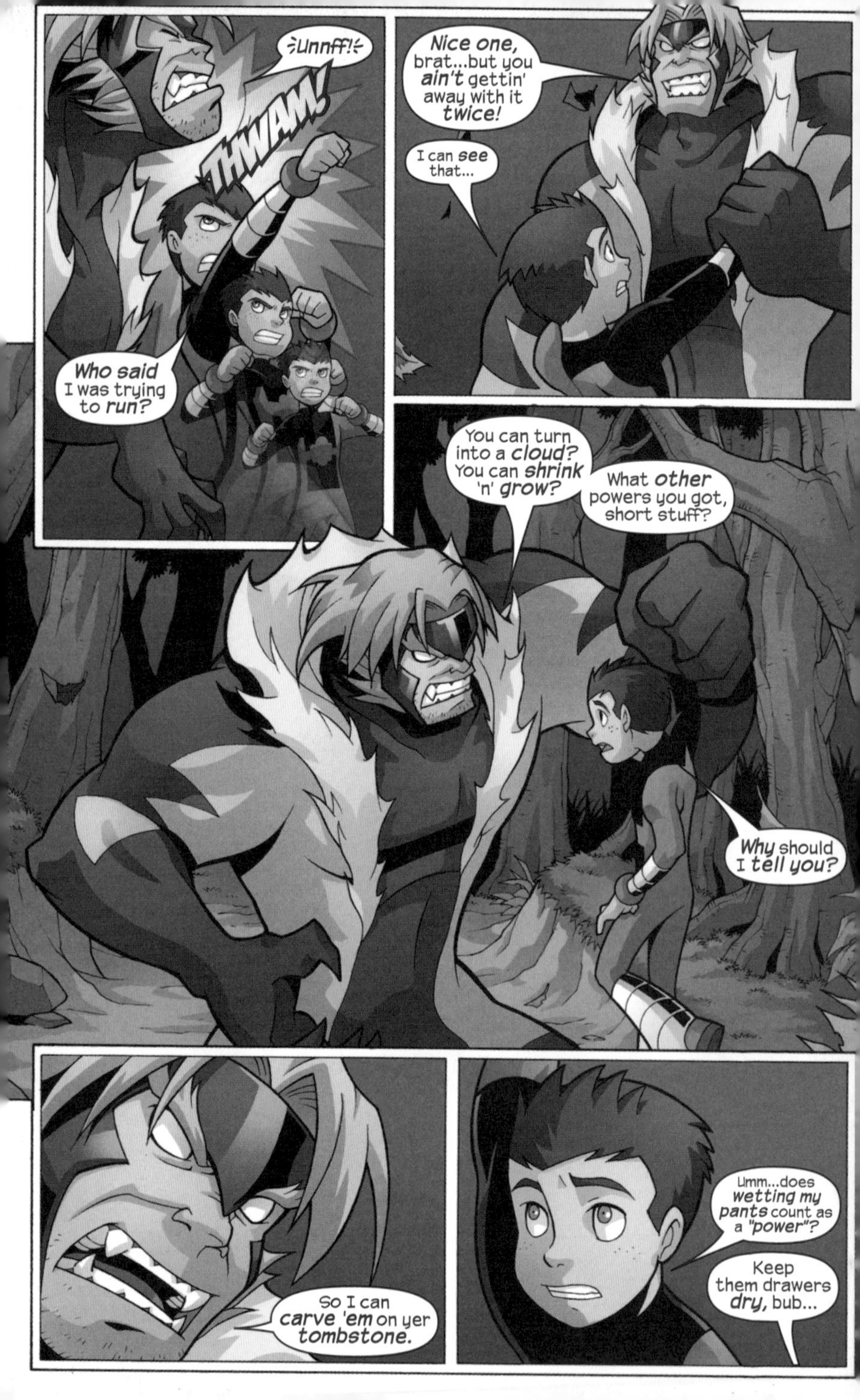
Unnff!
THWAM!
Who said I was trying to run?
Nice one, brat...but you ain't gettin' away with it twice!
I can see that...
You can turn into a cloud? You can shrink 'n' grow?
What other powers you got, short stuff?
Why should I tell you?
So I can carve 'em on yer tombstone.
Umm...does wetting my pants count as a "power"?
Keep them drawers dry, bub...

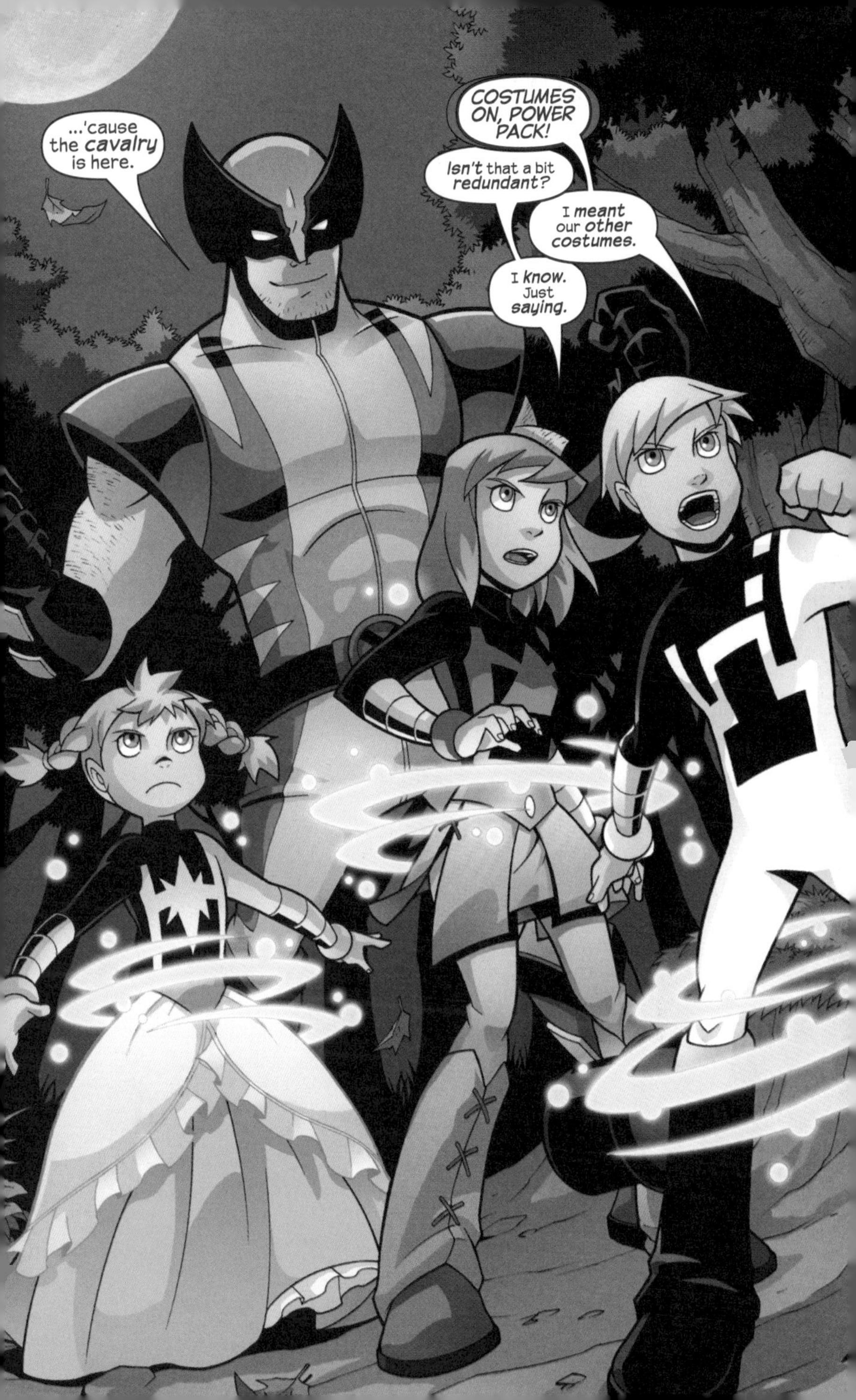
...'cause the cavalry is here.
COSTUMES ON, POWER PACK!
Isn't that a bit redundant?
I meant our other costumes.
I know. Just saying.

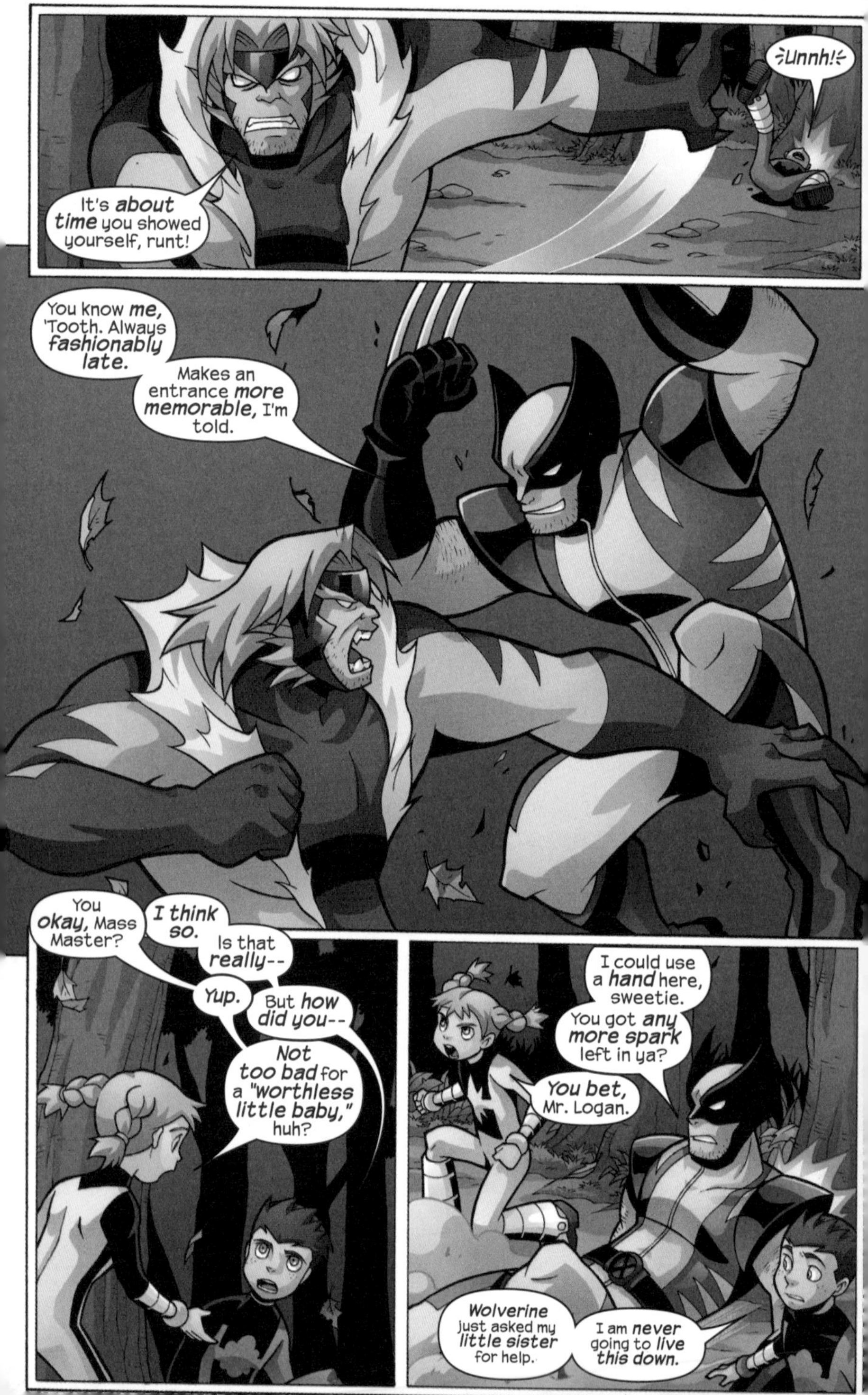

Unnh!
It's about time you showed yourself, runt!
You know me, 'Tooth. Always fashionably late.
Makes an entrance more memorable, I'm told.
You okay, Mass Master?
I think so.
Is that really--
Yup.
But how did you--
Not too bad for a "worthless little baby," huh?
I could use a hand here, sweetie.
You got any more spark left in ya?
You bet, Mr. Logan.
Wolverine just asked my little sister for help.
I am never going to live this down.

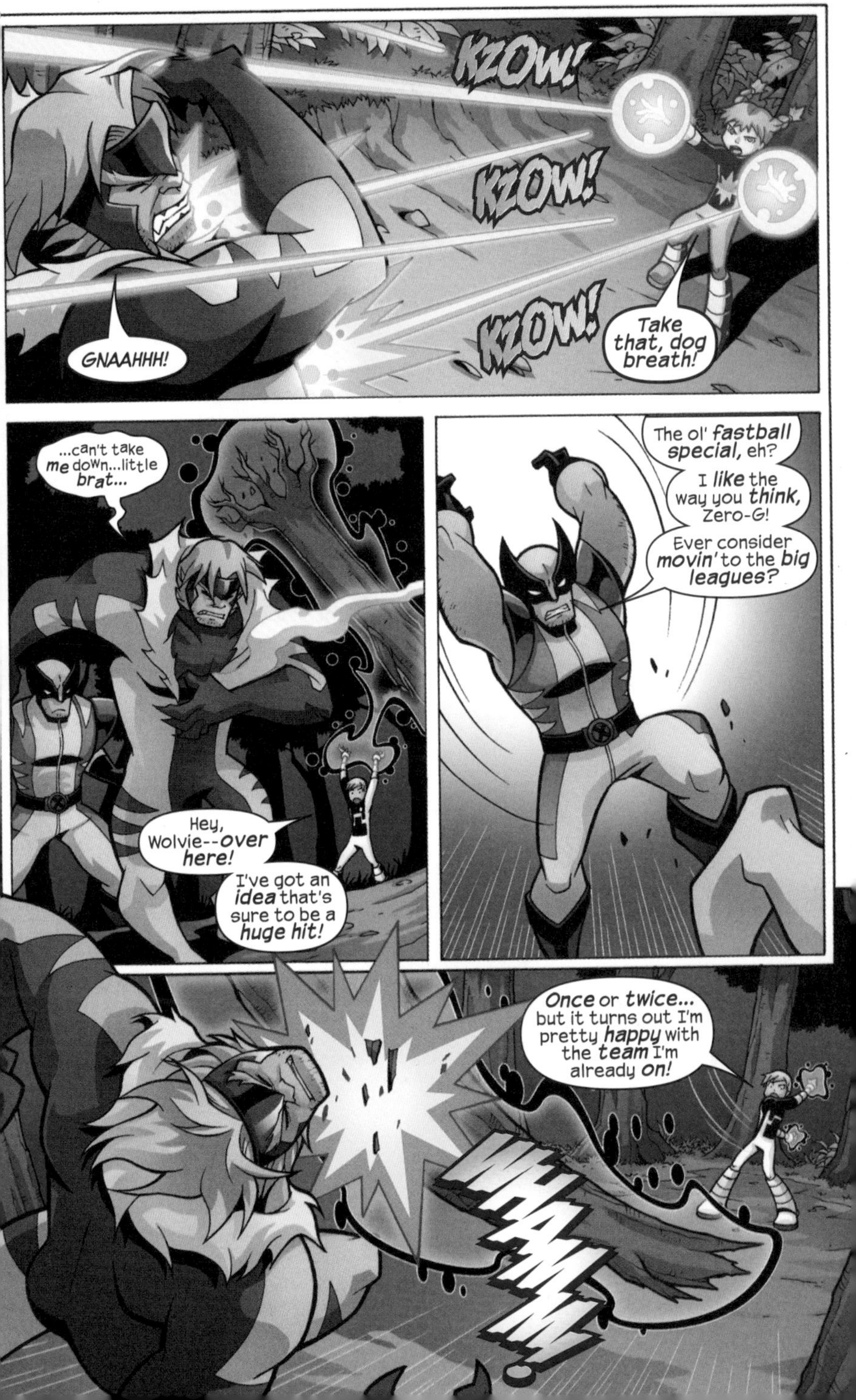
KZOW!
KZOW!
KZOW!
GNAAHHH!
Take that, dog breath!
...can't take me down...little brat...
Hey, Wolvie--over here!
I've got an idea that's sure to be a huge hit!
The ol' fastball special, eh?
I like the way you think, Zero-G!
Ever consider movin' to the big leagues?
Once or twice... but it turns out I'm pretty happy with the team I'm already on!
WHAM!

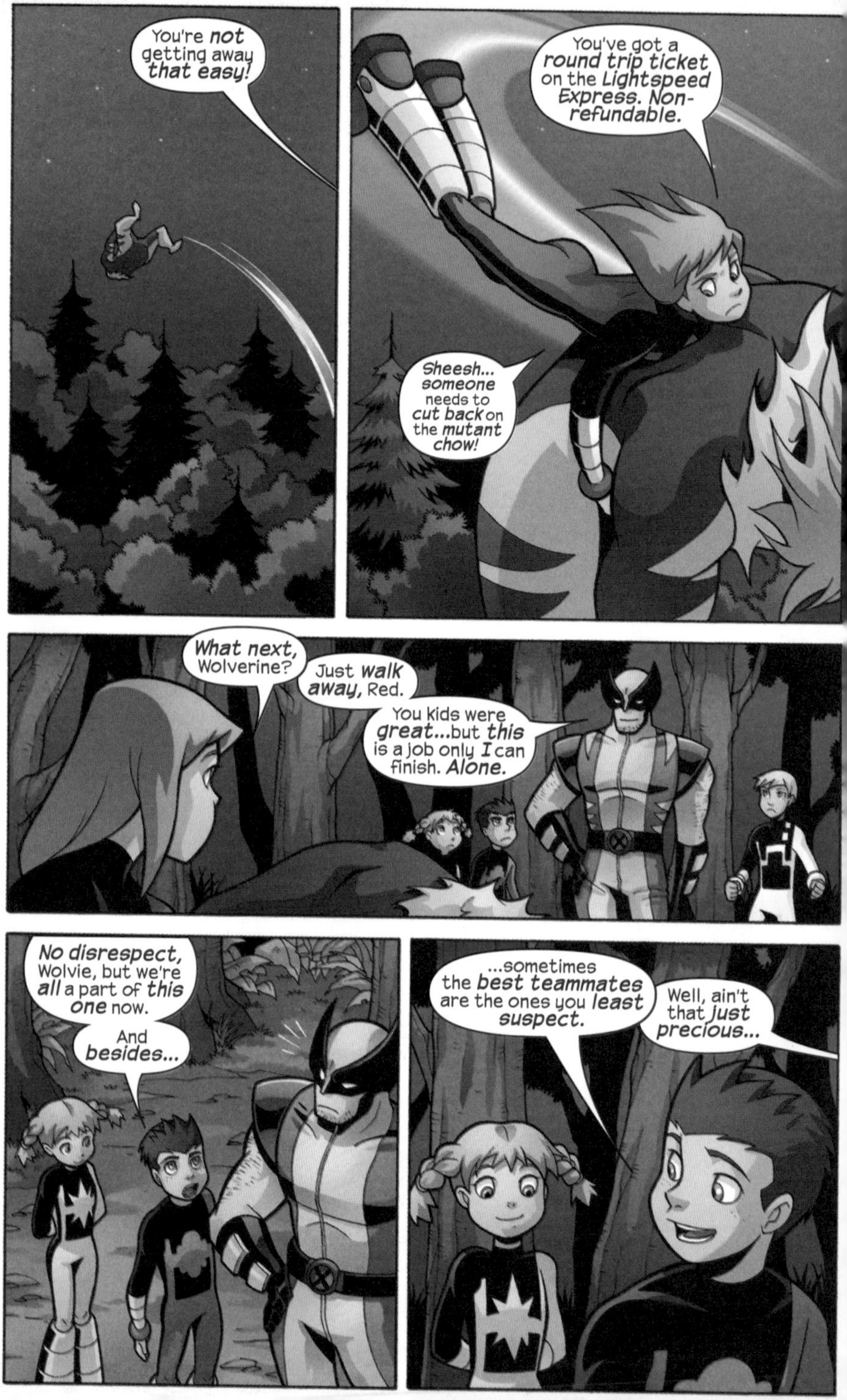
You're not getting away that easy!
You've got a round trip ticket on the Lightspeed Express. Non-refundable.
Sheesh... someone needs to cut back on the mutant chow!
What next, Wolverine?
Just walk away, Red.
You kids were great...but this is a job only I can finish. Alone.
No disrespect, Wolvie, but we're all a part of this one now.
And besides...
...sometimes the best teammates are the ones you least suspect.
Well, ain't that just precious...

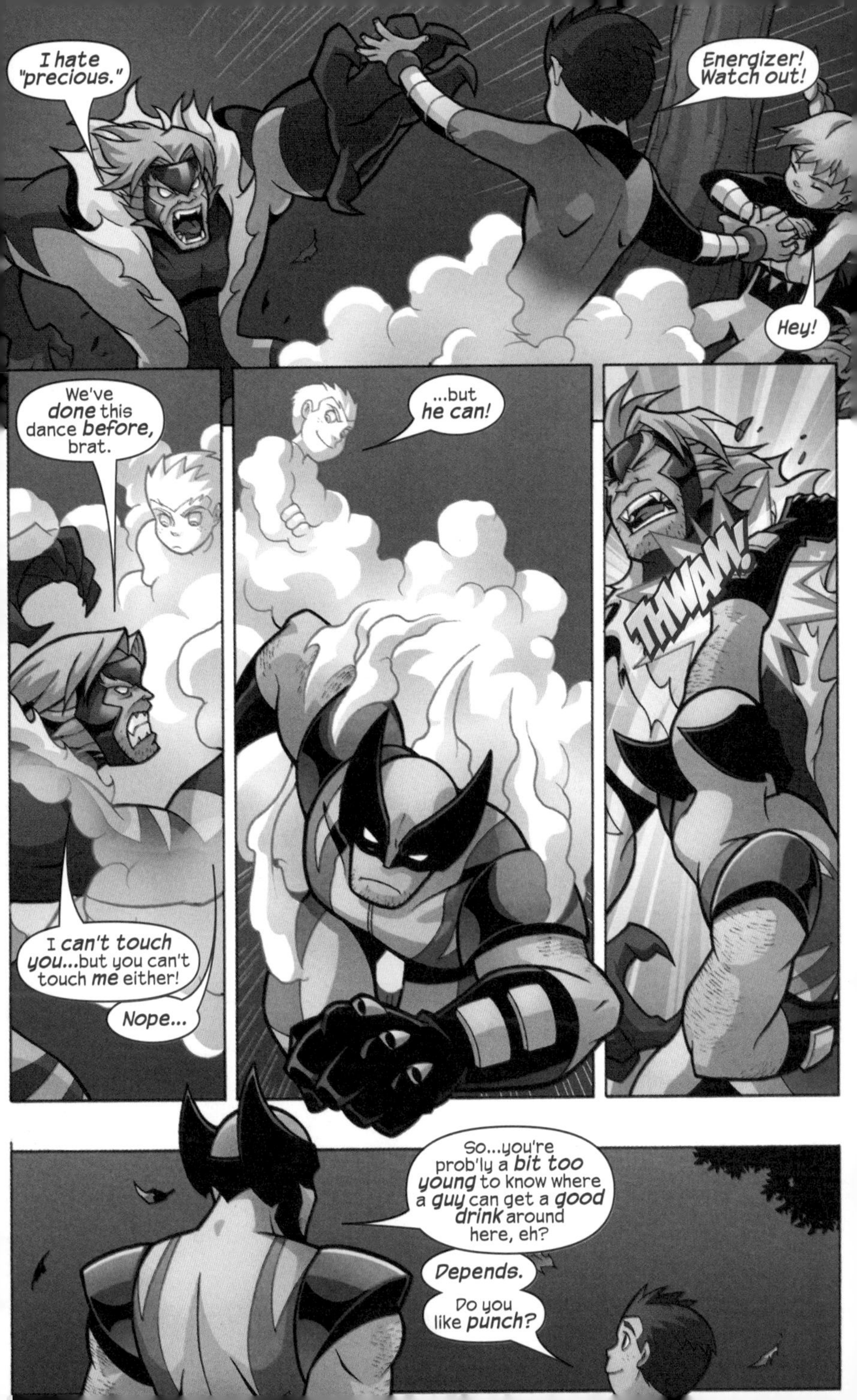
I hate "precious."
Energizer! Watch out!
Hey!
We've done this dance before, brat.
I can't touch you...but you can't touch me either!
Nope...
...but he can!
THWAM!
So...you're prob'ly a bit too young to know where a guy can get a good drink around here, eh?
Depends.
Do you like punch?

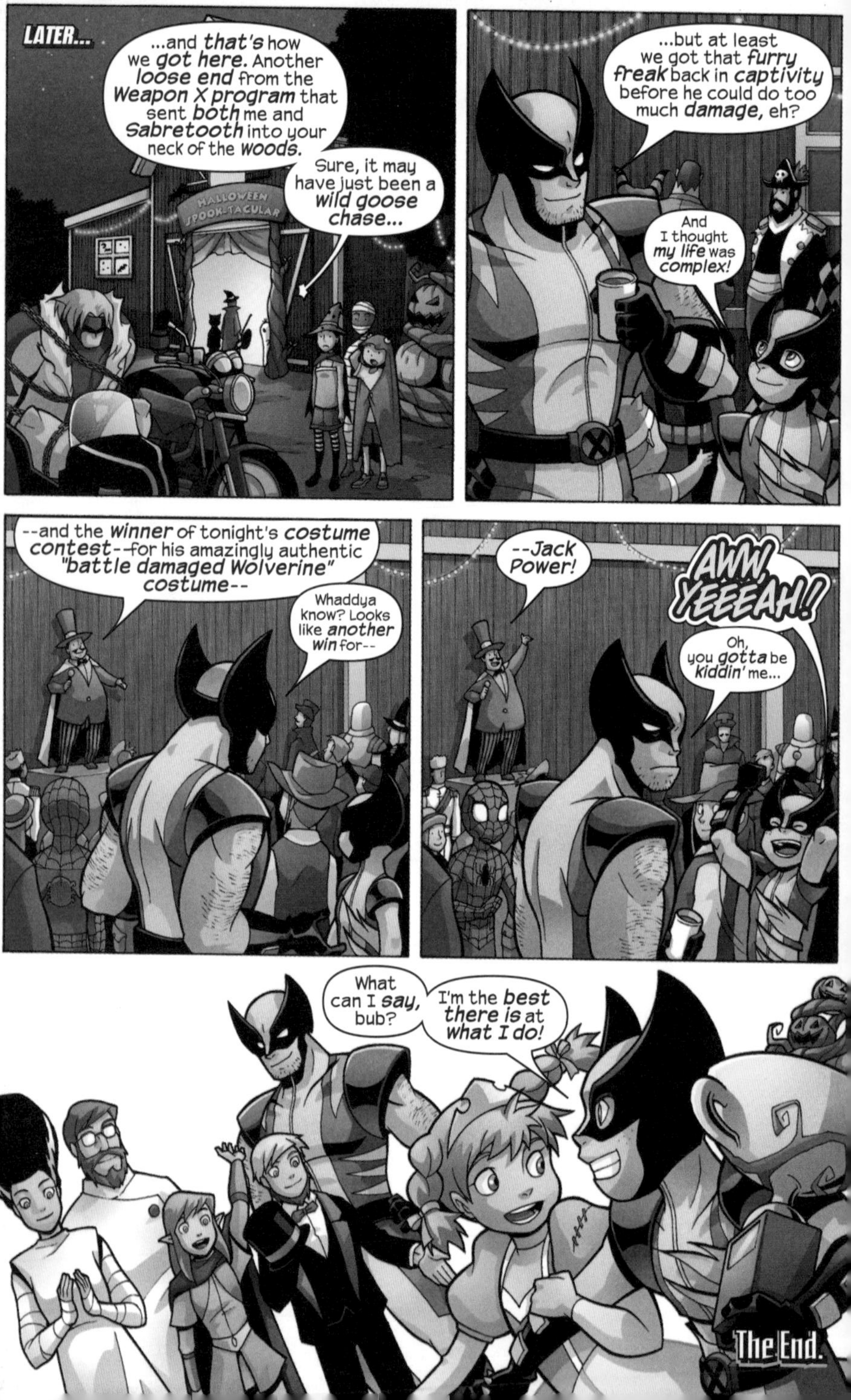
LATER...
...and that's how we got here. Another loose end from the Weapon X program that sent both me and Sabretooth into your neck of the woods.
Sure, it may have just been a wild goose chase...
HALLOWEEN SPOOK-TACULAR
...but at least we got that furry freak back in captivity before he could do too much damage, eh?
And I thought my life was complex!
--and the winner of tonight's costume contest--for his amazingly authentic "battle damaged Wolverine" costume--
Whaddya know? Looks like another win for--
--Jack Power!
AWW, YEEEAH!!
Oh, you gotta be kiddin' me...
What can I say, bub?
I'm the best there is at what I do!
The End.

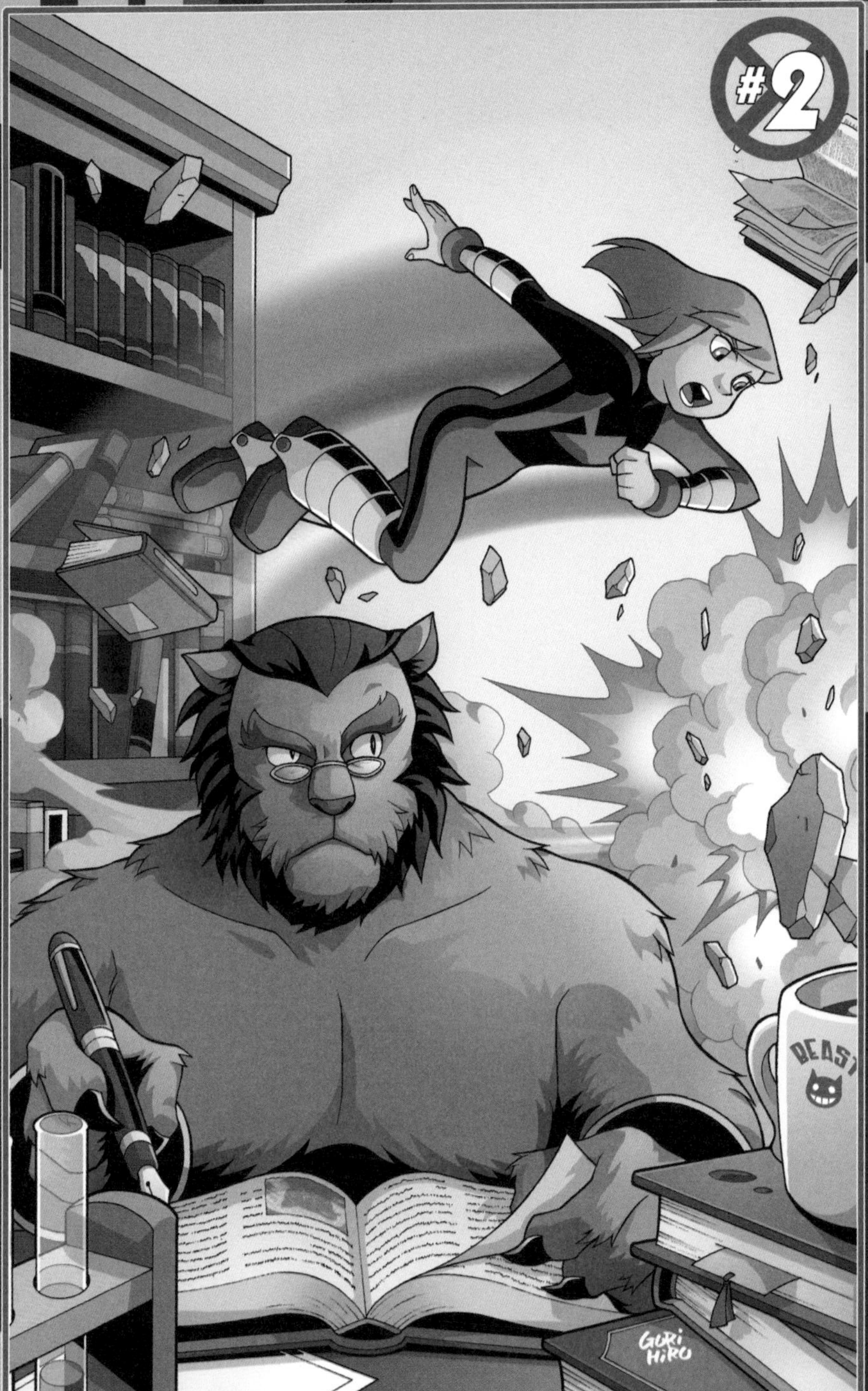
#2
BEAST
GURI HIRU

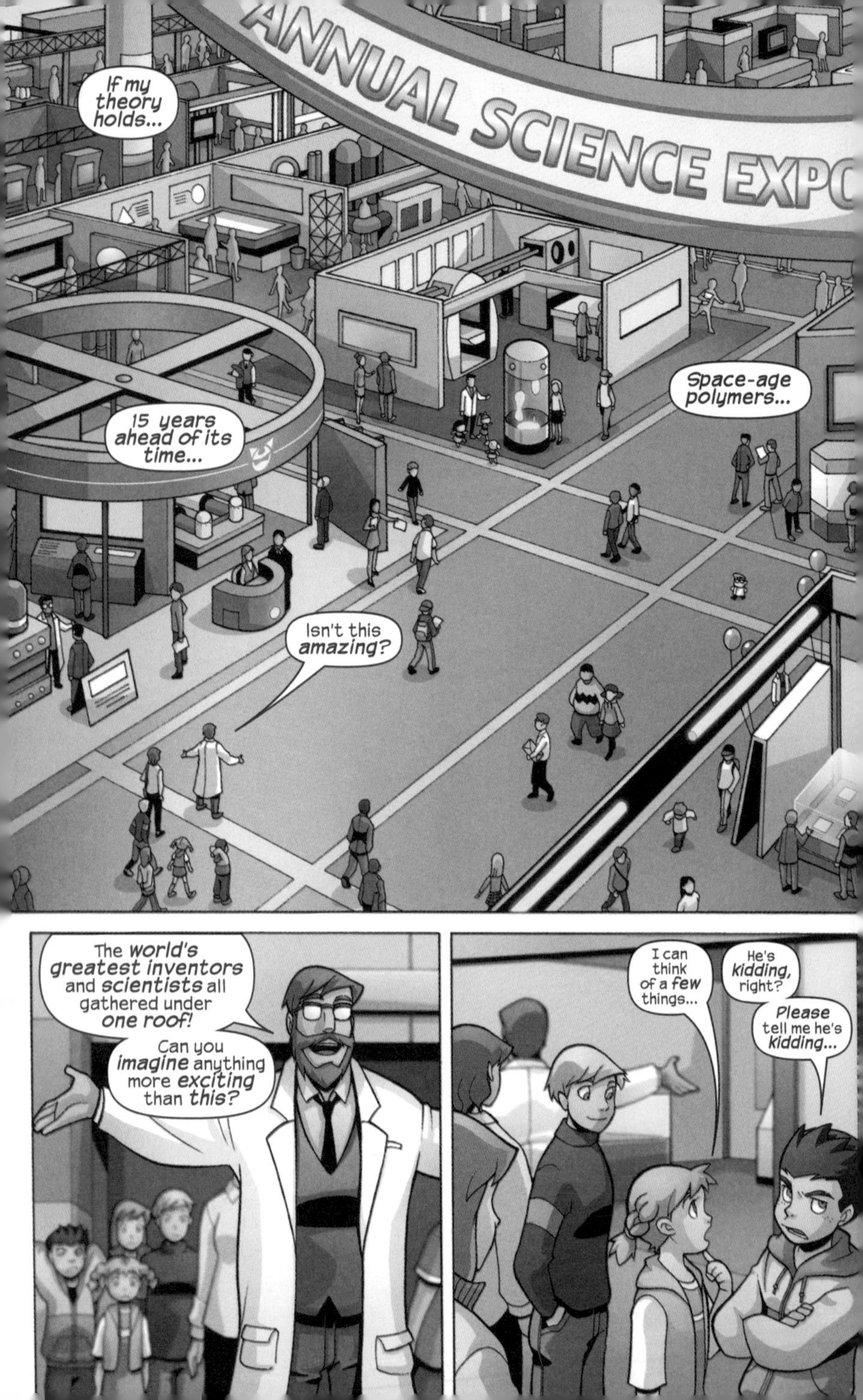
ANNUAL SCIENCE EXPO
If my theory holds...
15 years ahead of its time...
Space-age polymers...
Isn't this amazing?
The world's greatest inventors and scientists all gathered under one roof!
Can you imagine anything more exciting than this?
I can think of a few things...
He's kidding, right?
Please tell me he's kidding...

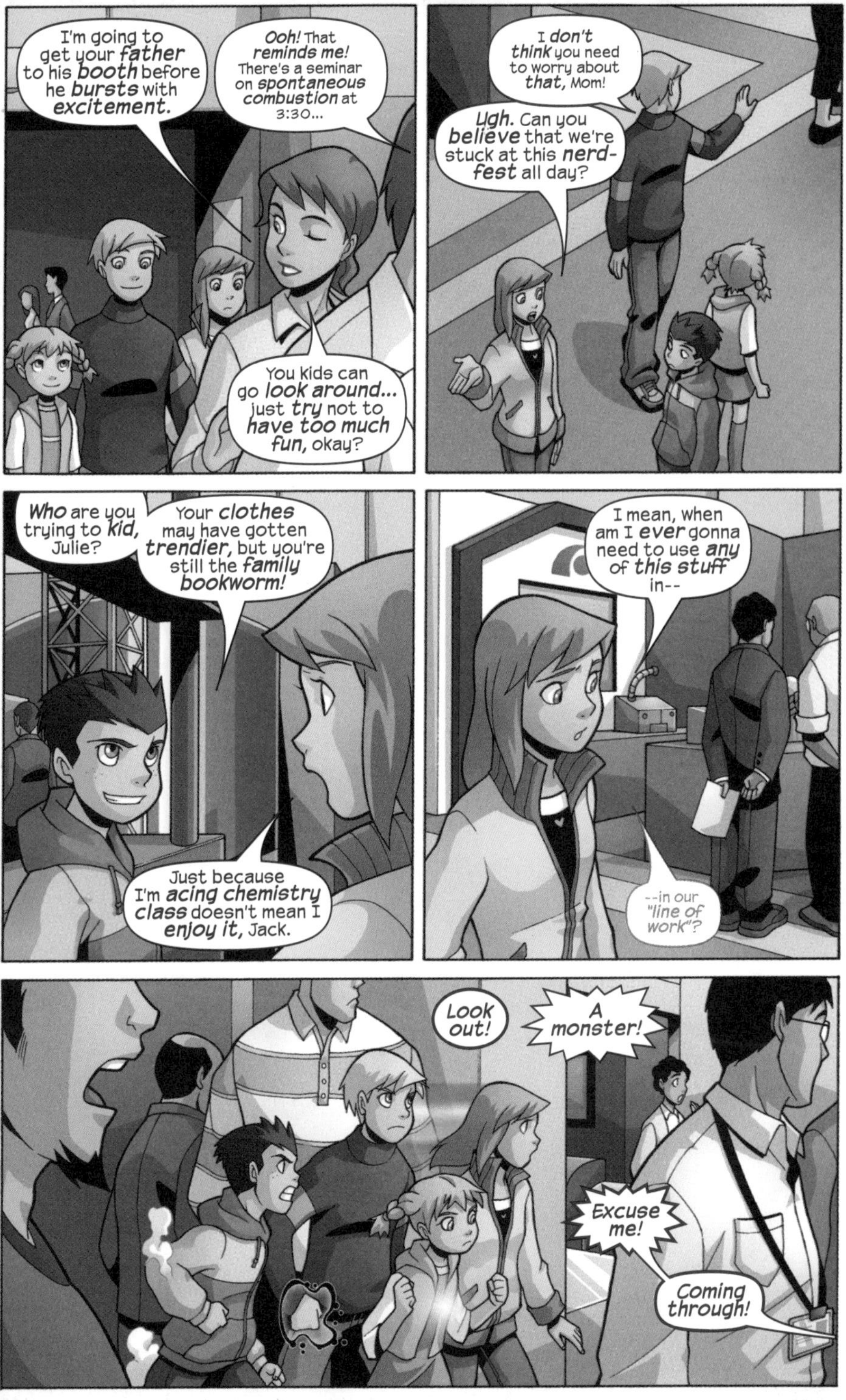
I'm going to get your father to his booth before he bursts with excitement.
Ooh! That reminds me! There's a seminar on spontaneous combustion at 3:30...
You kids can go look around... just try not to have too much fun, okay?
I don't think you need to worry about that, Mom!
Ugh. Can you believe that we're stuck at this nerd-fest all day?
Who are you trying to kid, Julie?
Your clothes may have gotten trendier, but you're still the family bookworm!
Just because I'm acing chemistry class doesn't mean I enjoy it, Jack.
I mean, when am I ever gonna need to use any of this stuff in--
--in our "line of work"?
Look out!
A monster!
Excuse me!
Coming through!

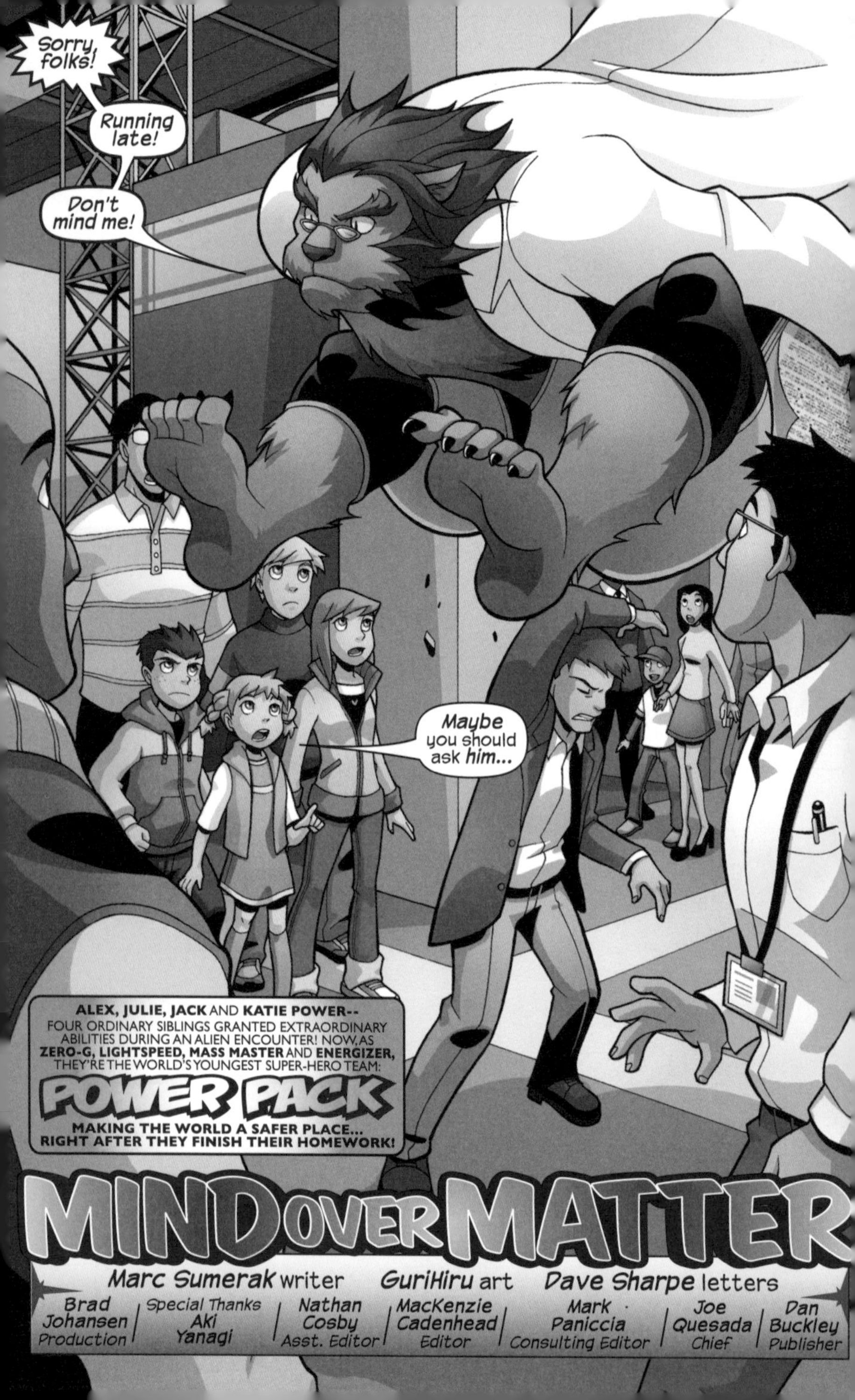
Sorry, folks!
Running late!
Don't mind me!
Maybe you should ask him...
ALEX, JULIE, JACK AND KATIE POWER-- FOUR ORDINARY SIBLINGS GRANTED EXTRAORDINARY ABILITIES DURING AN ALIEN ENCOUNTER! NOW, AS ZERO-G, LIGHTSPEED, MASS MASTER AND ENERGIZER, THEY'RE THE WORLD'S YOUNGEST SUPER-HERO TEAM:
POWER PACK
MAKING THE WORLD A SAFER PLACE... RIGHT AFTER THEY FINISH THEIR HOMEWORK!
MIND OVER MATTER
Marc Sumerak writer GuriHiru art Dave Sharpe letters
Brad Johansen Production
Special Thanks Aki Yanagi
Nathan Cosby Asst. Editor
MacKenzie Cadenhead Editor
Mark Paniccia Consulting Editor
Joe Quesada Chief
Dan Buckley Publisher

SOON...

--our keynote speaker, Dr. Henry McCoy!

Now *this* is *science!*

Greetings, friends and colleagues!

As our illustrious announcer *indicated,* my name is *Dr. Henry McCoy*--but many of you know me better as *"The Beast"!*

Over the years, I've been a *member* of the *X-Men,* the *Avengers,* the *Defenders*--the list goes *on* and *on...*

...but *today,* I take the *utmost pride* in being a *lifelong member* of *your* team--the *scientific community!*

And now, the worlds of *science* and *super heroics* find themselves once again *intertwined,* thanks to my *newest invention*--

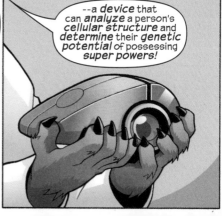

--a *device* that can *analyze* a person's *cellular structure* and *determine* their *genetic potential* of possessing *super powers!*

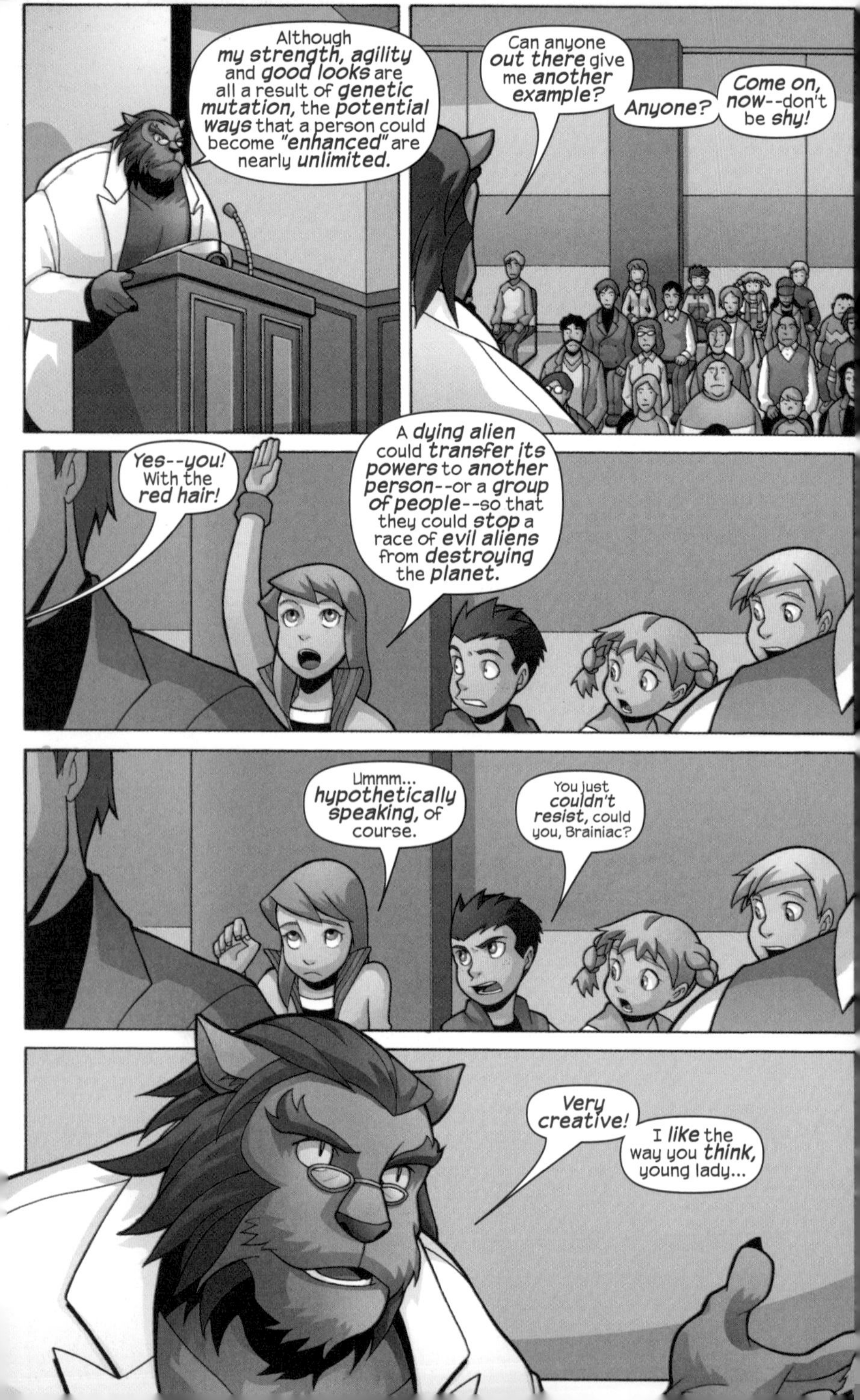
Although my strength, agility and good looks are all a result of genetic mutation, the potential ways that a person could become "enhanced" are nearly unlimited.
Can anyone out there give me another example?
Anyone?
Come on, now--don't be shy!
Yes--you! With the red hair!
A dying alien could transfer its powers to another person--or a group of people--so that they could stop a race of evil aliens from destroying the planet.
Ummm... hypothetically speaking, of course.
You just couldn't resist, could you, Brainiac?
Very creative!
I like the way you think, young lady...

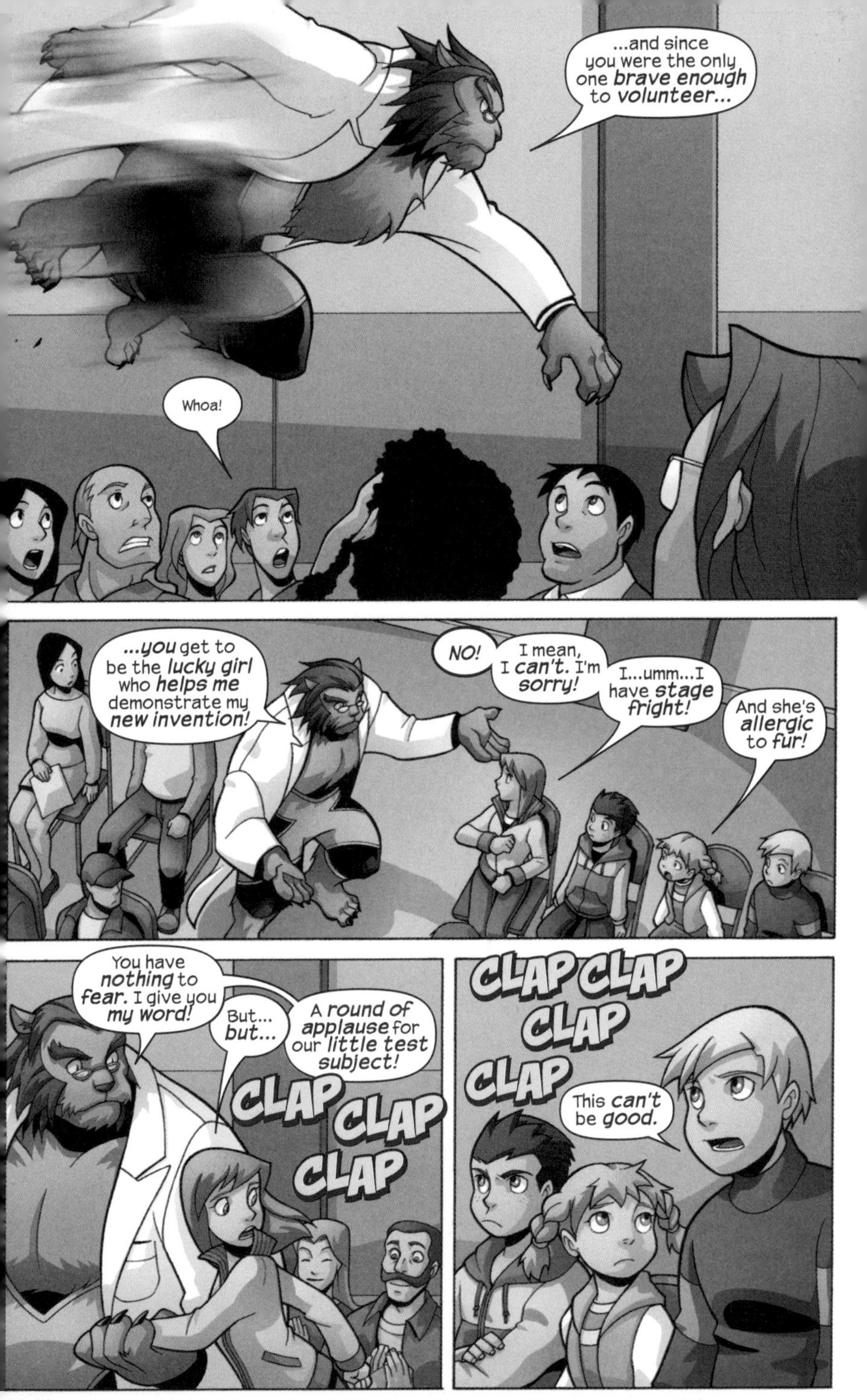

...and since you were the only one brave enough to volunteer...
Whoa!
...you get to be the lucky girl who helps me demonstrate my new invention!
NO!
I mean, I can't. I'm sorry!
I...umm...I have stage fright!
And she's allergic to fur!
You have nothing to fear. I give you my word!
But... but...
A round of applause for our little test subject!
CLAP CLAP CLAP
CLAP CLAP CLAP CLAP
This can't be good.

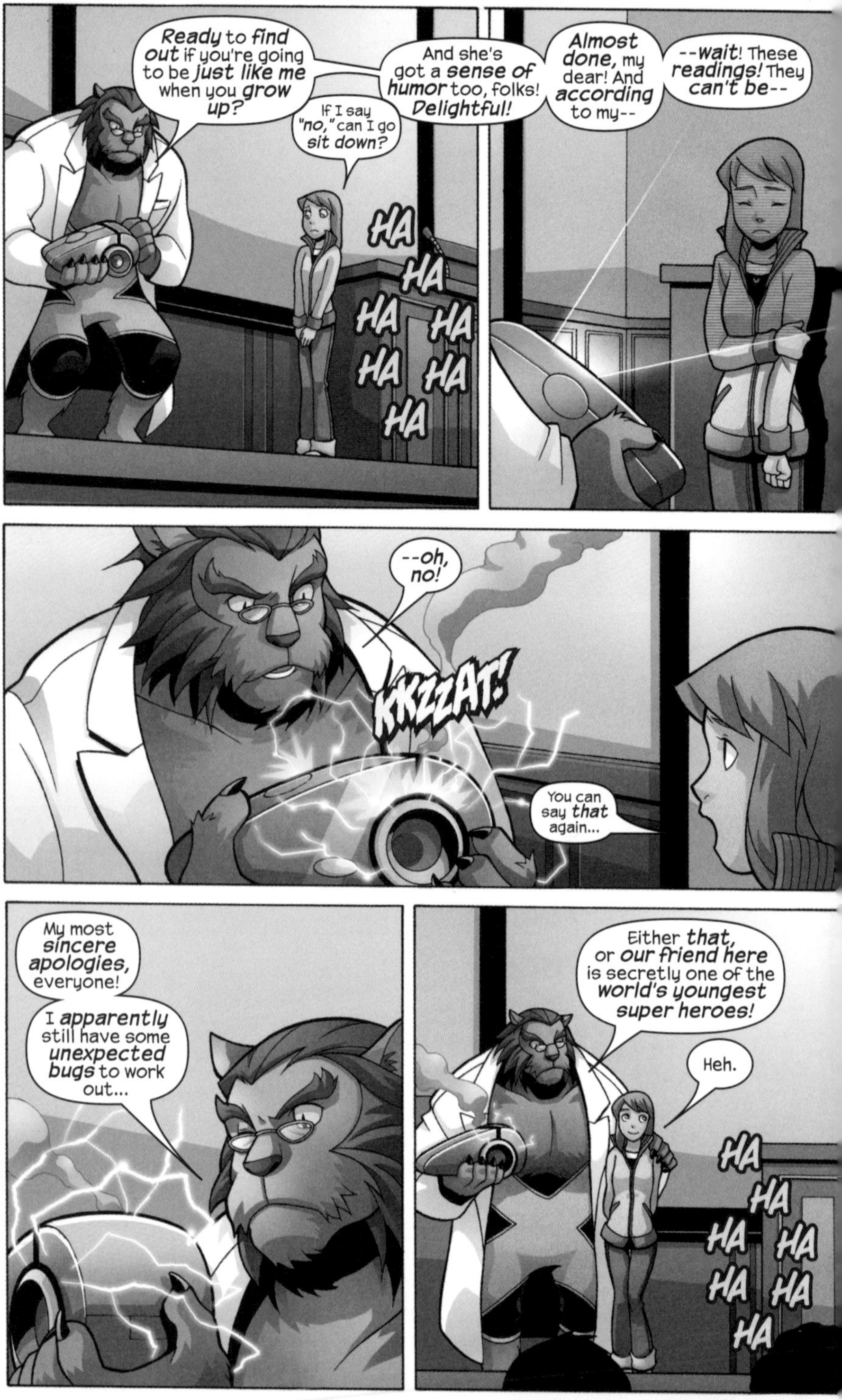
Ready to find out if you're going to be just like me when you grow up?
If I say "no," can I go sit down?
And she's got a sense of humor too, folks! Delightful!
HA HA HA HA HA HA HA
Almost done, my dear! And according to my--
--wait! These readings! They can't be--
--oh, no!
KKZZAT!
You can say that again...
My most sincere apologies, everyone!
I apparently still have some unexpected bugs to work out...
Either that, or our friend here is secretly one of the world's youngest super heroes!
Heh.
HA HA HA HA HA HA HA

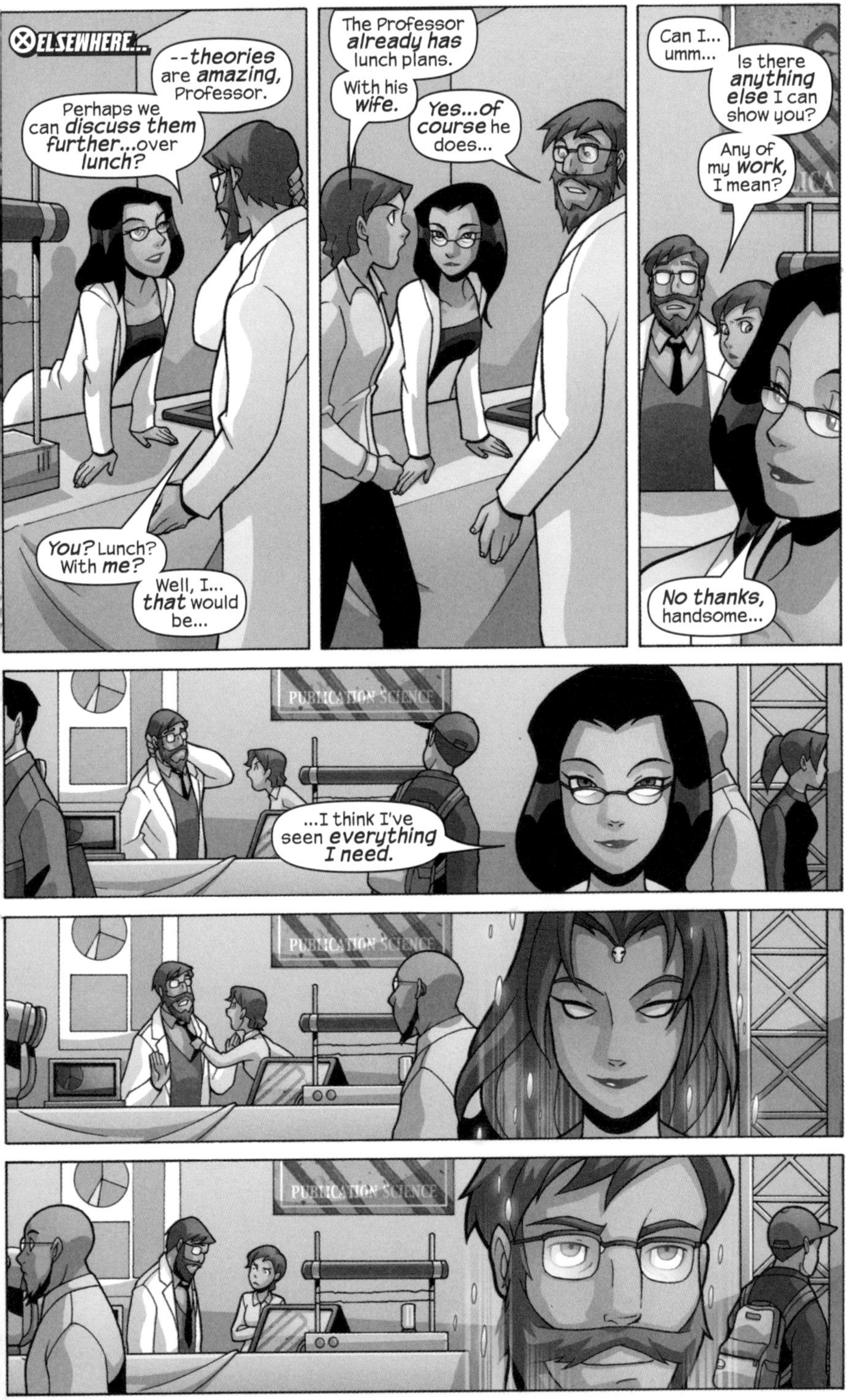
ELSEWHERE...
--theories are amazing, Professor.
Perhaps we can discuss them further...over lunch?
You? Lunch? With me?
Well, I... that would be...
The Professor already has lunch plans.
With his wife.
Yes...of course he does...
Can I... umm...
Is there anything else I can show you?
Any of my work, I mean?
No thanks, handsome...
PUBLICATION SCIENCE
...I think I've seen everything I need.
PUBLICATION SCIENCE
PUBLICATION SCIENCE

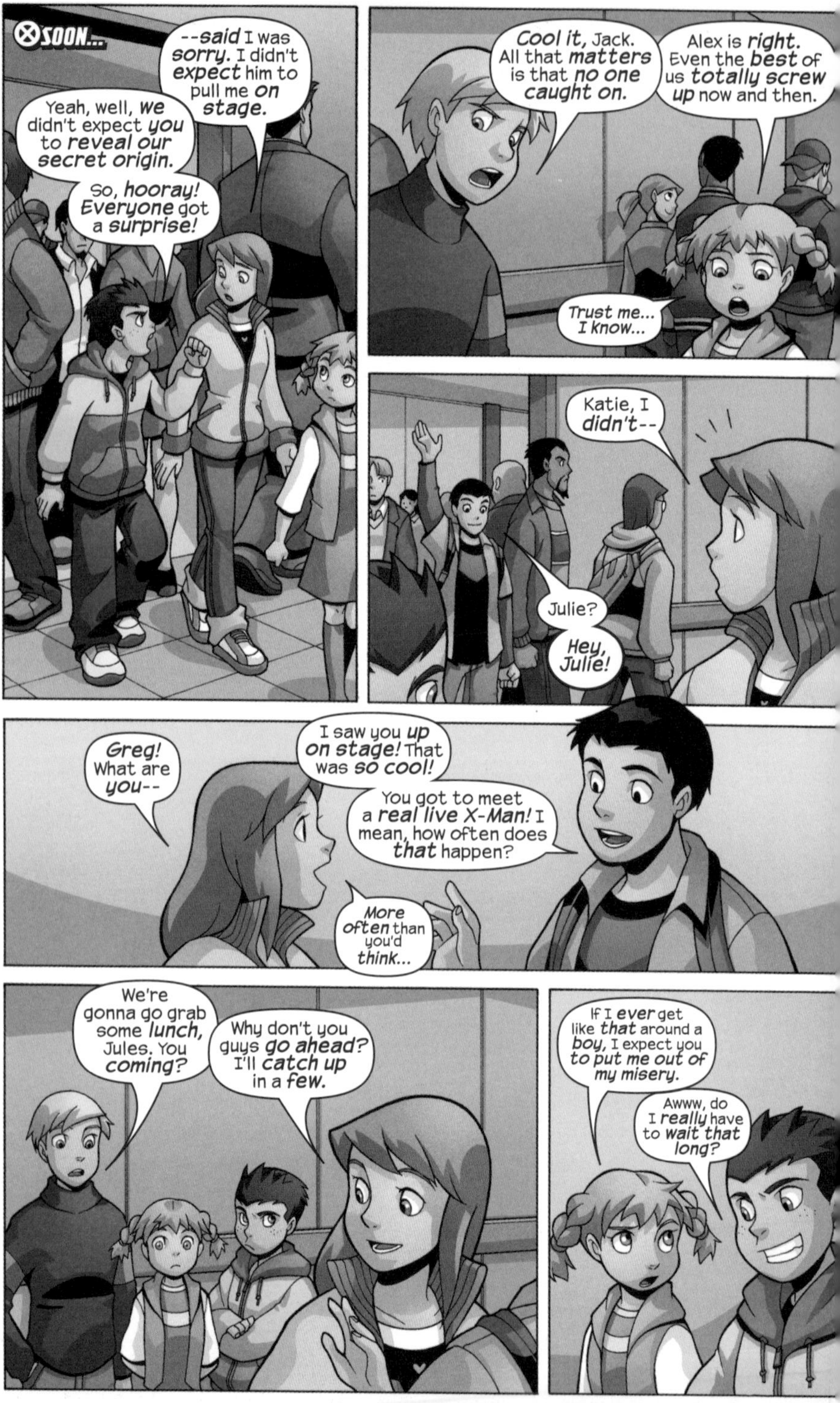
SOON...
--said I was sorry. I didn't expect him to pull me on stage.
Yeah, well, we didn't expect you to reveal our secret origin.
So, hooray! Everyone got a surprise!
Cool it, Jack. All that matters is that no one caught on.
Alex is right. Even the best of us totally screw up now and then.
Trust me... I know...
Katie, I didn't--
Julie?
Hey, Julie!
Greg! What are you--
I saw you up on stage! That was so cool!
You got to meet a real live X-Man! I mean, how often does that happen?
More often than you'd think...
We're gonna go grab some lunch, Jules. You coming?
Why don't you guys go ahead? I'll catch up in a few.
If I ever get like that around a boy, I expect you to put me out of my misery.
Awww, do I really have to wait that long?

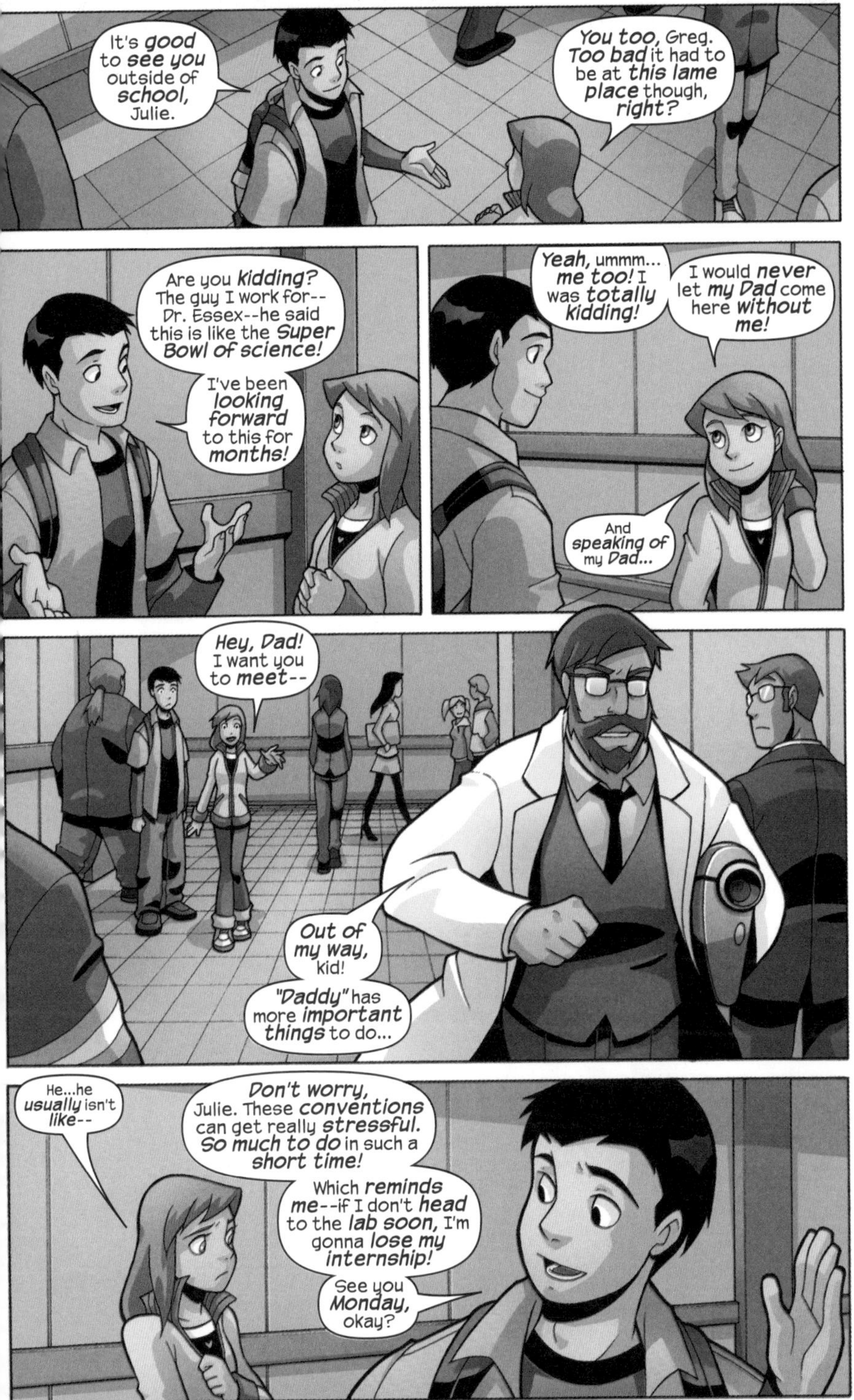
It's good to see you outside of school, Julie.
You too, Greg. Too bad it had to be at this lame place though, right?
Are you kidding? The guy I work for--Dr. Essex--he said this is like the Super Bowl of science!
I've been looking forward to this for months!
Yeah, ummm... me too! I was totally kidding!
I would never let my Dad come here without me!
And speaking of my Dad...
Hey, Dad! I want you to meet--
Out of my way, kid!
"Daddy" has more important things to do...
He...he usually isn't like--
Don't worry, Julie. These conventions can get really stressful. So much to do in such a short time!
Which reminds me--if I don't head to the lab soon, I'm gonna lose my internship!
See you Monday, okay?

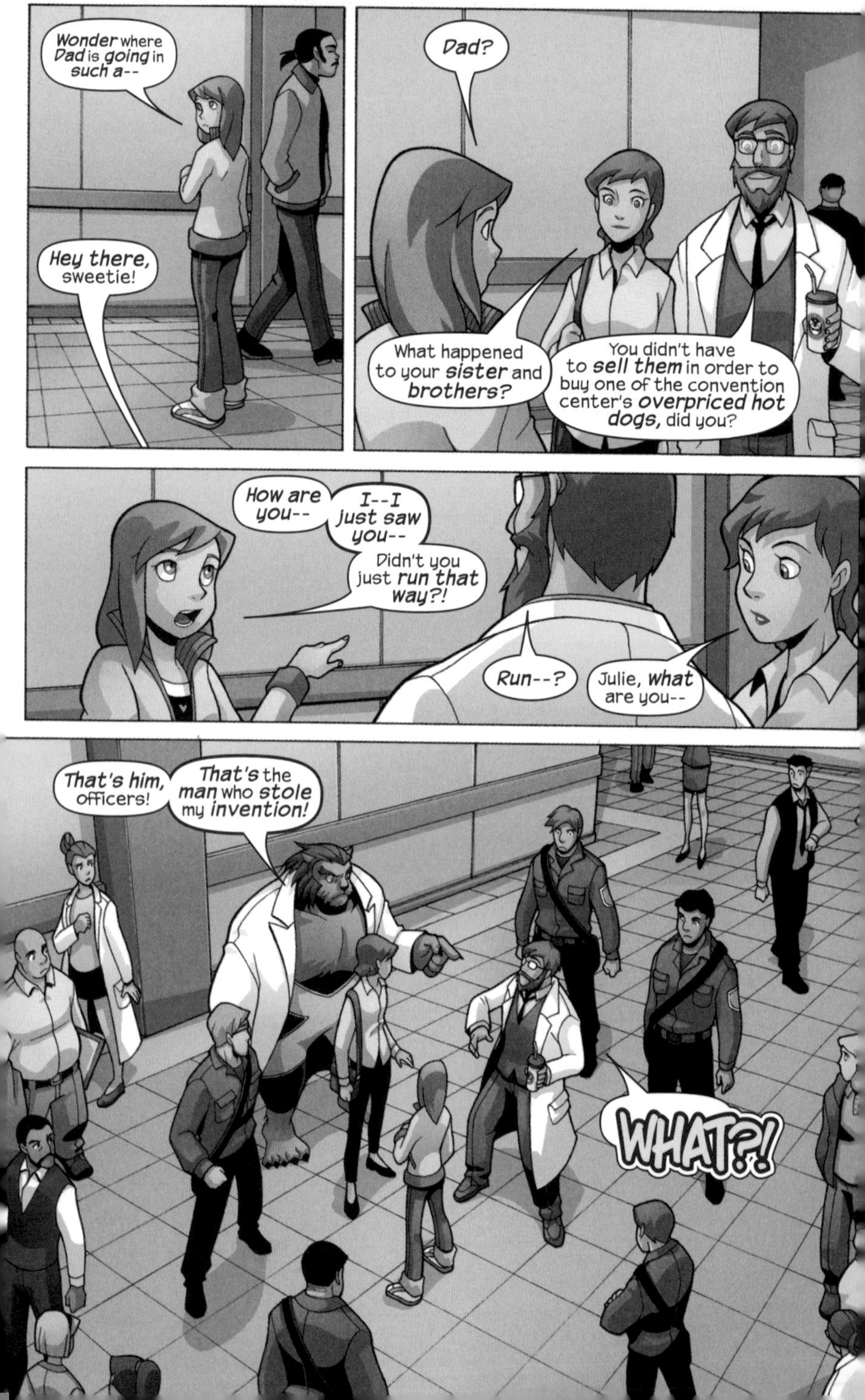

Wonder where Dad is going in such a--
Hey there, sweetie!
Dad?
What happened to your sister and brothers?
You didn't have to sell them in order to buy one of the convention center's overpriced hot dogs, did you?
How are you--
I--I just saw you--
Didn't you just run that way?!
Run--?
Julie, what are you--
That's him, officers!
That's the man who stole my invention!
WHAT?!

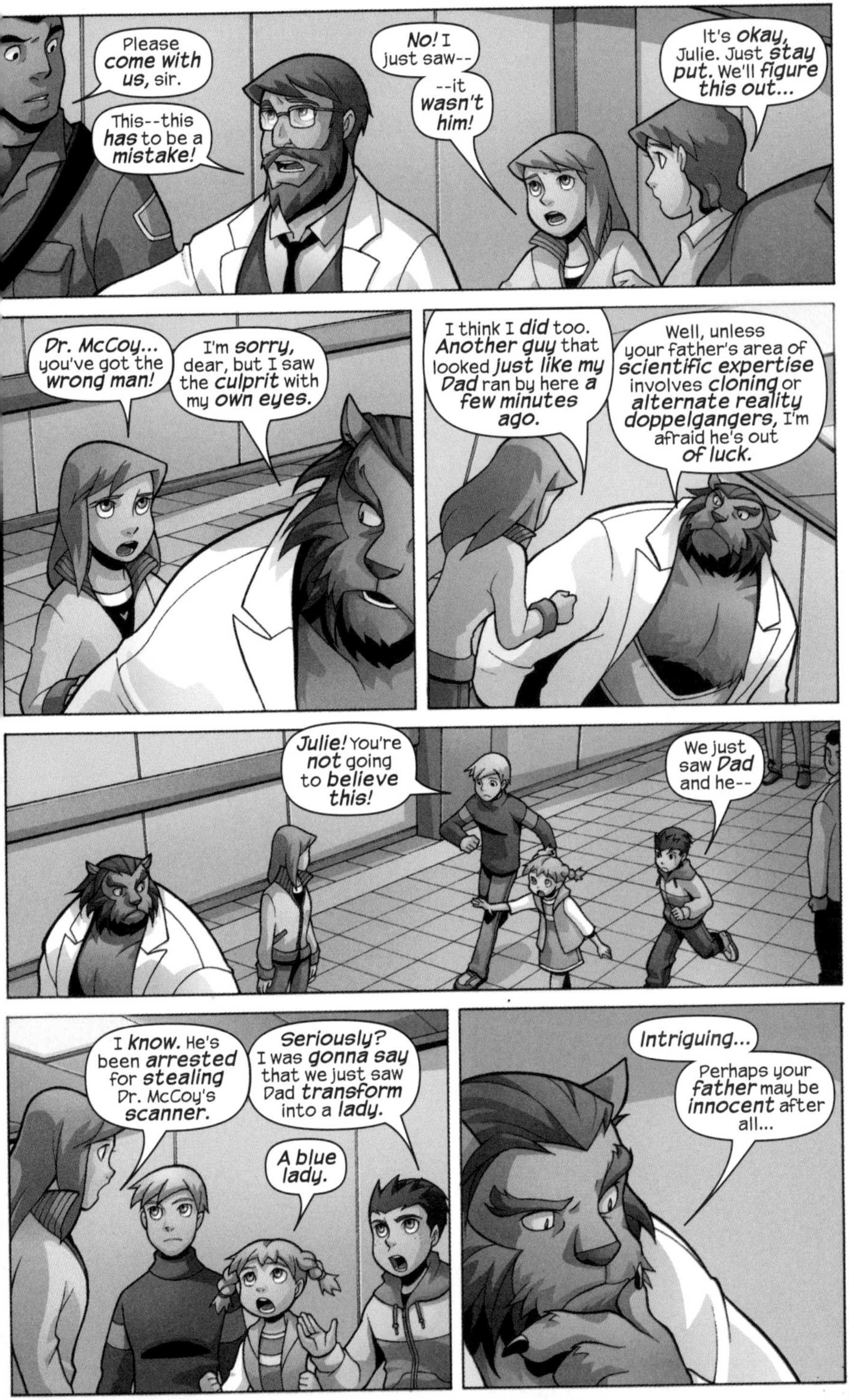

Please come with us, sir.
This--this has to be a mistake!
No! I just saw--
--it wasn't him!
It's okay, Julie. Just stay put. We'll figure this out...
Dr. McCoy... you've got the wrong man!
I'm sorry, dear, but I saw the culprit with my own eyes.
I think I did too. Another guy that looked just like my Dad ran by here a few minutes ago.
Well, unless your father's area of scientific expertise involves cloning or alternate reality doppelgangers, I'm afraid he's out of luck.
Julie! You're not going to believe this!
We just saw Dad and he--
I know. He's been arrested for stealing Dr. McCoy's scanner.
Seriously? I was gonna say that we just saw Dad transform into a lady.
A blue lady.
Intriguing...
Perhaps your father may be innocent after all...

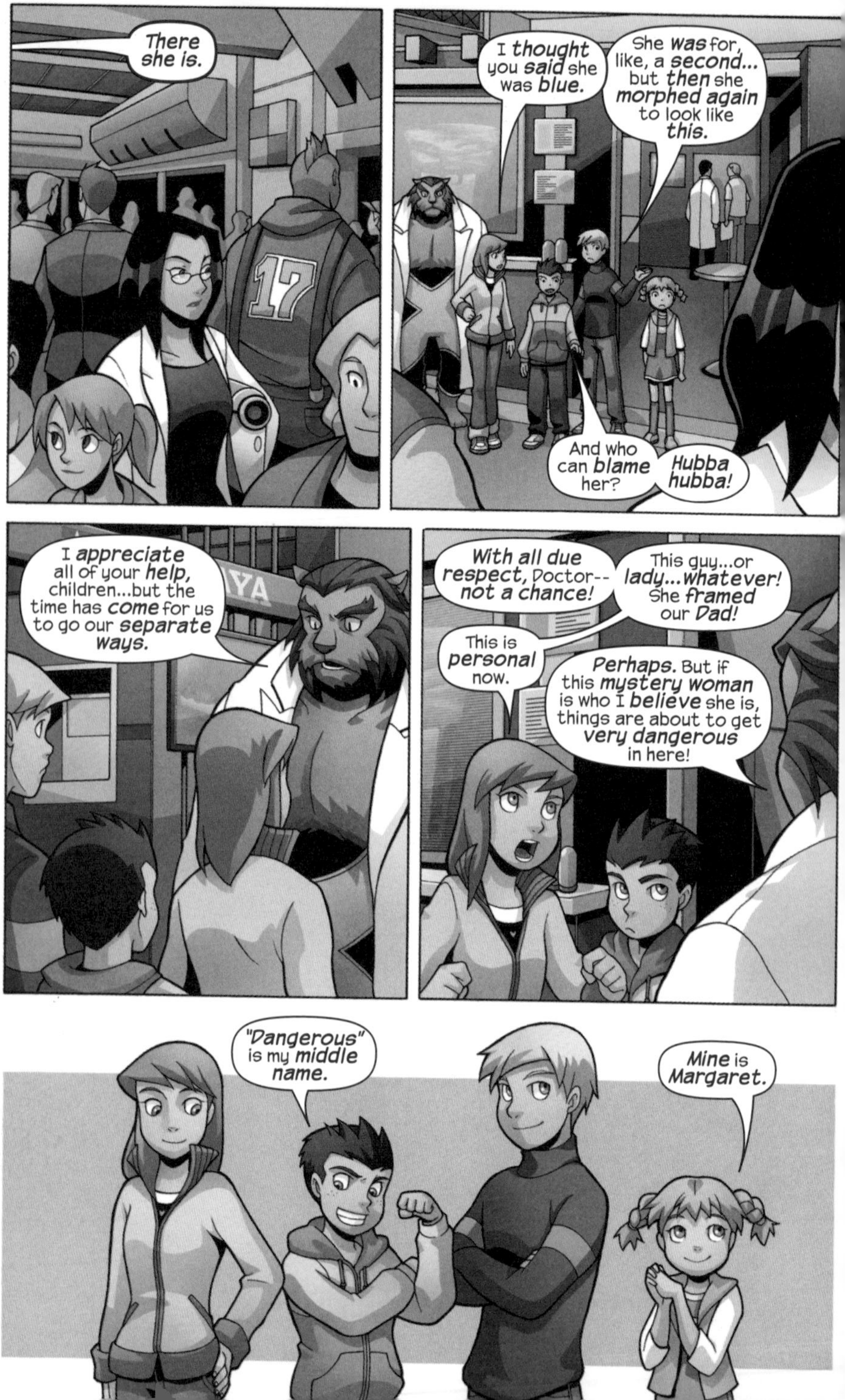
There she is.
I thought you said she was blue.
She was for, like, a second... but then she morphed again to look like this.
And who can blame her?
Hubba hubba!
I appreciate all of your help, children...but the time has come for us to go our separate ways.
With all due respect, Doctor-- not a chance!
This guy...or lady...whatever! She framed our Dad!
This is personal now.
Perhaps. But if this mystery woman is who I believe she is, things are about to get very dangerous in here!
"Dangerous" is my middle name.
Mine is Margaret.

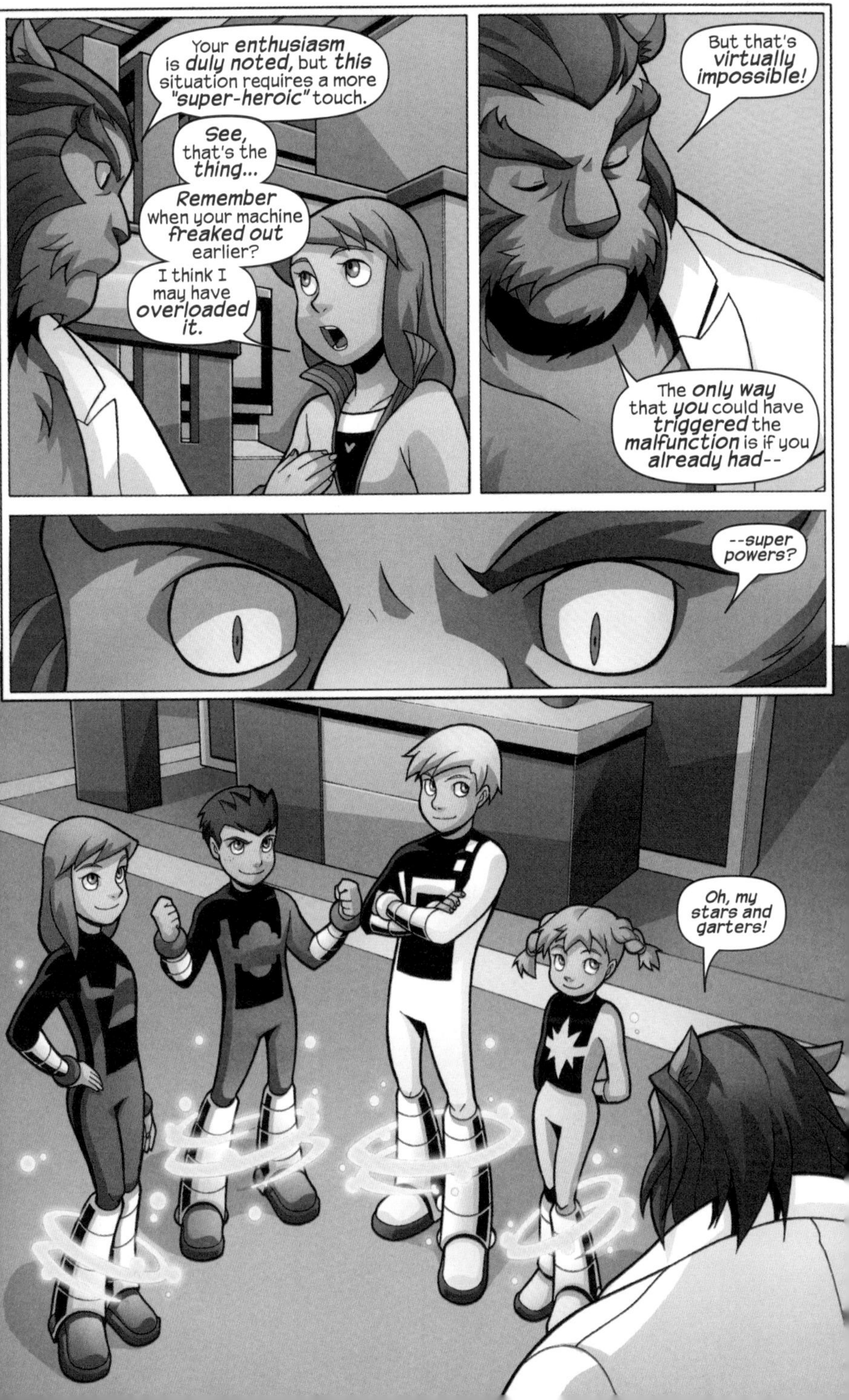

Your enthusiasm is duly noted, but this situation requires a more "super-heroic" touch.
See, that's the thing...
Remember when your machine freaked out earlier?
I think I may have overloaded it.
But that's virtually impossible!
The only way that you could have triggered the malfunction is if you already had--
--super powers?
Oh, my stars and garters!

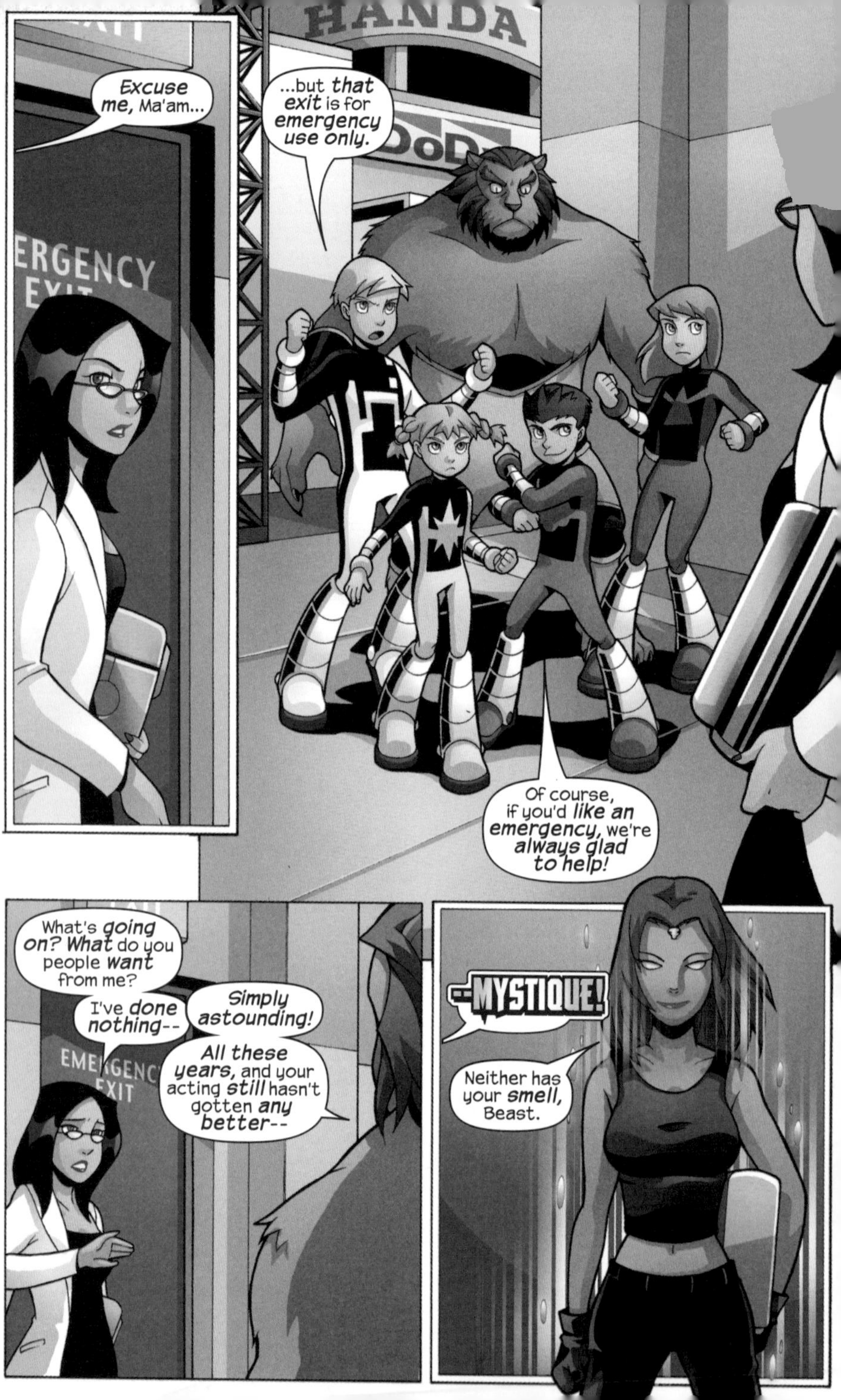
Excuse me, Ma'am...
...but that exit is for emergency use only.
Of course, if you'd like an emergency, we're always glad to help!
What's going on? What do you people want from me?
I've done nothing--
Simply astounding!
All these years, and your acting still hasn't gotten any better--
--MYSTIQUE!
Neither has your smell, Beast.

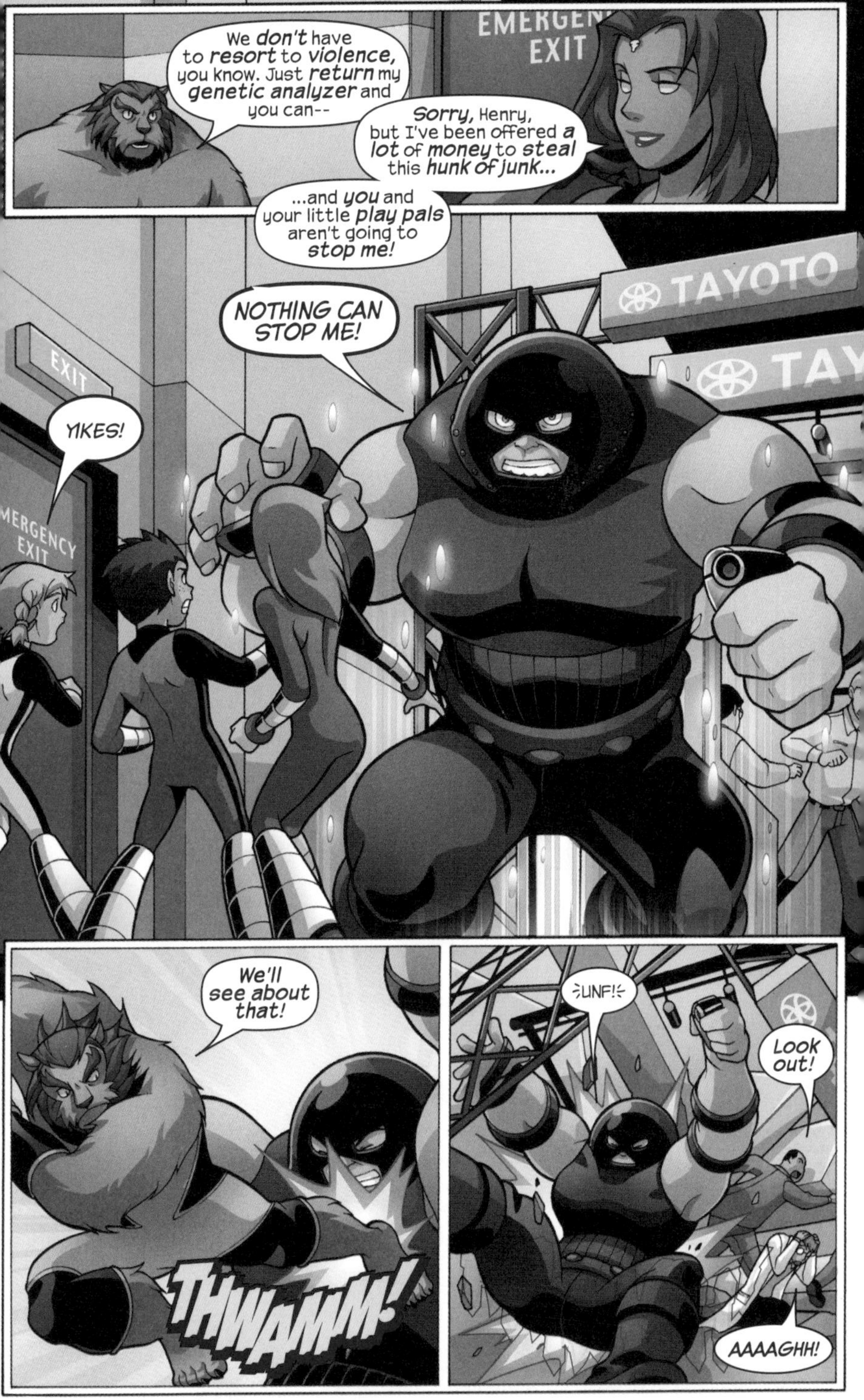
We don't have to resort to violence, you know. Just return my genetic analyzer and you can--
Sorry, Henry, but I've been offered a lot of money to steal this hunk of junk...
...and you and your little play pals aren't going to stop me!
EMERGENCY EXIT
TAYOTO
NOTHING CAN STOP ME!
EXIT
YIKES!
EMERGENCY EXIT
We'll see about that!
THWAMM!
UNF!
Look out!
AAAAGHH!

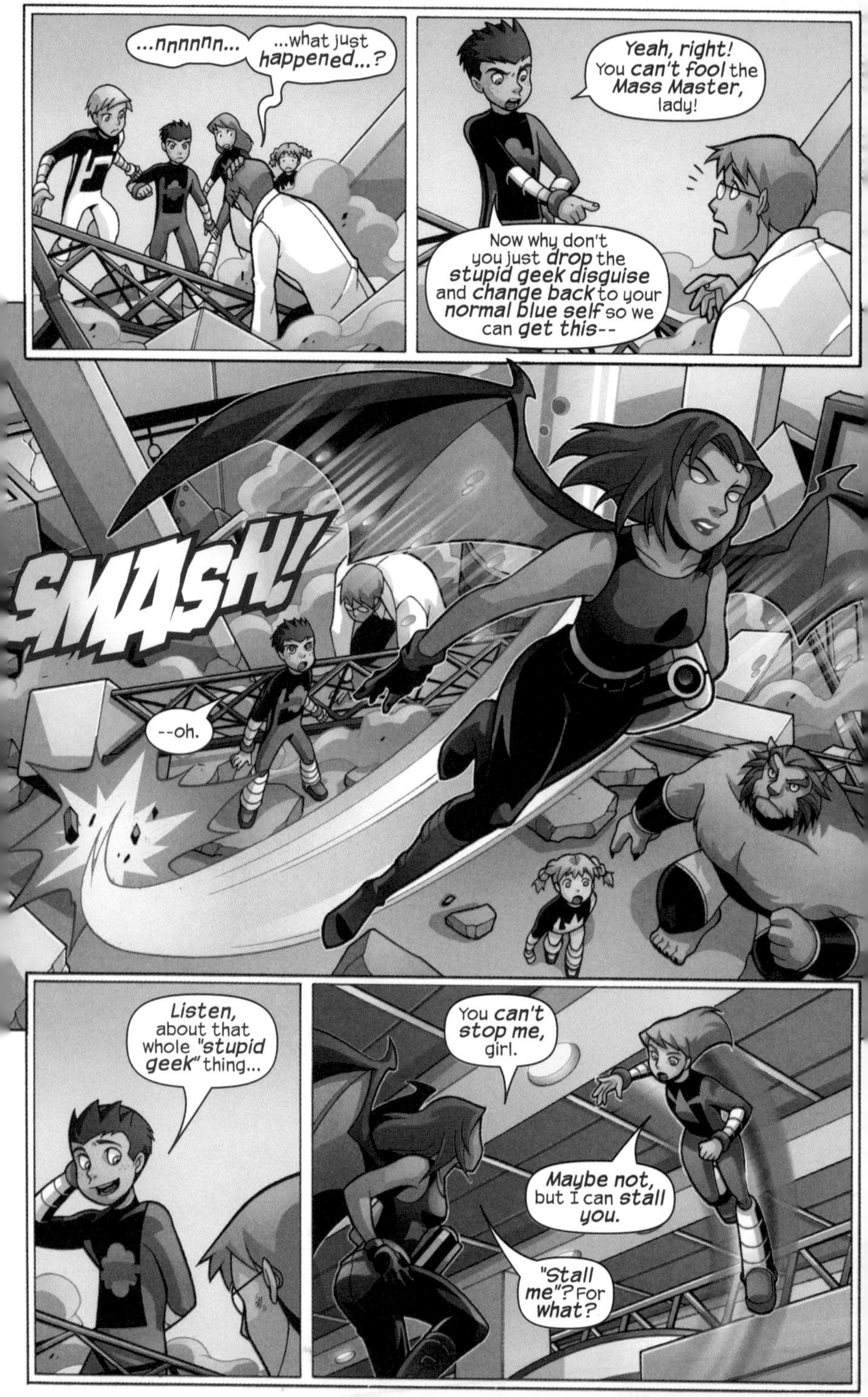
...nnnnnn...
...what just happened...?
Yeah, right! You can't fool the Mass Master, lady!
Now why don't you just drop the stupid geek disguise and change back to your normal blue self so we can get this--
SMASH!
--oh.
Listen, about that whole "stupid geek" thing...
You can't stop me, girl.
Maybe not, but I can stall you.
"Stall me"? For what?

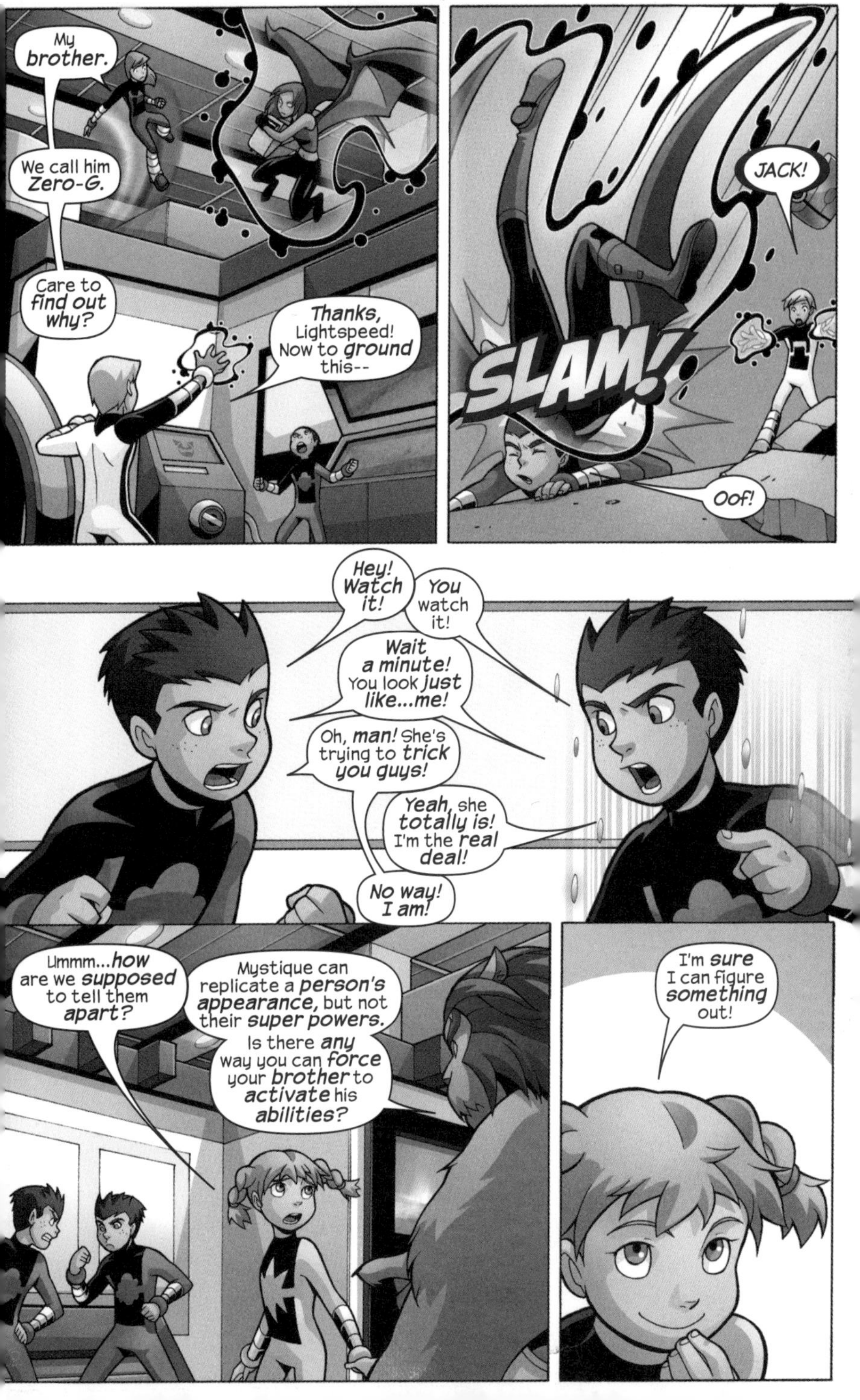
My brother.
We call him Zero-G.
Care to find out why?
Thanks, Lightspeed! Now to ground this--
JACK!
SLAM!
Oof!
Hey! Watch it!
You watch it!
Wait a minute! You look just like...me!
Oh, man! She's trying to trick you guys!
Yeah, she totally is! I'm the real deal!
No way! I am!
Ummm...how are we supposed to tell them apart?
Mystique can replicate a person's appearance, but not their super powers.
Is there any way you can force your brother to activate his abilities?
I'm sure I can figure something out!

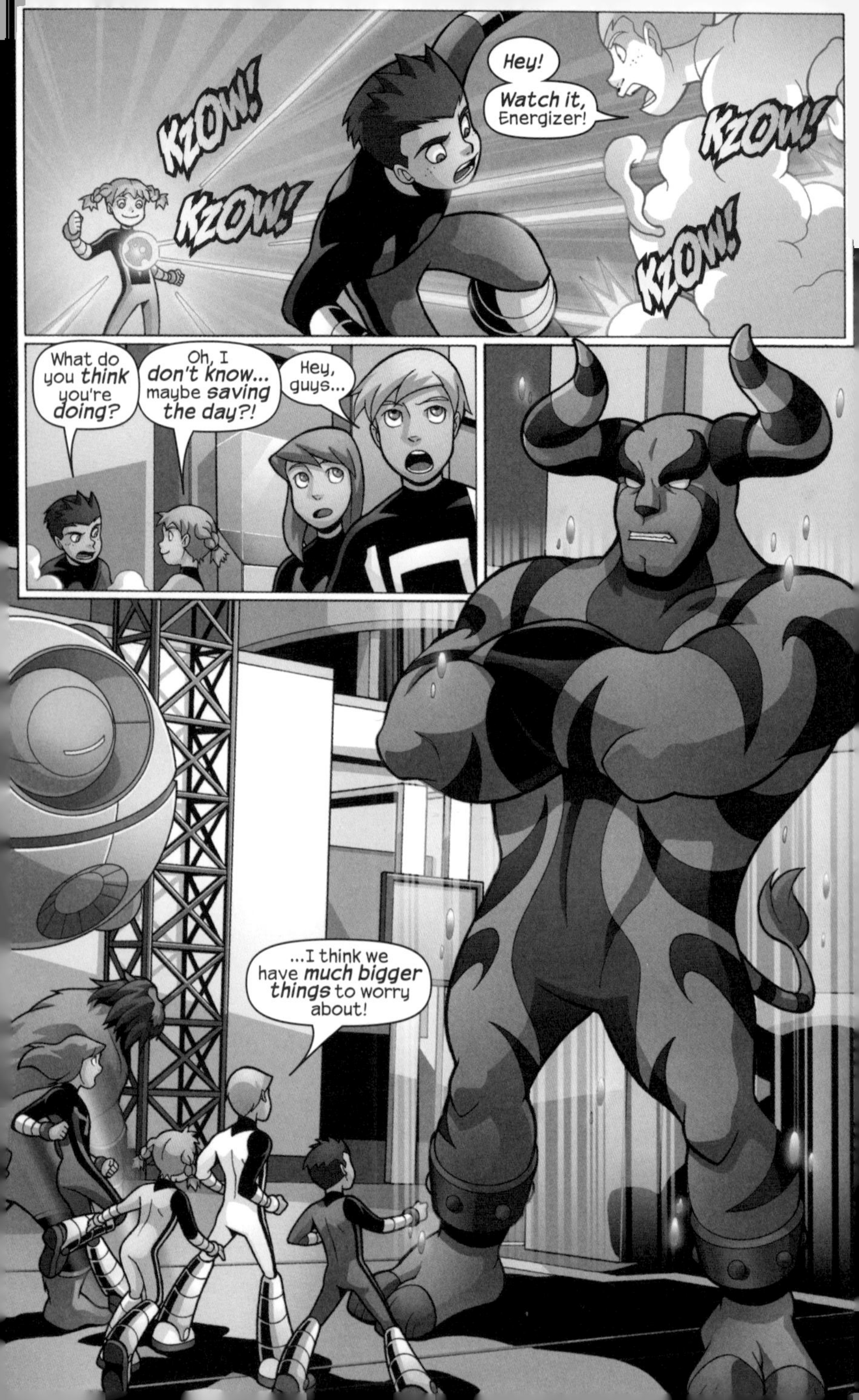
KZOW!
KZOW!
Hey!
Watch it, Energizer!
KZOW!
KZOW!
What do you think you're doing?
Oh, I don't know... maybe saving the day?!
Hey, guys...
...I think we have much bigger things to worry about!

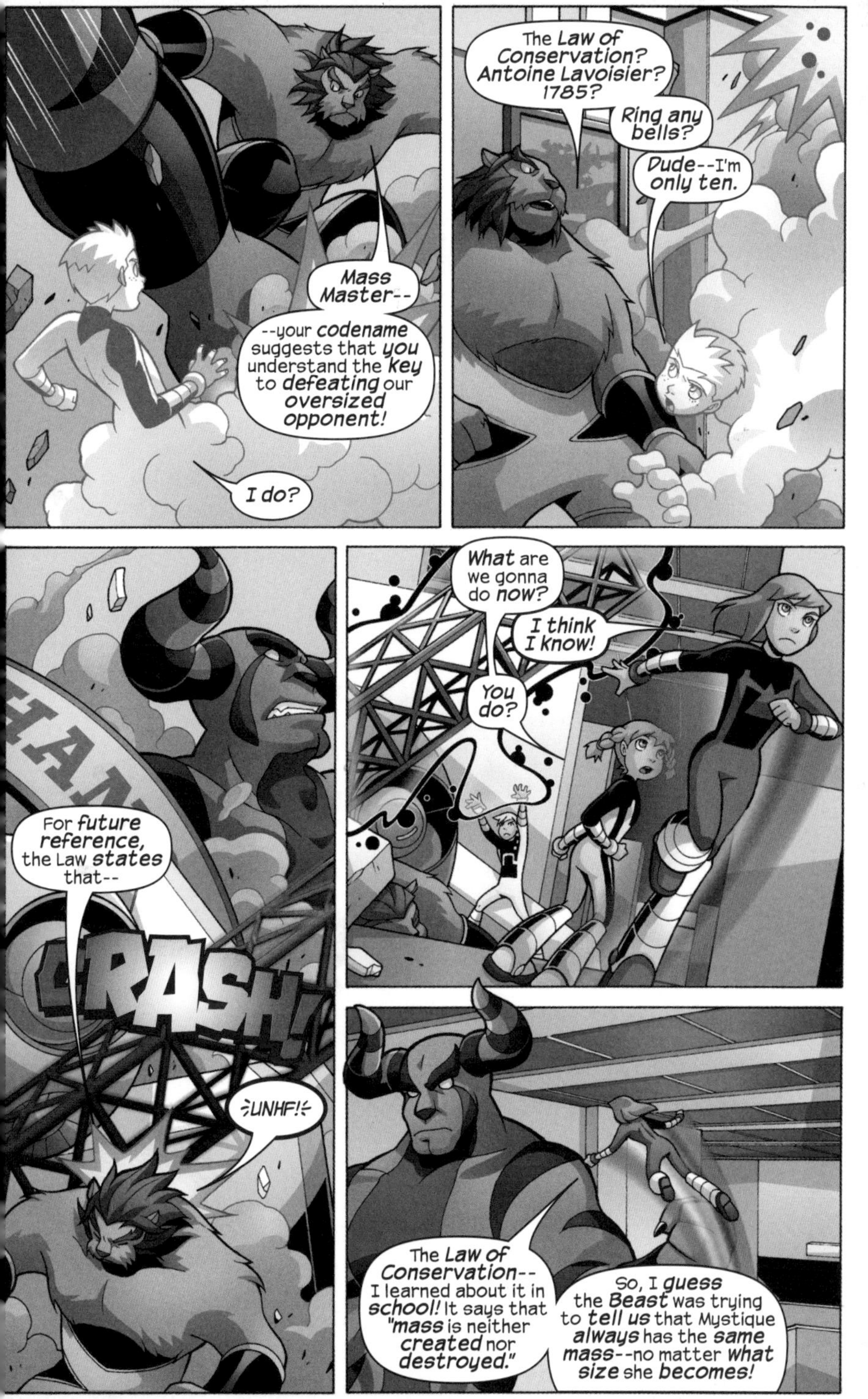

Mass Master--
--your codename suggests that you understand the key to defeating our oversized opponent!
I do?
The Law of Conservation? Antoine Lavoisier? 1785?
Ring any bells?
Dude--I'm only ten.
For future reference, the Law states that--
CRASH!
UNHF!
What are we gonna do now?
I think I know!
You do?
The Law of Conservation-- I learned about it in school! It says that "mass is neither created nor destroyed."
So, I guess the Beast was trying to tell us that Mystique always has the same mass--no matter what size she becomes!

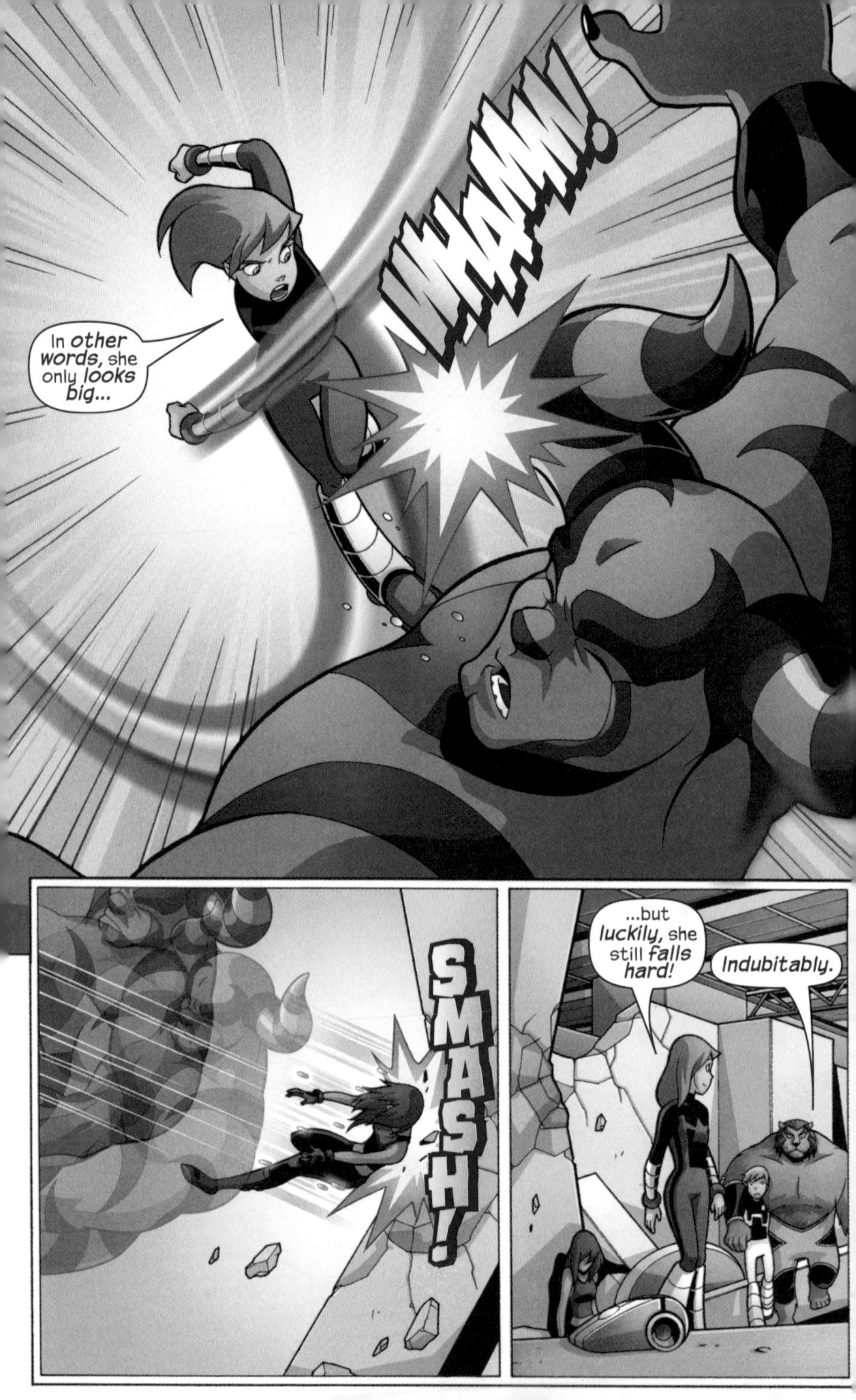

WHAMM!
In other words, she only looks big...
SMASH!
...but luckily, she still falls hard!
Indubitably.

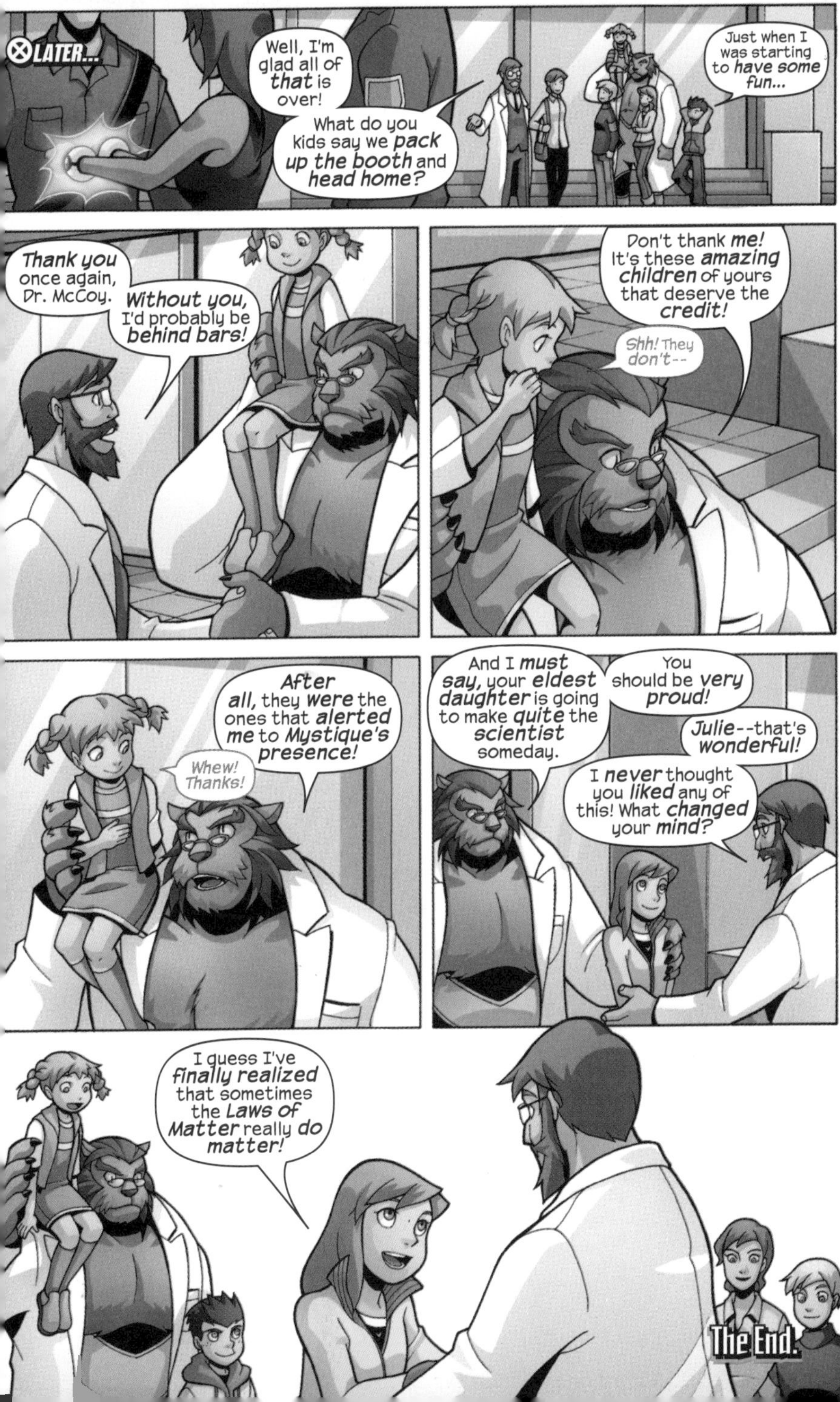
LATER...
Well, I'm glad all of that is over!
What do you kids say we pack up the booth and head home?
Just when I was starting to have some fun...
Thank you once again, Dr. McCoy.
Without you, I'd probably be behind bars!
Don't thank me! It's these amazing children of yours that deserve the credit!
Shh! They don't--
After all, they were the ones that alerted me to Mystique's presence!
Whew! Thanks!
And I must say, your eldest daughter is going to make quite the scientist someday.
You should be very proud!
Julie--that's wonderful!
I never thought you liked any of this! What changed your mind?
I guess I've finally realized that sometimes the Laws of Matter really do matter!
The End.

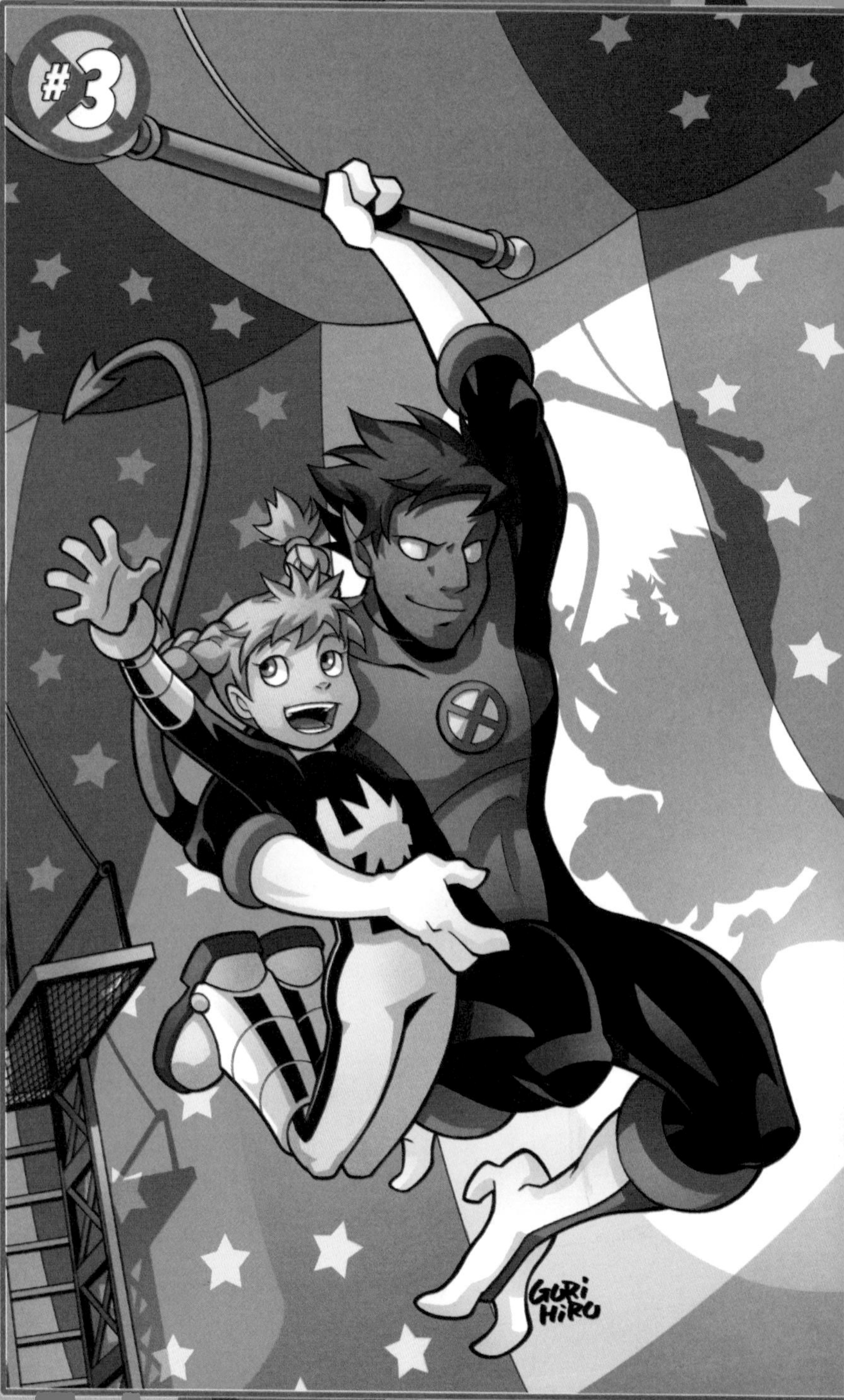
#3
GURIHIRU

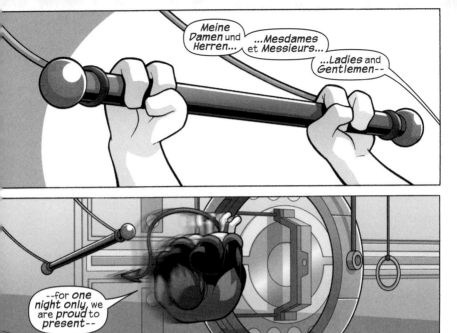

Meine Damen und Herren...

...Mesdames et Messieurs...

...Ladies and Gentlemen--

--for one night only, we are proud to present--

--the sensational--

--the inspirational--

--the teleportational--

BAMF!

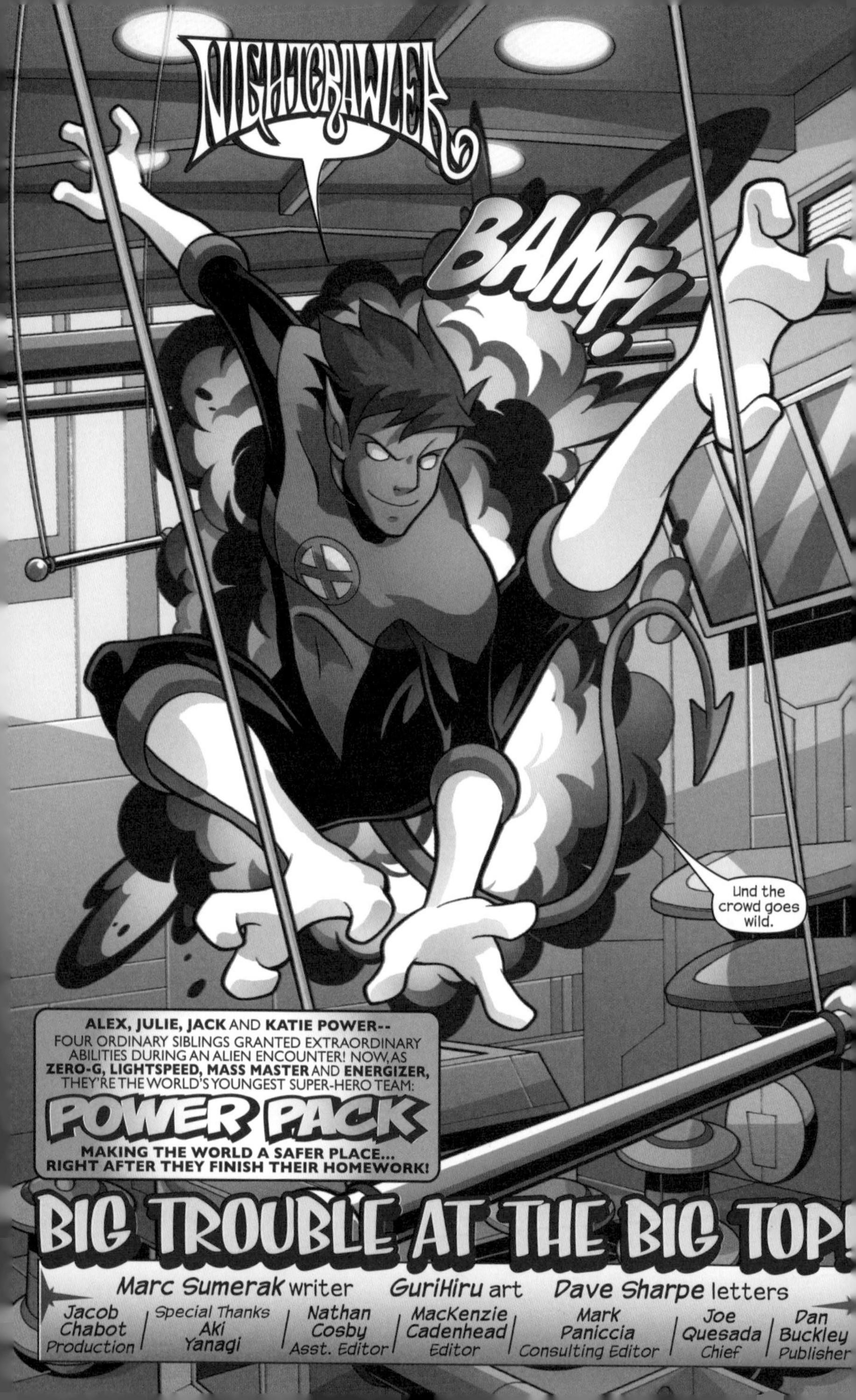
NIGHTCRAWLER
BAMF!
Und the crowd goes wild.
ALEX, JULIE, JACK AND KATIE POWER-- FOUR ORDINARY SIBLINGS GRANTED EXTRAORDINARY ABILITIES DURING AN ALIEN ENCOUNTER! NOW, AS ZERO-G, LIGHTSPEED, MASS MASTER AND ENERGIZER, THEY'RE THE WORLD'S YOUNGEST SUPER-HERO TEAM:
POWER PACK
MAKING THE WORLD A SAFER PLACE... RIGHT AFTER THEY FINISH THEIR HOMEWORK!
BIG TROUBLE AT THE BIG TOP!
Marc Sumerak writer GuriHiru art Dave Sharpe letters
Jacob Chabot Production | Special Thanks Aki Yanagi | Nathan Cosby Asst. Editor | MacKenzie Cadenhead Editor | Mark Paniccia Consulting Editor | Joe Quesada Chief | Dan Buckley Publisher

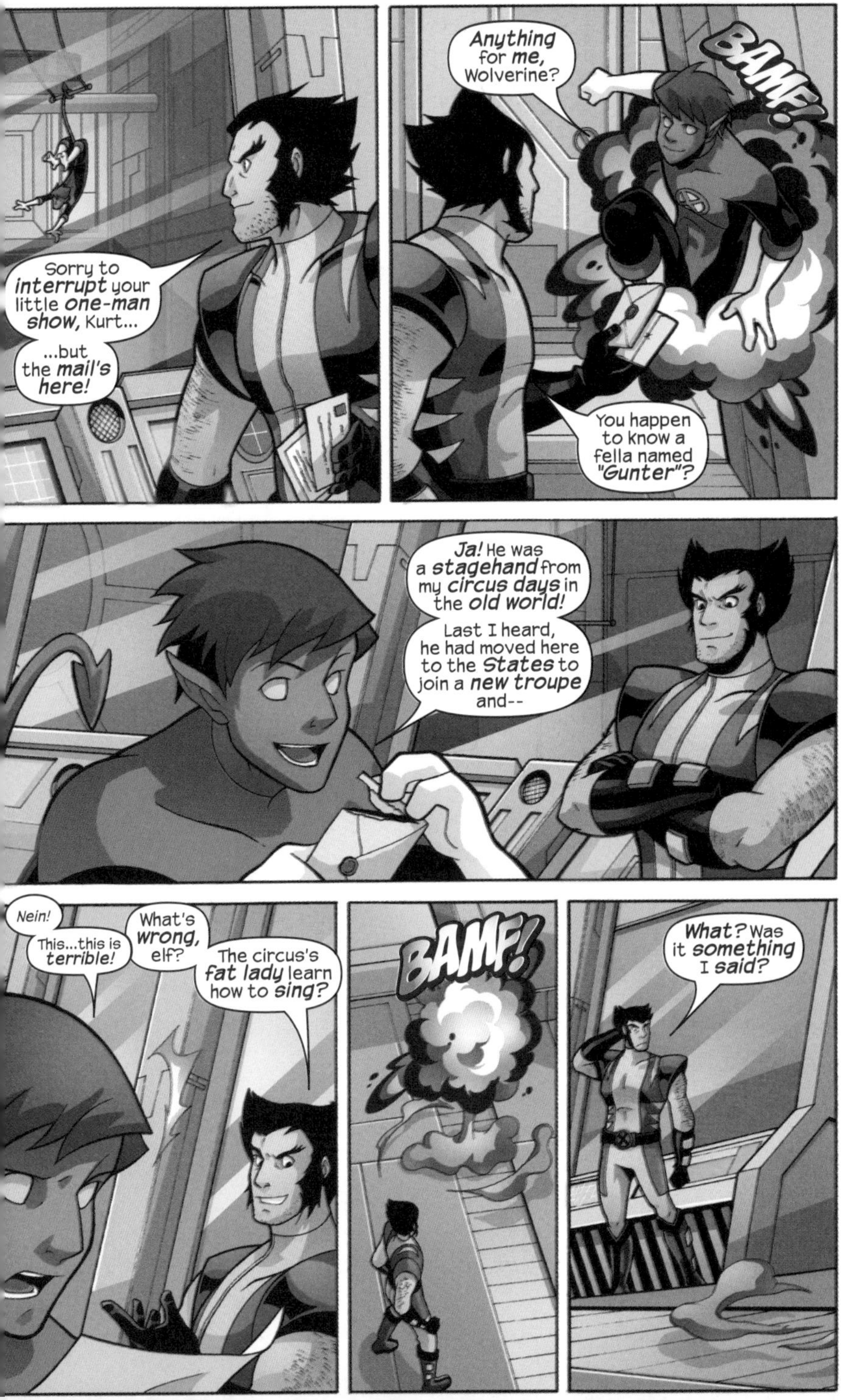
Sorry to interrupt your little one-man show, Kurt...
...but the mail's here!
BAMF!
Anything for me, Wolverine?
You happen to know a fella named "Gunter"?
Ja! He was a stagehand from my circus days in the old world!
Last I heard, he had moved here to the States to join a new troupe and--
Nein!
This...this is terrible!
What's wrong, elf?
The circus's fat lady learn how to sing?
BAMF!
What? Was it something I said?

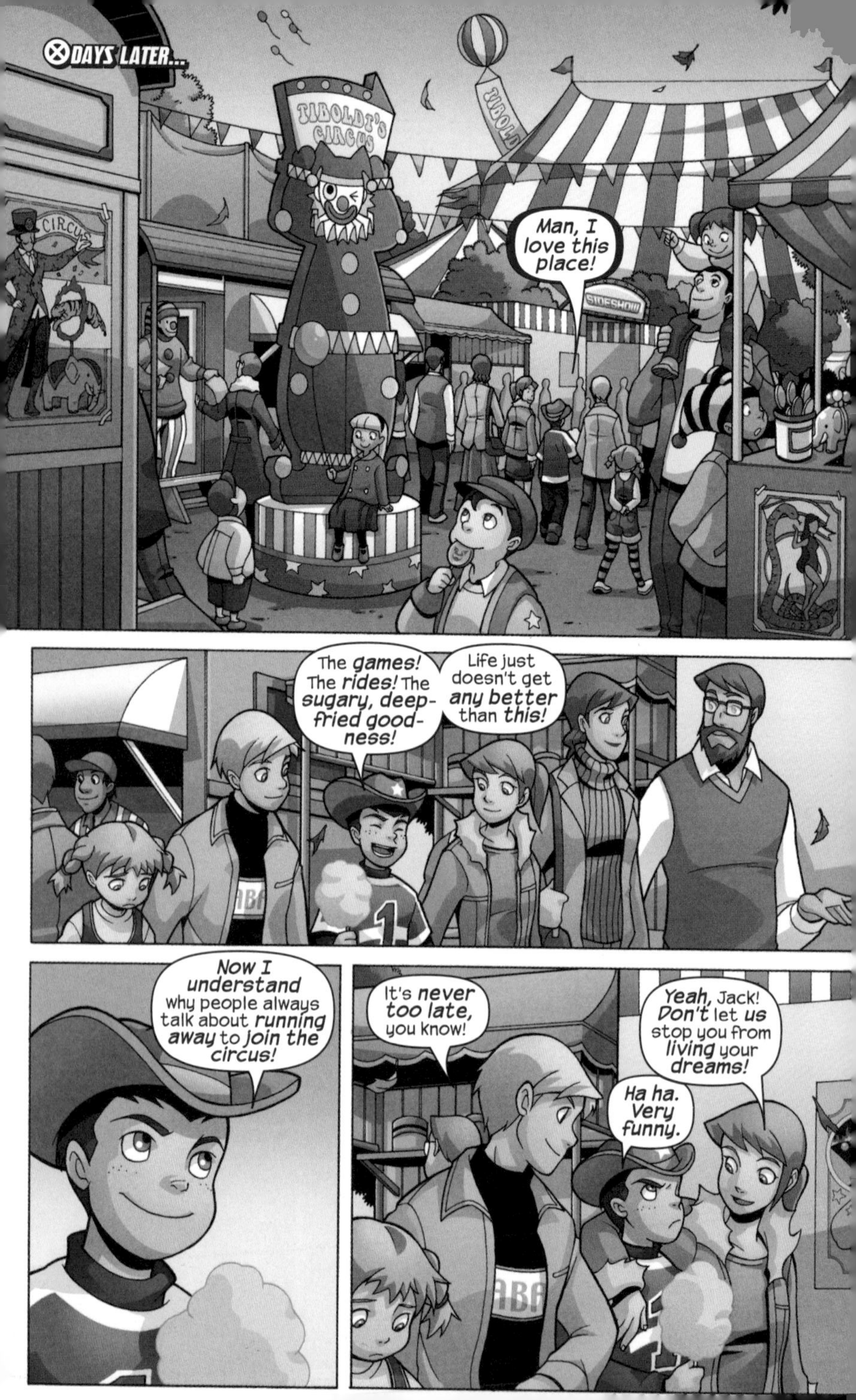
DAYS LATER...
TIBOLDI'S CIRCUS
CIRCUS
SIDESHOW
Man, I love this place!
The games! The rides! The sugary, deep-fried good-ness!
Life just doesn't get any better than this!
Now I understand why people always talk about running away to join the circus!
It's never too late, you know!
Yeah, Jack! Don't let us stop you from living your dreams!
Ha ha. Very funny.

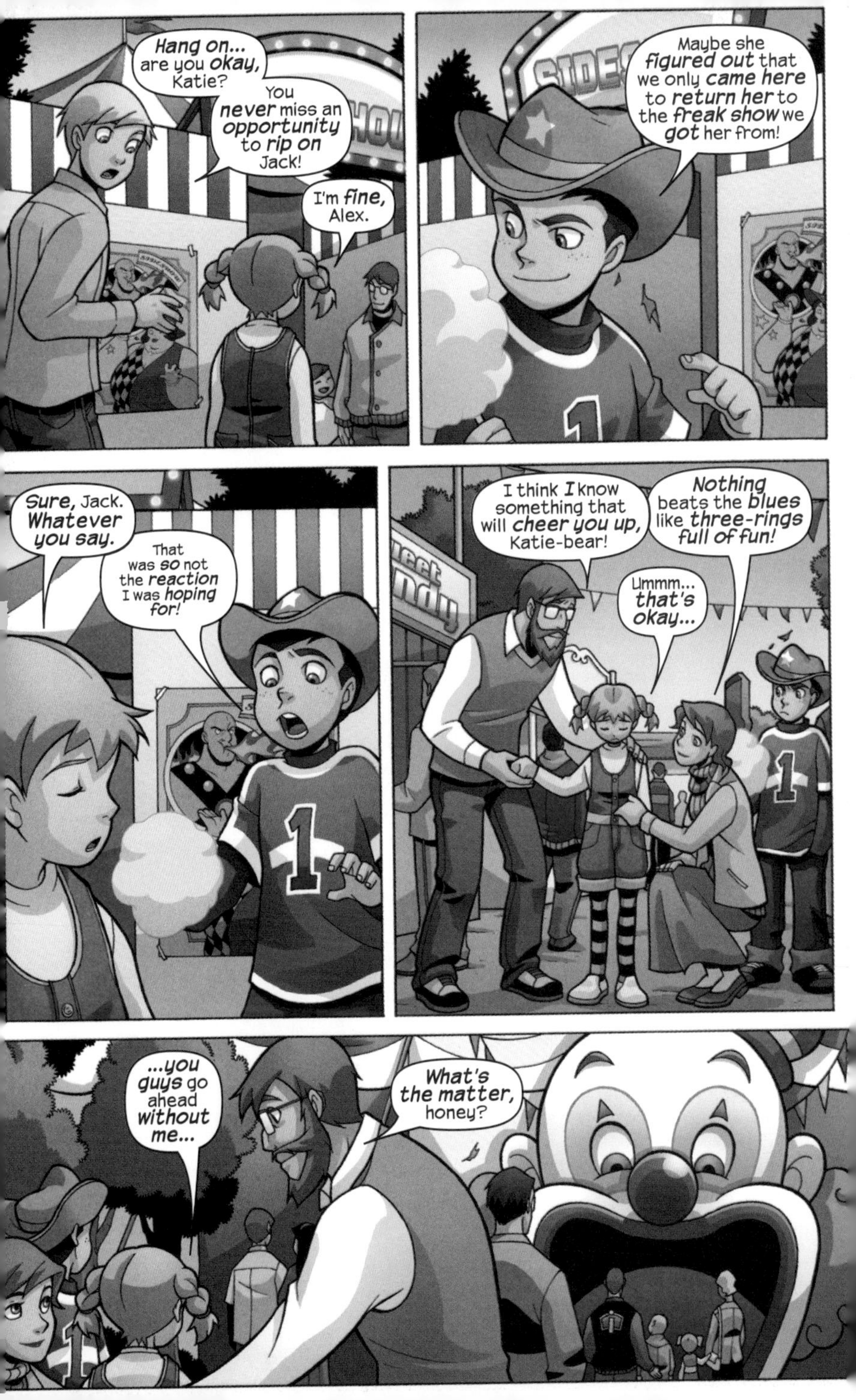
Hang on... are you okay, Katie?
You never miss an opportunity to rip on Jack!
I'm fine, Alex.
Maybe she figured out that we only came here to return her to the freak show we got her from!
Sure, Jack. Whatever you say.
That was so not the reaction I was hoping for!
I think I know something that will cheer you up, Katie-bear!
Nothing beats the blues like three-rings full of fun!
Ummm... that's okay...
...you guys go ahead without me...
What's the matter, honey?

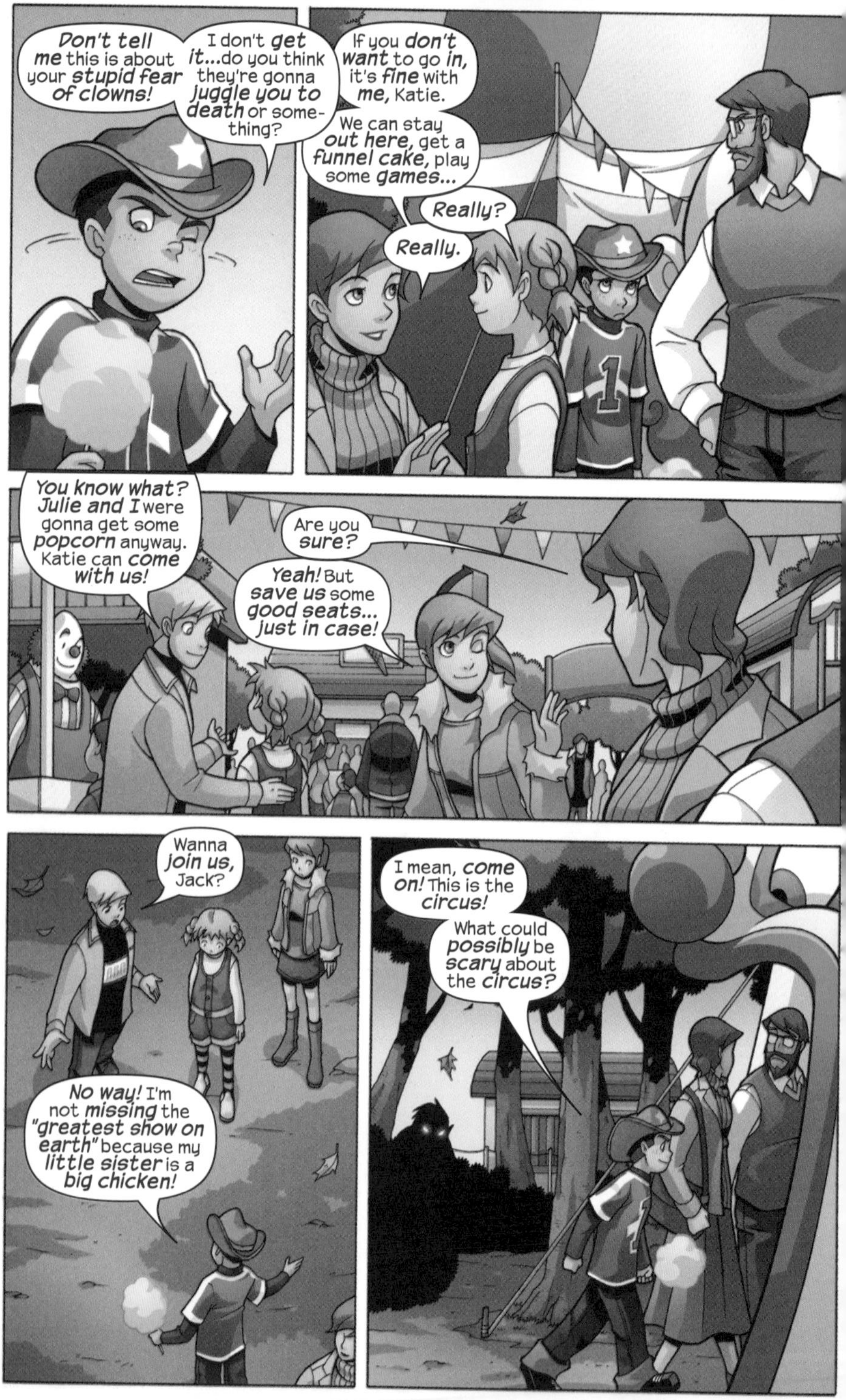
Don't tell me this is about your stupid fear of clowns!
I don't get it...do you think they're gonna juggle you to death or something?
If you don't want to go in, it's fine with me, Katie.
We can stay out here, get a funnel cake, play some games...
Really?
Really.
You know what? Julie and I were gonna get some popcorn anyway. Katie can come with us!
Are you sure?
Yeah! But save us some good seats... just in case!
Wanna join us, Jack?
No way! I'm not missing the "greatest show on earth" because my little sister is a big chicken!
I mean, come on! This is the circus!
What could possibly be scary about the circus?

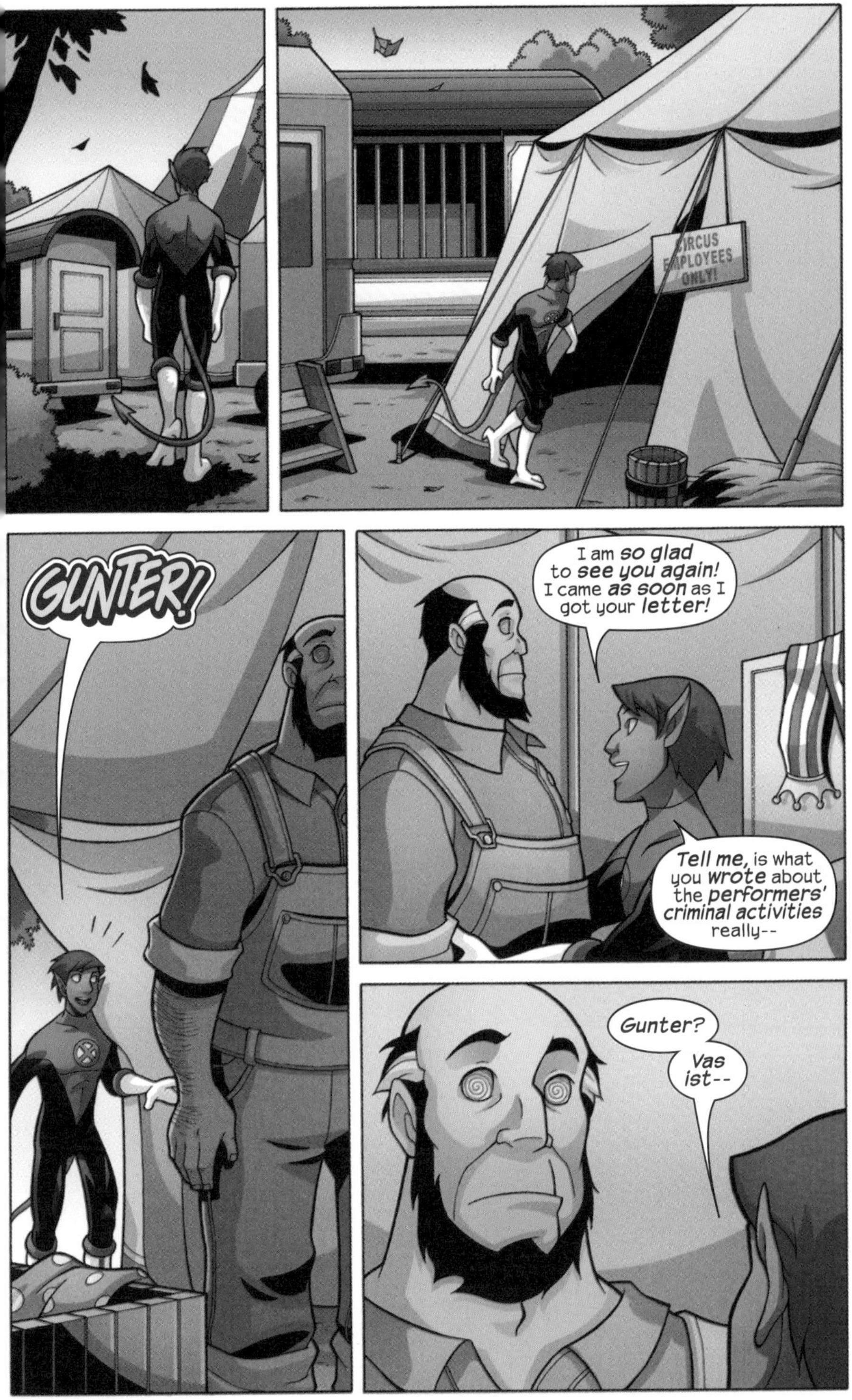
CIRCUS EMPLOYEES ONLY!
GUNTER!
I am so glad to see you again! I came as soon as I got your letter!
Tell me, is what you wrote about the performers' criminal activities really--
Gunter?
Vas ist--

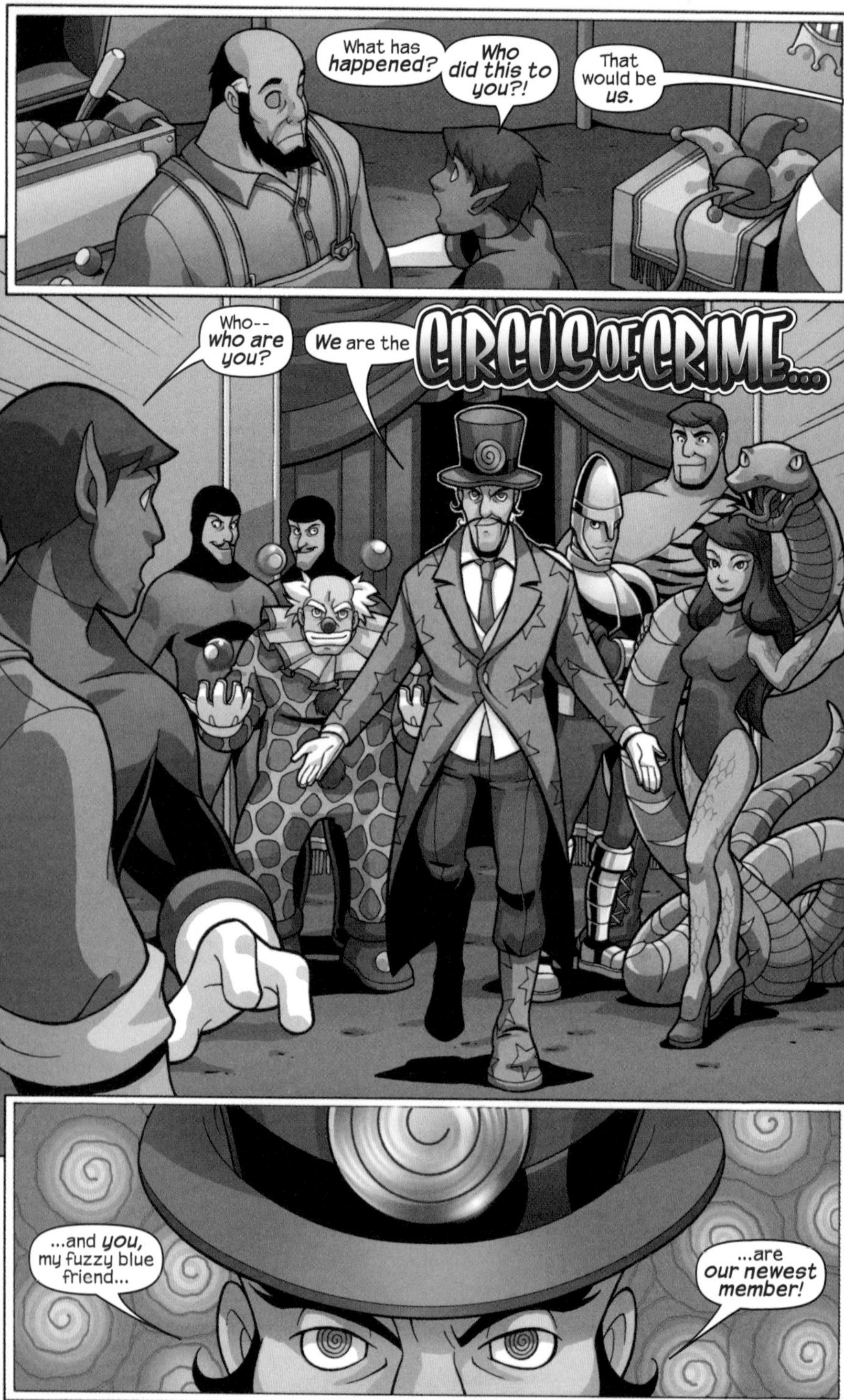
What has happened?
Who did this to you?!
That would be us.
Who-- who are you?
We are the
CIRCUS OF CRIME...
...and you, my fuzzy blue friend...
...are our newest member!

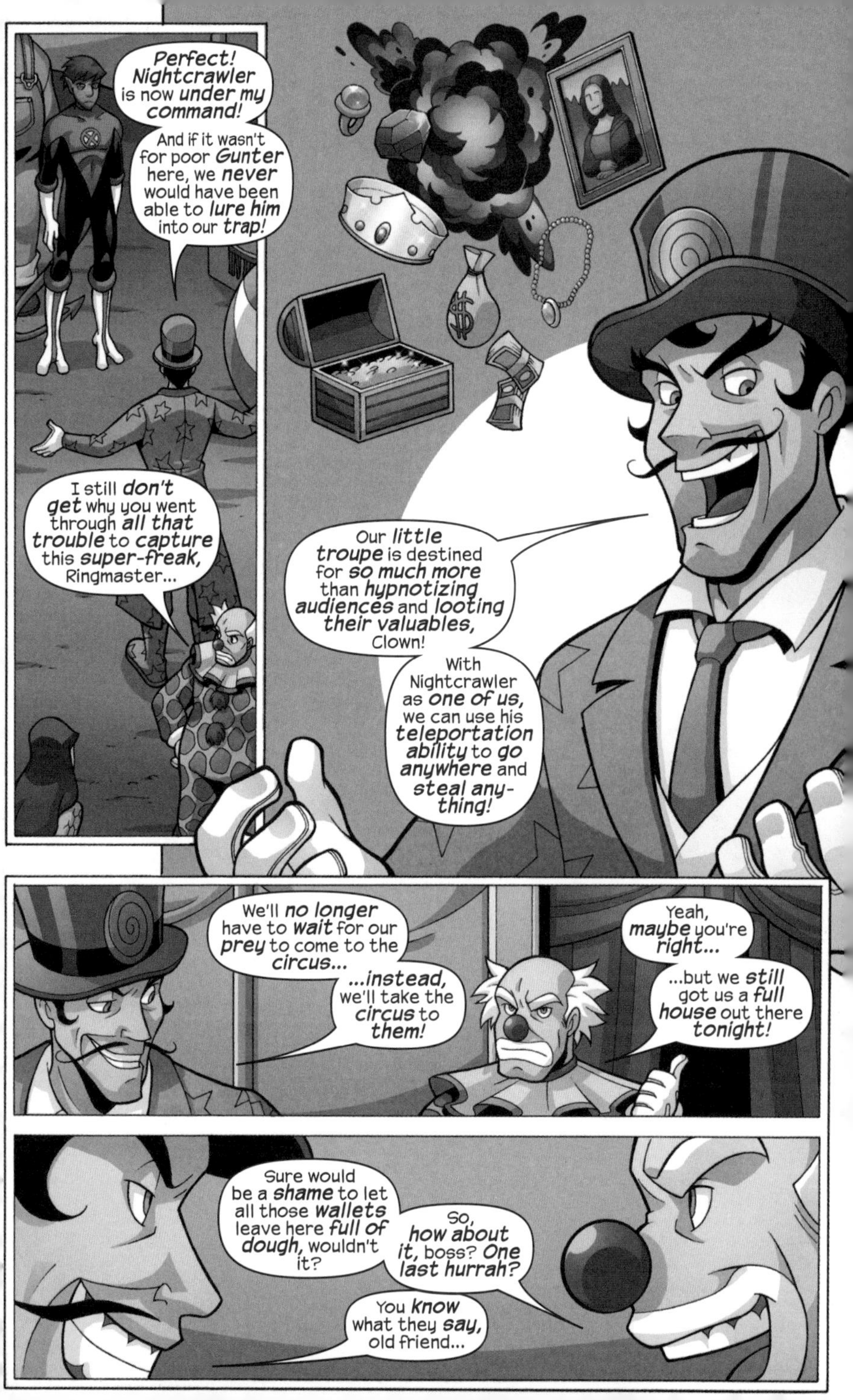
Perfect! Nightcrawler is now under my command!
And if it wasn't for poor Gunter here, we never would have been able to lure him into our trap!
I still don't get why you went through all that trouble to capture this super-freak, Ringmaster...
Our little troupe is destined for so much more than hypnotizing audiences and looting their valuables, Clown!
With Nightcrawler as one of us, we can use his teleportation ability to go anywhere and steal any-thing!
We'll no longer have to wait for our prey to come to the circus...
...instead, we'll take the circus to them!
Yeah, maybe you're right...
...but we still got us a full house out there tonight!
Sure would be a shame to let all those wallets leave here full of dough, wouldn't it?
So, how about it, boss? One last hurrah?
You know what they say, old friend...

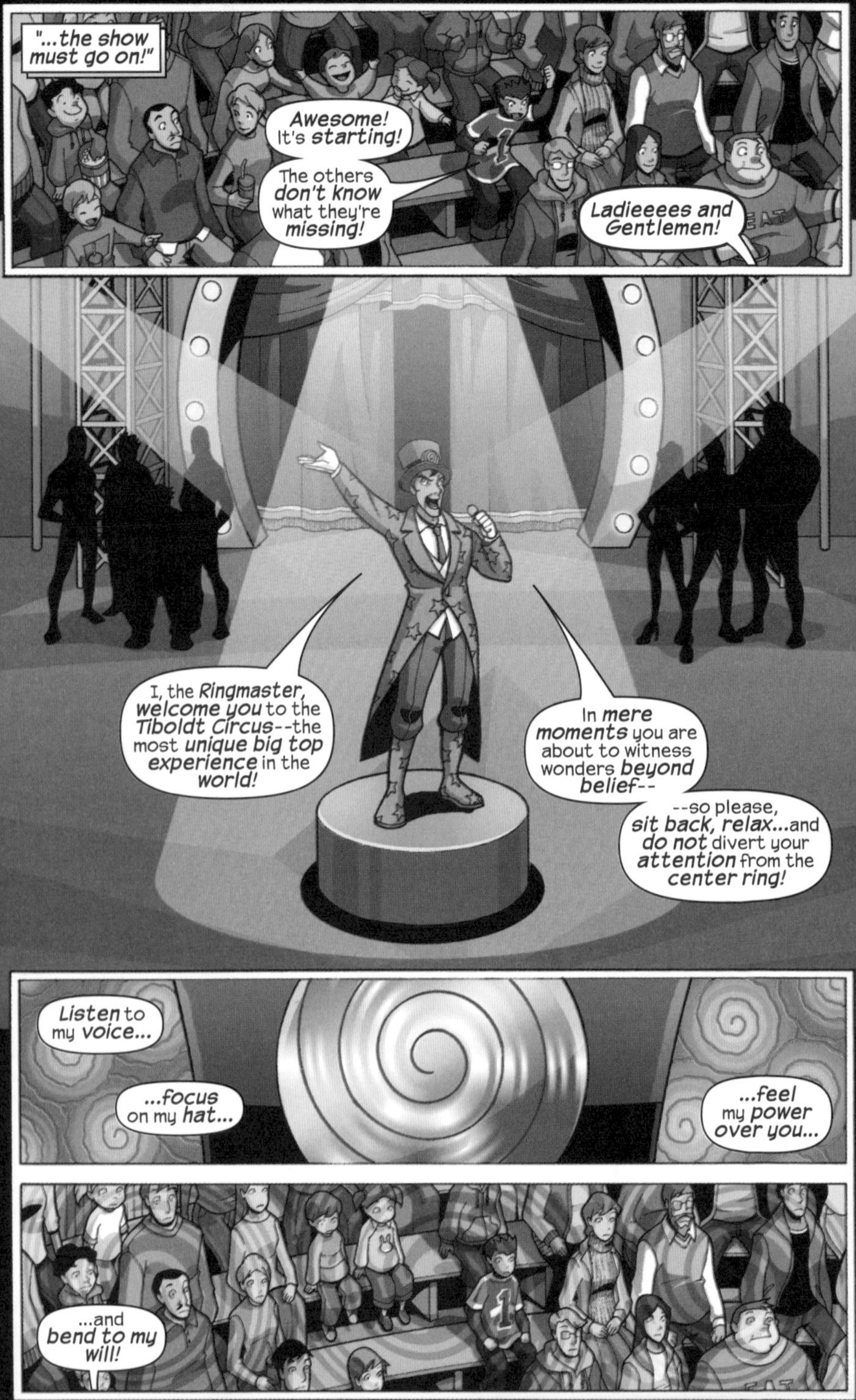
"...the show must go on!"
Awesome! It's starting!
The others don't know what they're missing!
Ladieeees and Gentlemen!
I, the Ringmaster, welcome you to the Tiboldt Circus--the most unique big top experience in the world!
In mere moments you are about to witness wonders beyond belief--
--so please, sit back, relax...and do not divert your attention from the center ring!
Listen to my voice...
...focus on my hat...
...feel my power over you...
...and bend to my will!

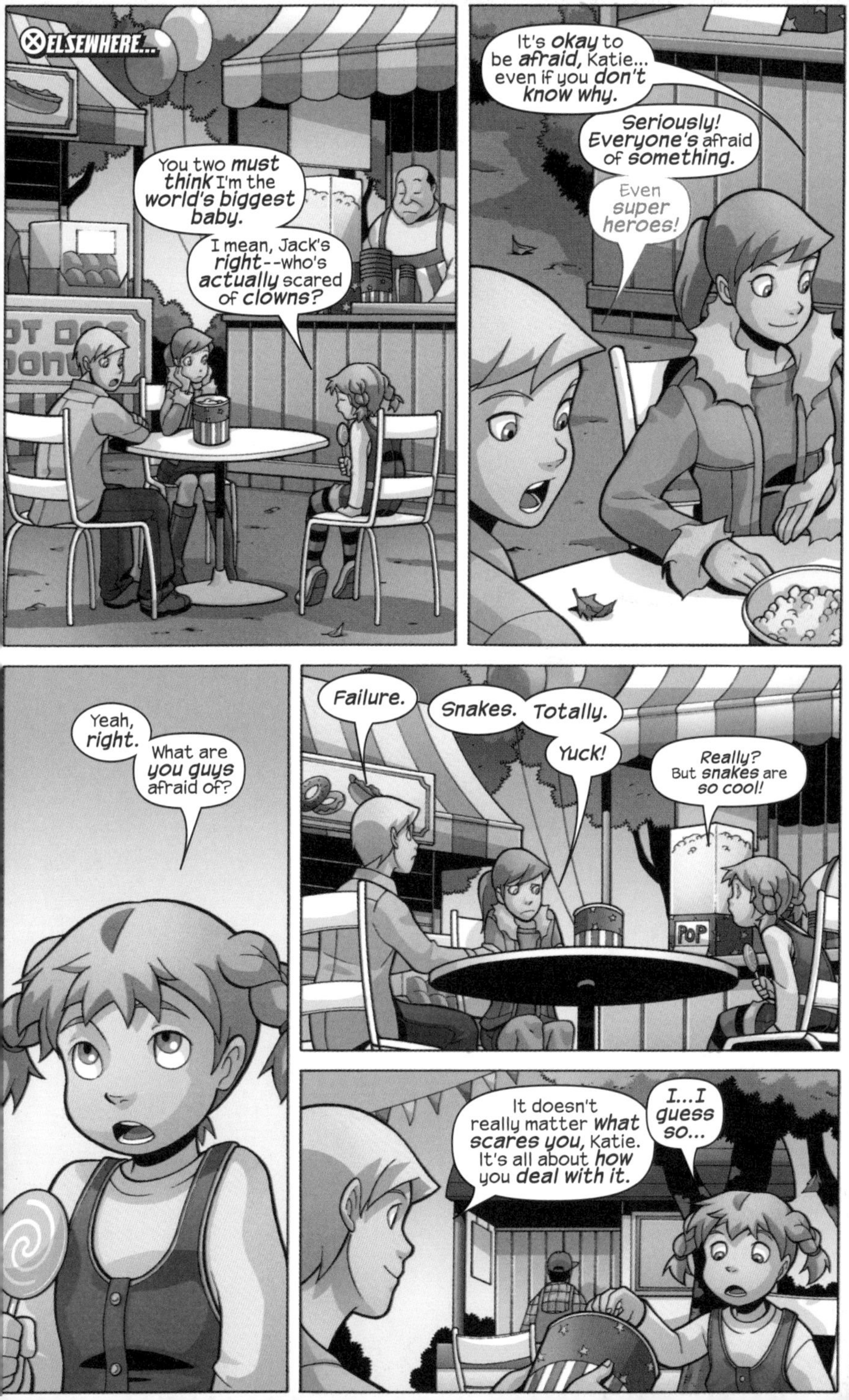
ELSEWHERE...
You two must think I'm the world's biggest baby.
I mean, Jack's right--who's actually scared of clowns?
It's okay to be afraid, Katie... even if you don't know why.
Seriously! Everyone's afraid of something.
Even super heroes!
Yeah, right.
What are you guys afraid of?
Failure.
Snakes.
Totally.
Yuck!
Really? But snakes are so cool!
POP
It doesn't really matter what scares you, Katie. It's all about how you deal with it.
I...I guess so...

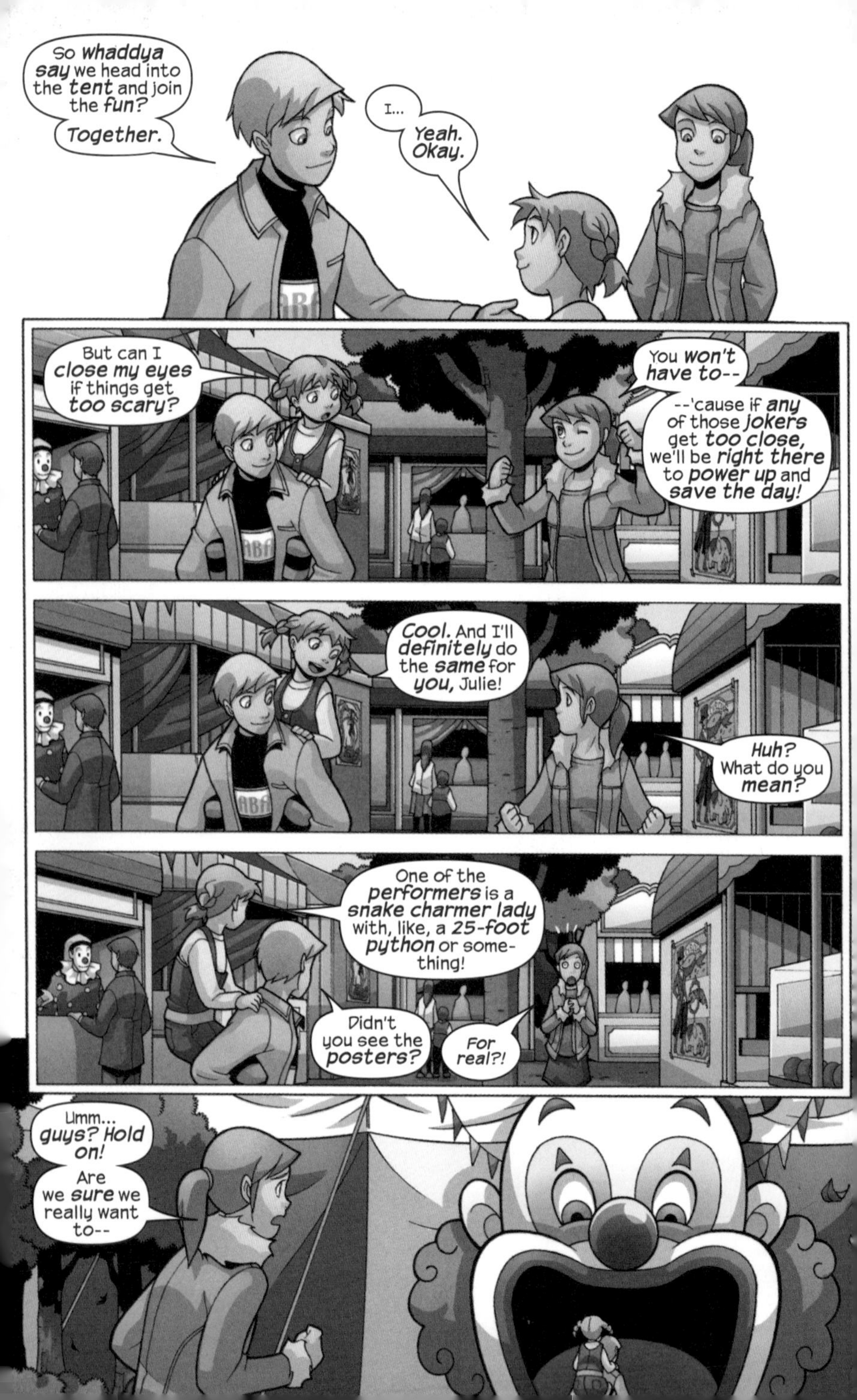
So whaddya say we head into the tent and join the fun?
Together.
I...
Yeah. Okay.
But can I close my eyes if things get too scary?
You won't have to--
--'cause if any of those jokers get too close, we'll be right there to power up and save the day!
Cool. And I'll definitely do the same for you, Julie!
Huh? What do you mean?
One of the performers is a snake charmer lady with, like, a 25-foot python or something!
Didn't you see the posters?
For real?!
Umm... guys? Hold on!
Are we sure we really want to--

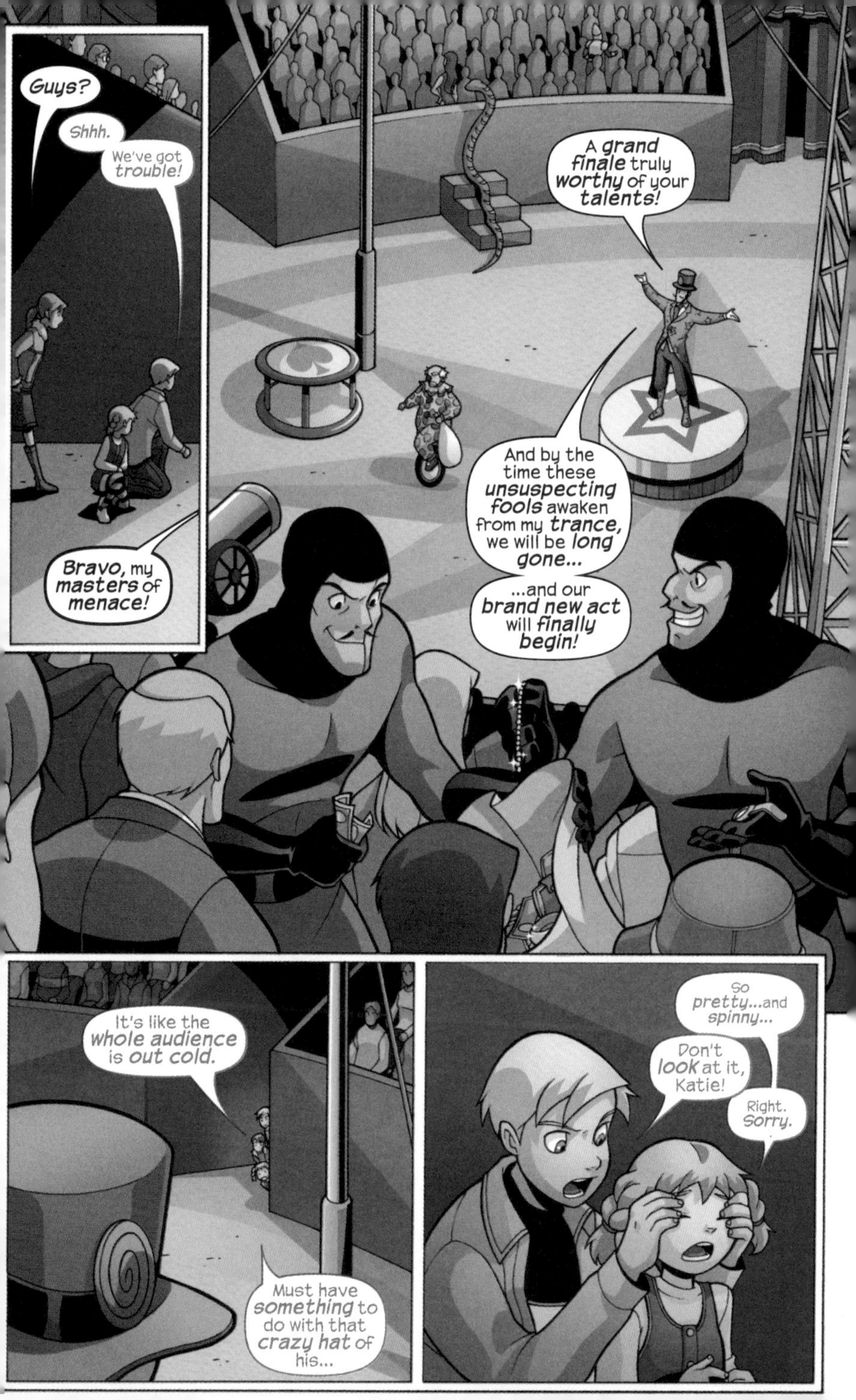
Guys?
Shhh.
We've got trouble!
A grand finale truly worthy of your talents!
And by the time these unsuspecting fools awaken from my trance, we will be long gone...
...and our brand new act will finally begin!
Bravo, my masters of menace!
It's like the whole audience is out cold.
Must have something to do with that crazy hat of his...
So pretty...and spinny...
Don't look at it, Katie!
Right. Sorry.

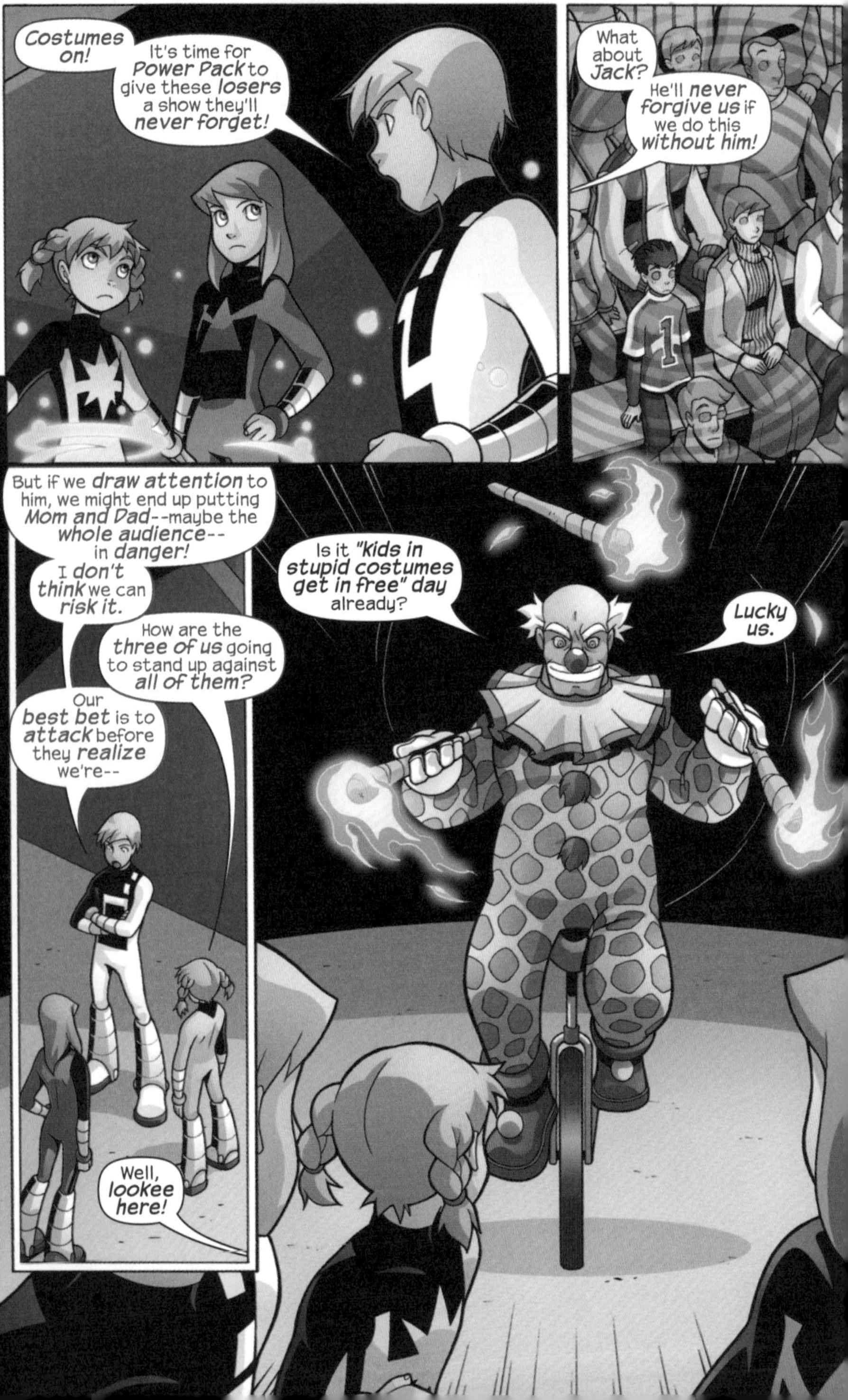
Costumes on!
It's time for Power Pack to give these losers a show they'll never forget!
What about Jack?
He'll never forgive us if we do this without him!
But if we draw attention to him, we might end up putting Mom and Dad--maybe the whole audience--in danger!
I don't think we can risk it.
How are the three of us going to stand up against all of them?
Our best bet is to attack before they realize we're--
Well, lookee here!
Is it "kids in stupid costumes get in free" day already?
Lucky us.

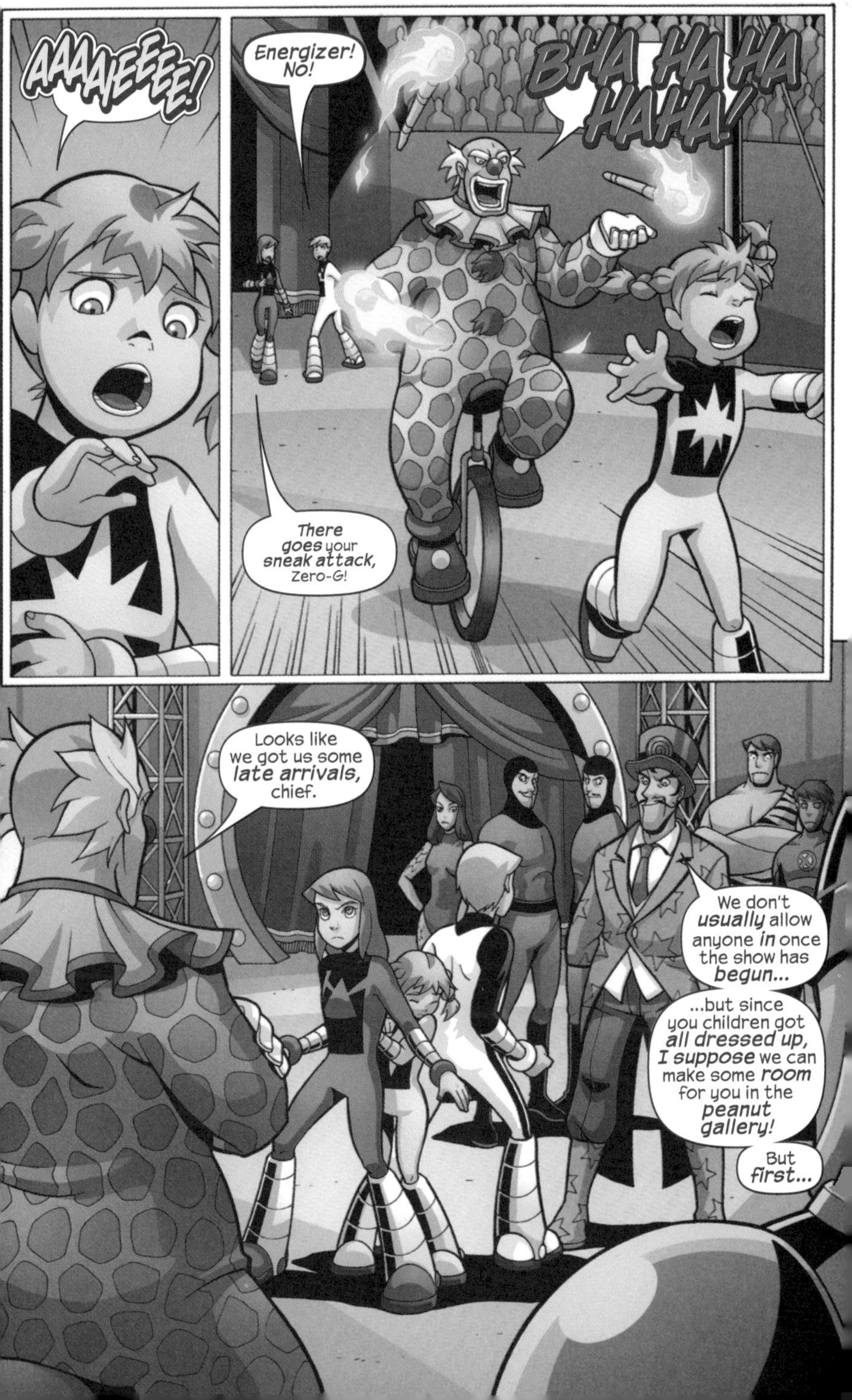
AAAAIEEEEE!
Energizer! No!
BHA HA HA HAHA!
There goes your sneak attack, Zero-G!
Looks like we got us some late arrivals, chief.
We don't usually allow anyone in once the show has begun...
...but since you children got all dressed up, I suppose we can make some room for you in the peanut gallery!
But first...

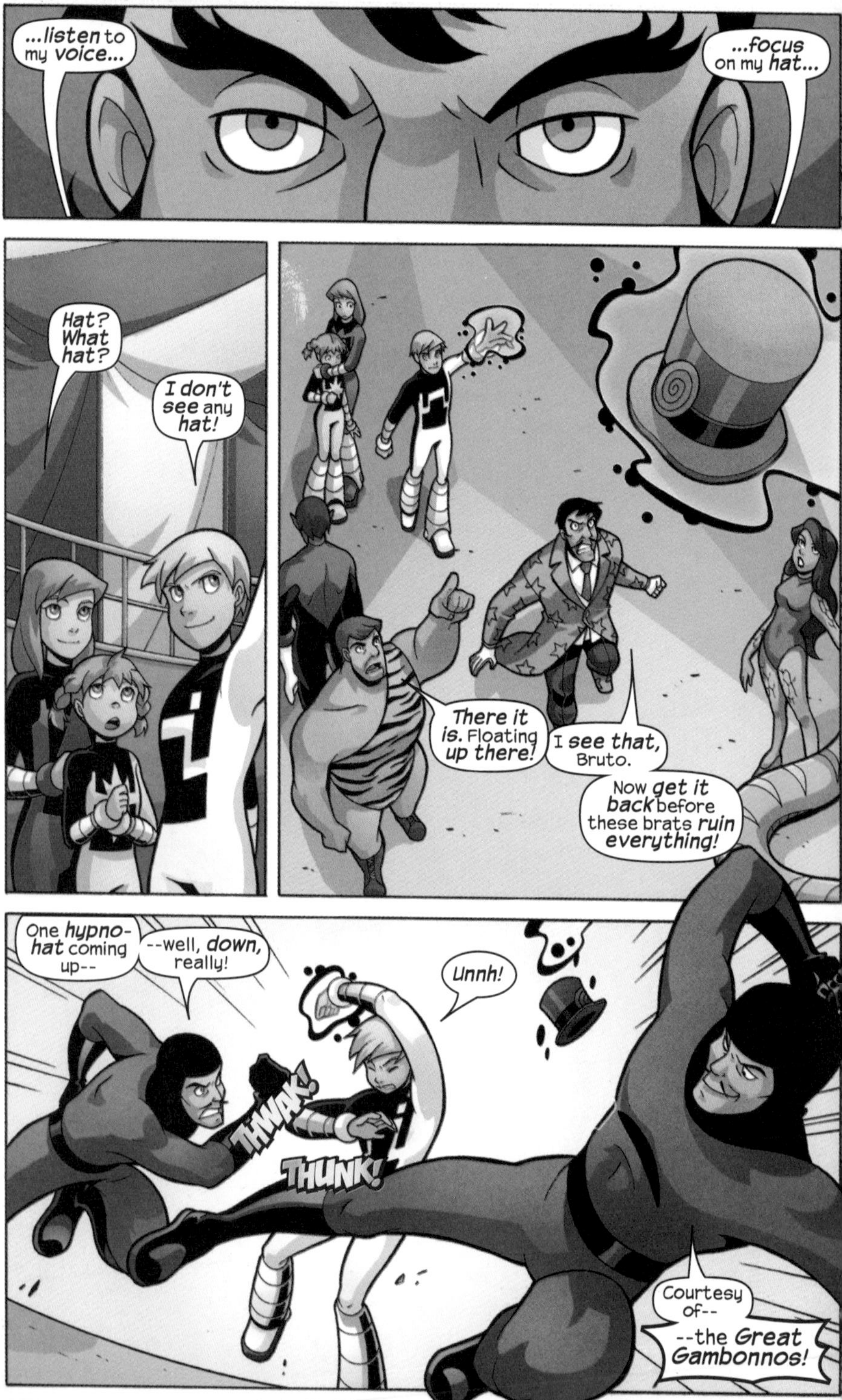
...listen to my voice...
...focus on my hat...
Hat? What hat?
I don't see any hat!
There it is. Floating up there!
I see that, Bruto.
Now get it back before these brats ruin everything!
One hypno-hat coming up--
--well, down, really!
Unnh!
THWAK!
THUNK!
Courtesy of--
--the Great Gambonnos!

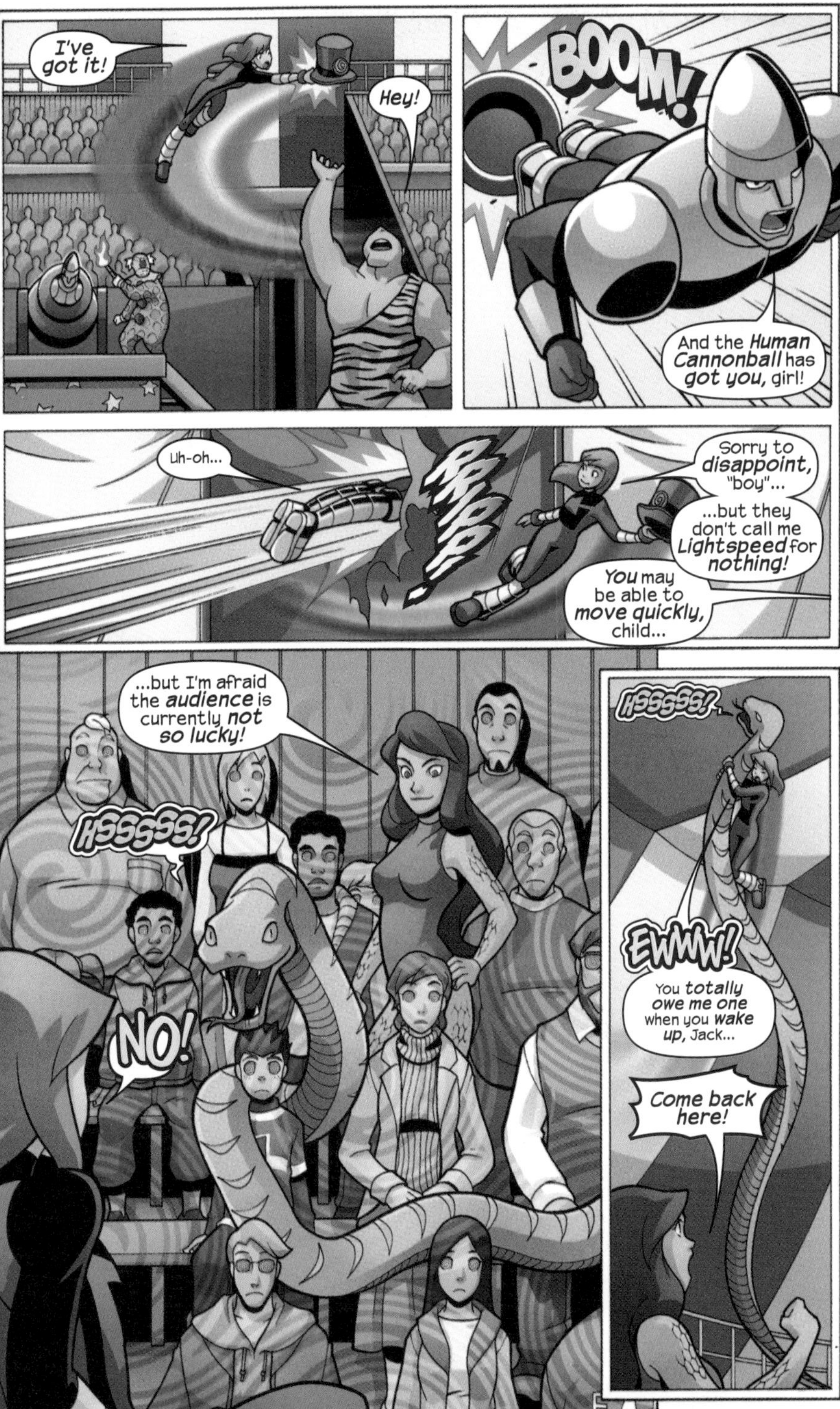

I've got it!
Hey!
BOOM!
And the Human Cannonball has got you, girl!
Uh-oh...
RRRIP!
Sorry to disappoint, "boy"...
...but they don't call me Lightspeed for nothing!
You may be able to move quickly, child...
...but I'm afraid the audience is currently not so lucky!
HSSSSS!
NO!
HSSSSS!
EWWW!
You totally owe me one when you wake up, Jack...
Come back here!

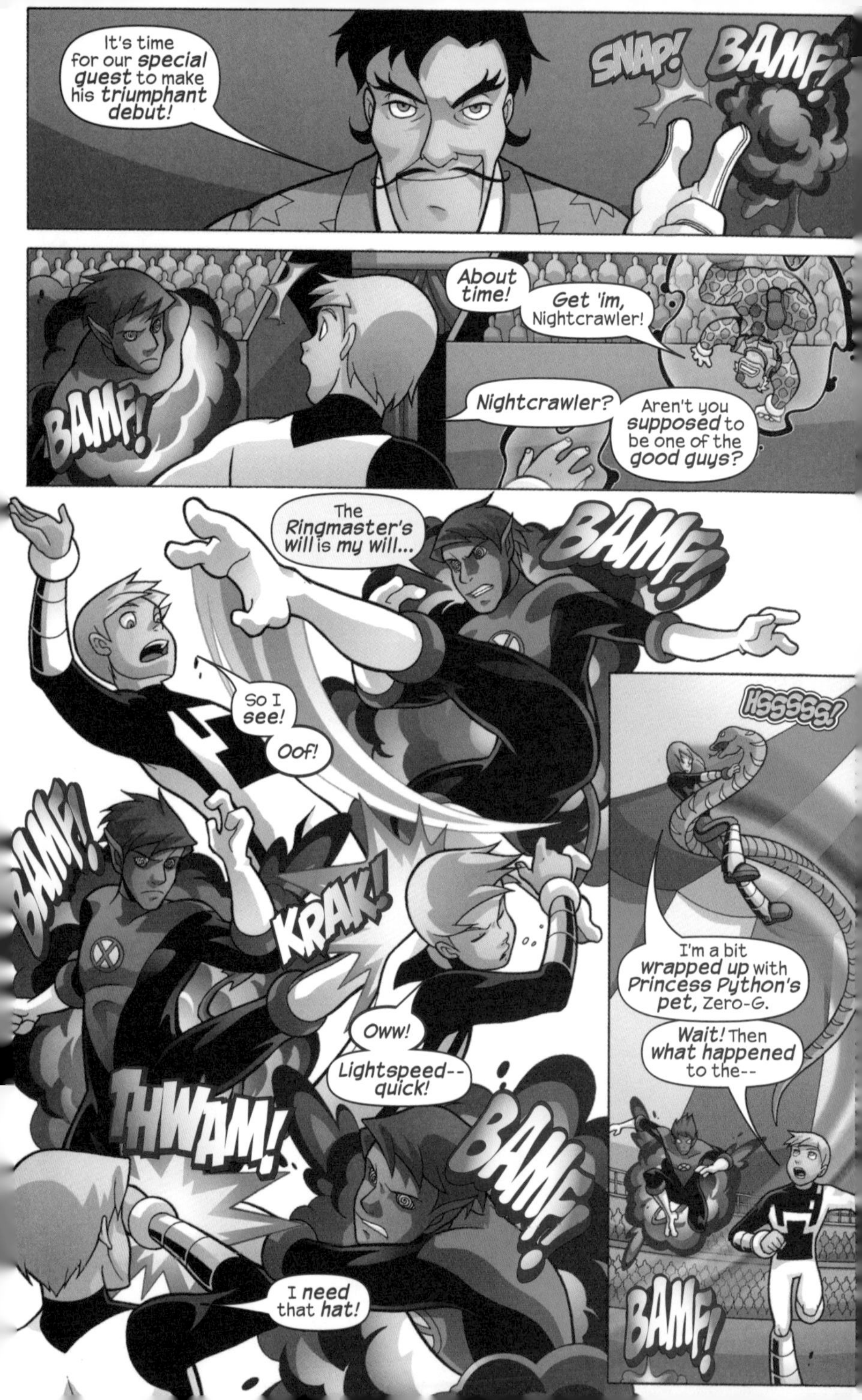

It's time for our special guest to make his triumphant debut!
SNAP!
BAMF!
About time!
Get 'im, Nightcrawler!
BAMF!
Nightcrawler?
Aren't you supposed to be one of the good guys?
The Ringmaster's will is my will...
BAMF!
So I see!
Oof!
HSSSSS!
BAMF!
KRAK!
Oww!
Lightspeed--quick!
I'm a bit wrapped up with Princess Python's pet, Zero-G.
Wait! Then what happened to the--
THWAM!
BAMF!
I need that hat!
BAMF!

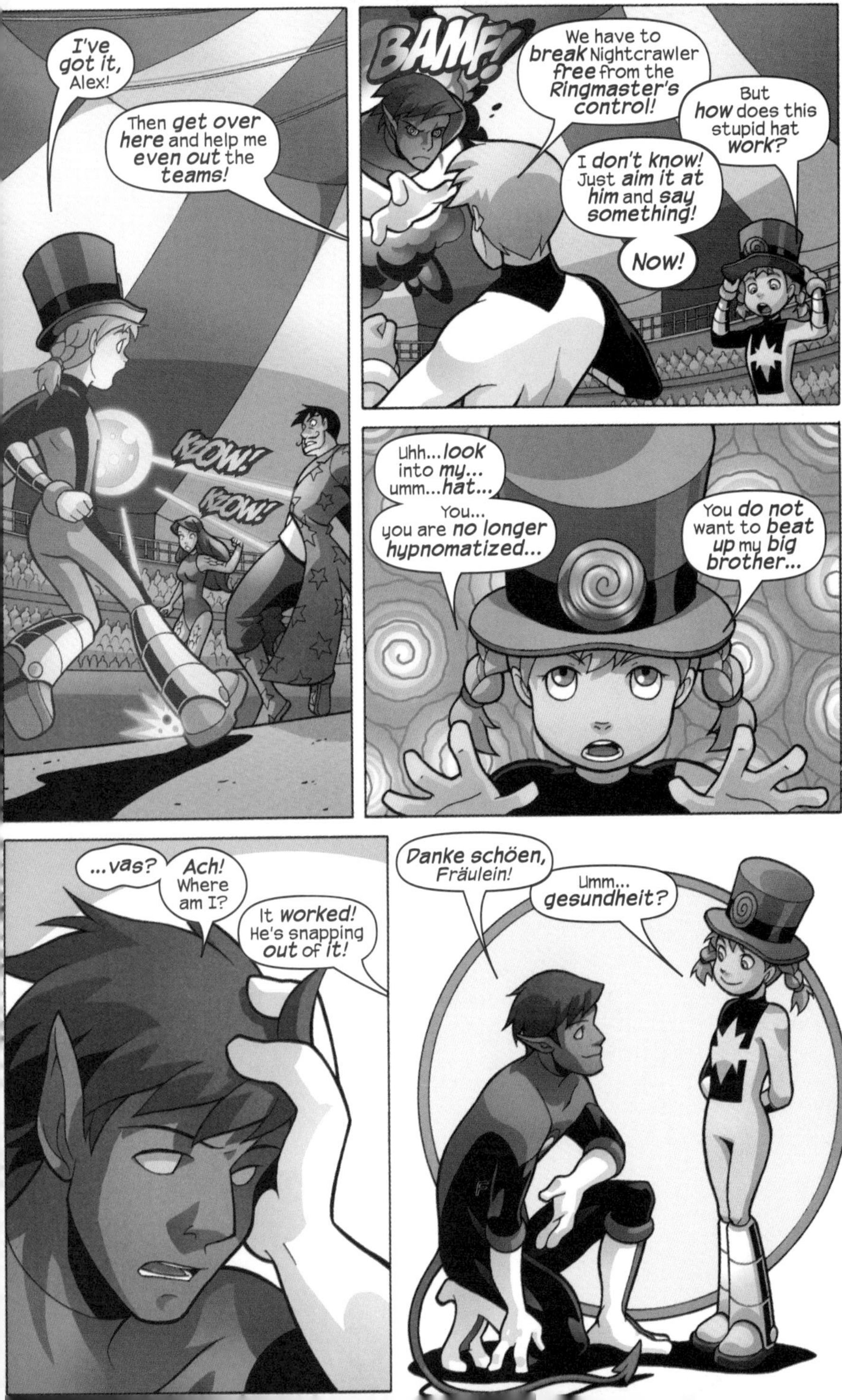
I've got it, Alex!
Then get over here and help me even out the teams!
KZOW!
KZOW!
BAMF!
We have to break Nightcrawler free from the Ringmaster's control!
But how does this stupid hat work?
I don't know! Just aim it at him and say something!
Now!
Uhh...look into my... umm...hat...
You... you are no longer hypnomatized...
You do not want to beat up my big brother...
...vas?
Ach! Where am I?
It worked! He's snapping out of it!
Danke schöen, Fräulein!
Umm... gesundheit?

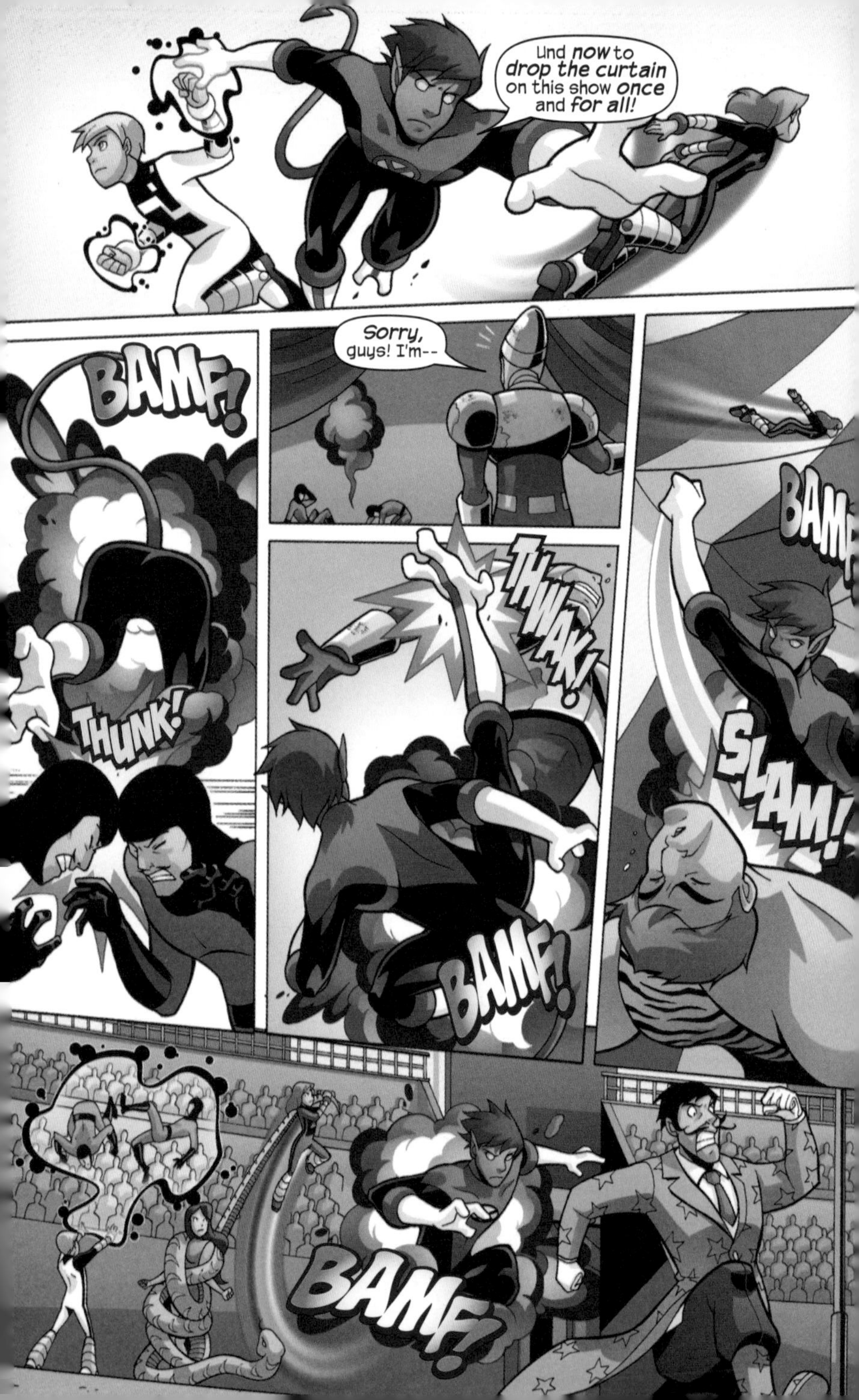
Und now to drop the curtain on this show once and for all!
BAMF!
THUNK!
Sorry, guys! I'm--
THWAK!
BAMF!
BAMF
SLAM!
BAMF!

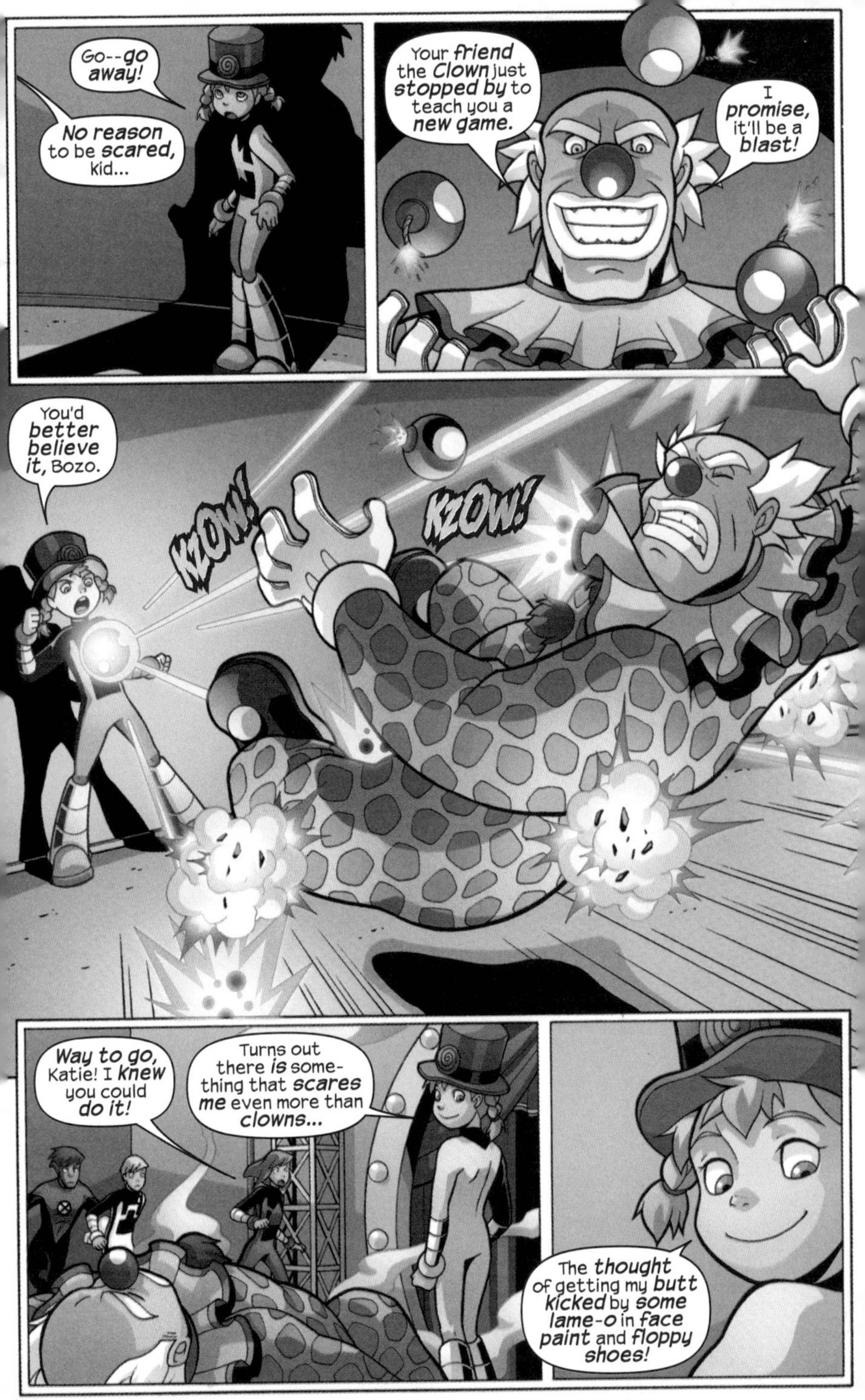
Go--go away!
No reason to be scared, kid...
Your friend the Clown just stopped by to teach you a new game.
I promise, it'll be a blast!
You'd better believe it, Bozo.
KZOW!
KZOW!
Way to go, Katie! I knew you could do it!
Turns out there is something that scares me even more than clowns...
The thought of getting my butt kicked by some lame-o in face paint and floppy shoes!

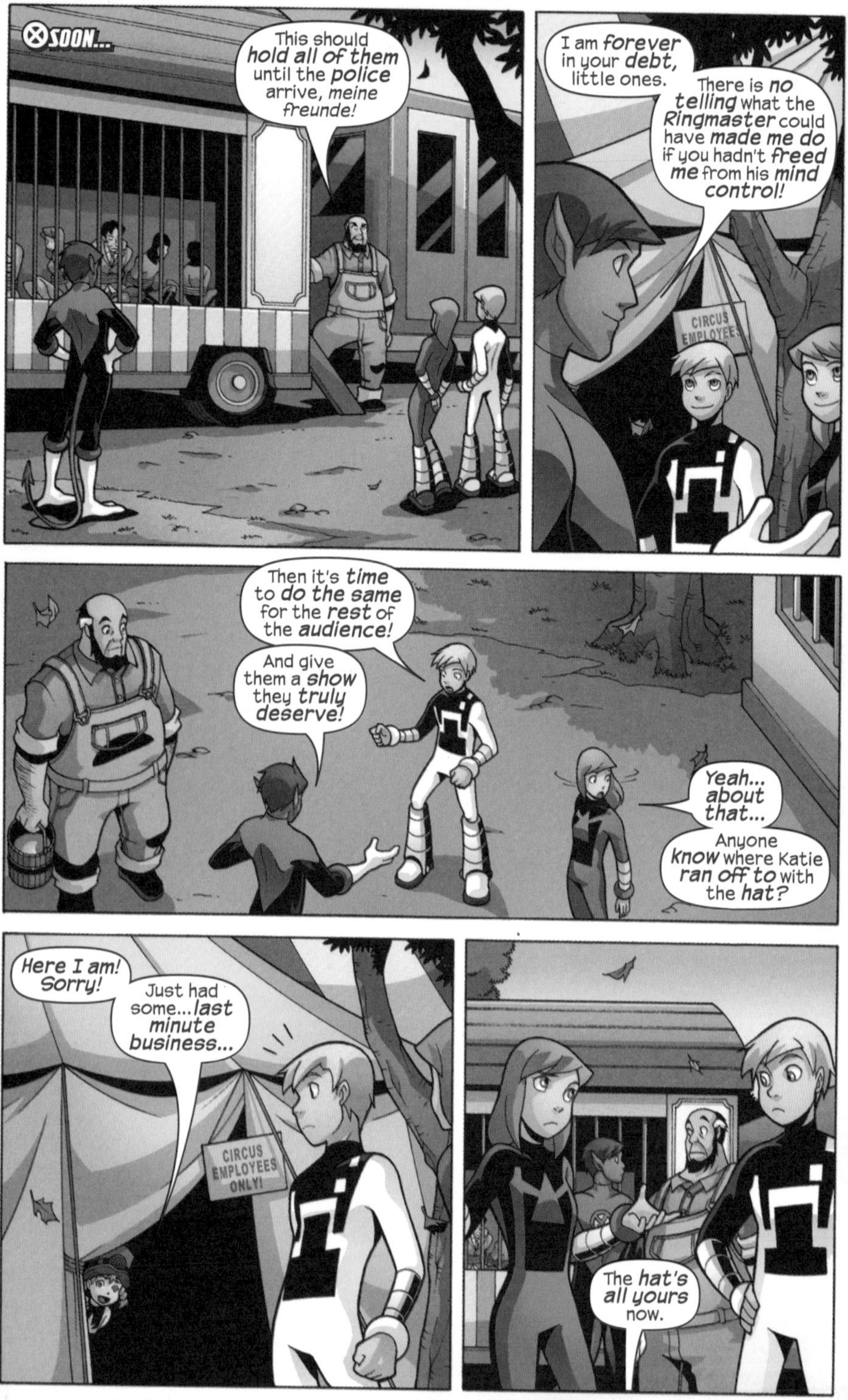
SOON...
This should hold all of them until the police arrive, meine freunde!
I am forever in your debt, little ones.
There is no telling what the Ringmaster could have made me do if you hadn't freed me from his mind control!
CIRCUS EMPLOYEES
Then it's time to do the same for the rest of the audience!
And give them a show they truly deserve!
Yeah... about that...
Anyone know where Katie ran off to with the hat?
Here I am! Sorry!
Just had some...last minute business...
CIRCUS EMPLOYEES ONLY!
The hat's all yours now.

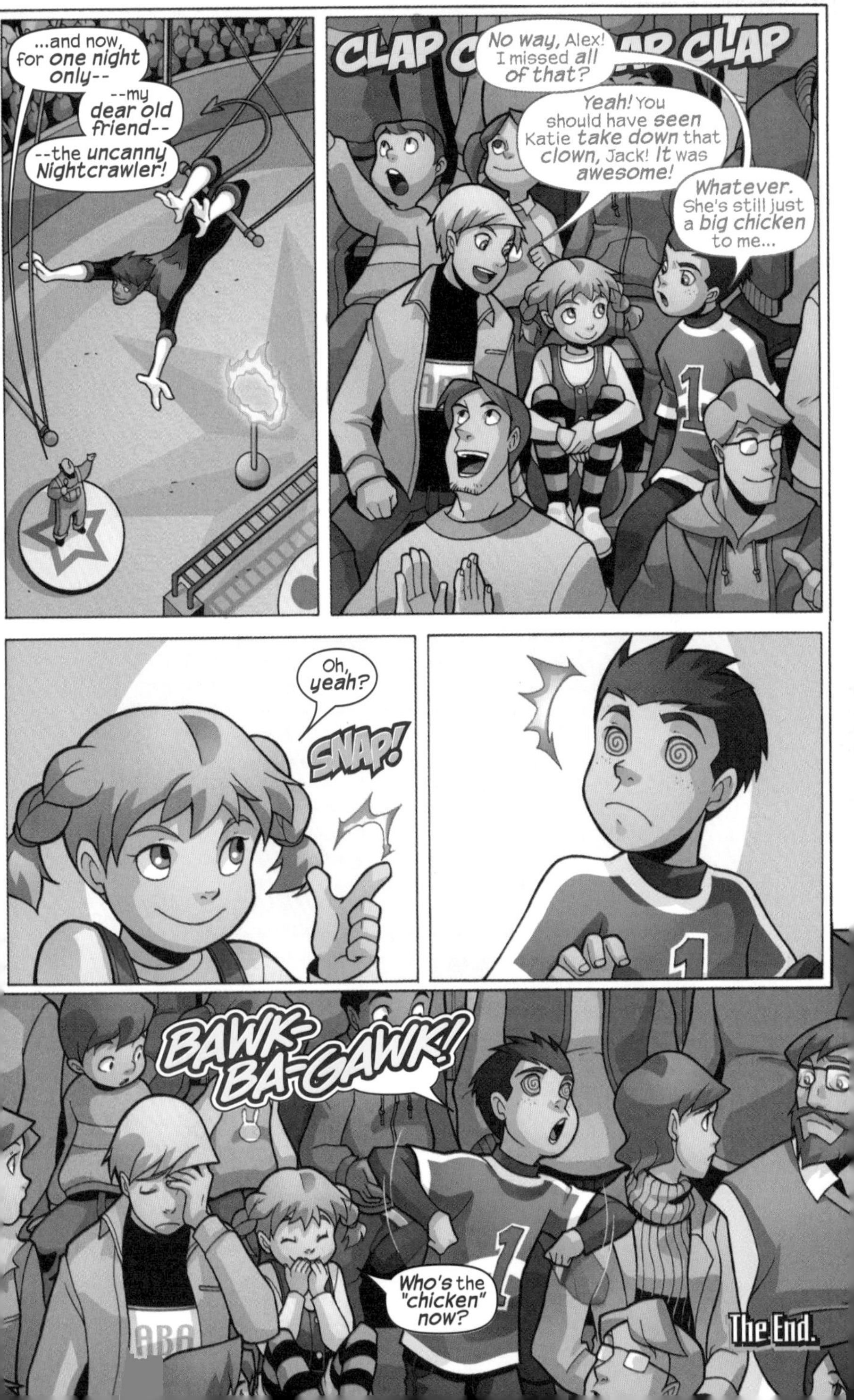
...and now, for one night only--
--my dear old friend--
--the uncanny Nightcrawler!
CLAP
No way, Alex! I missed all of that?
Yeah! You should have seen Katie take down that clown, Jack! It was awesome!
Whatever. She's still just a big chicken to me...
Oh, yeah?
SNAP!
BAWK-BA-GAWK!
Who's the "chicken" now?
The End.

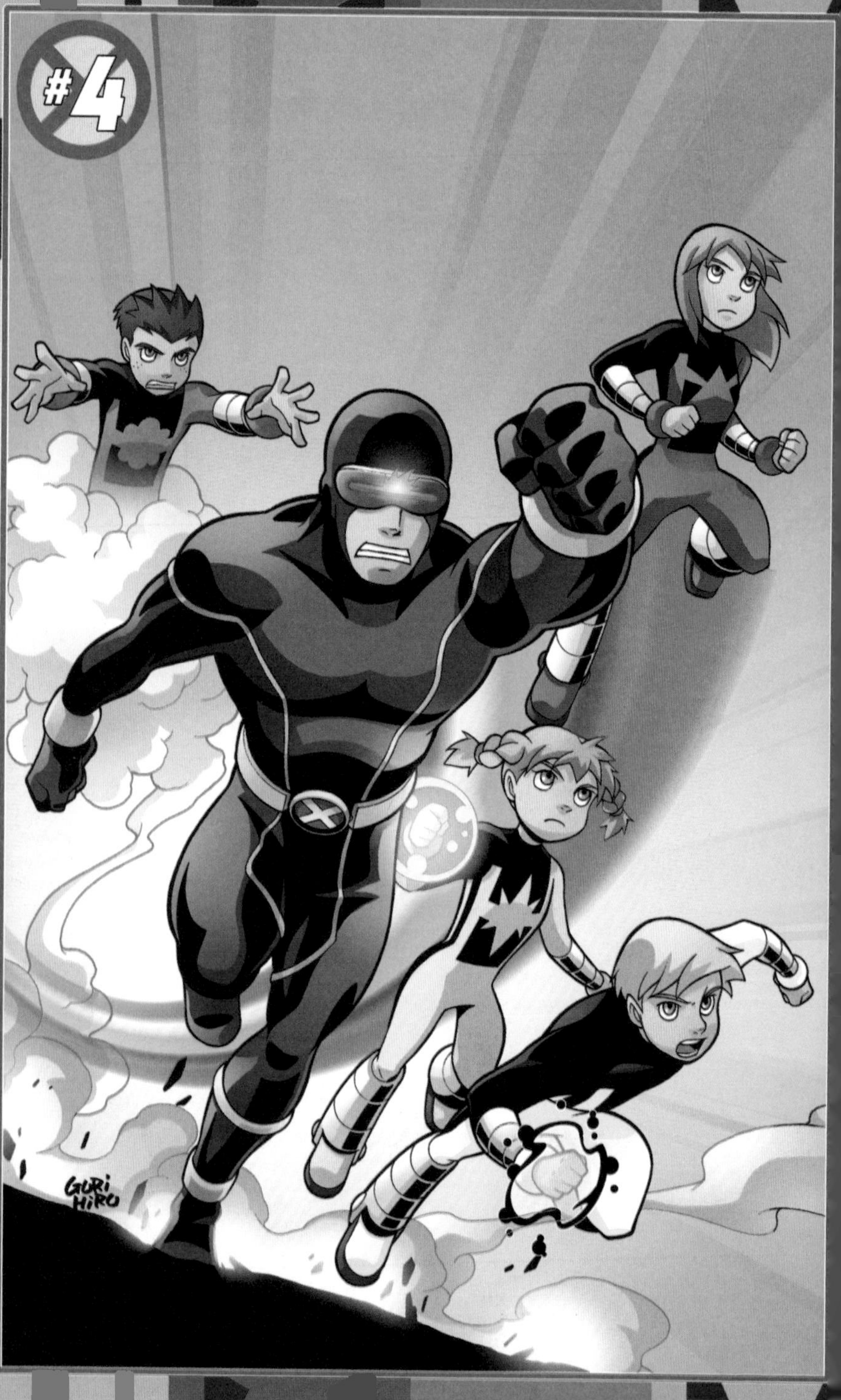
#4
GURI HIRO

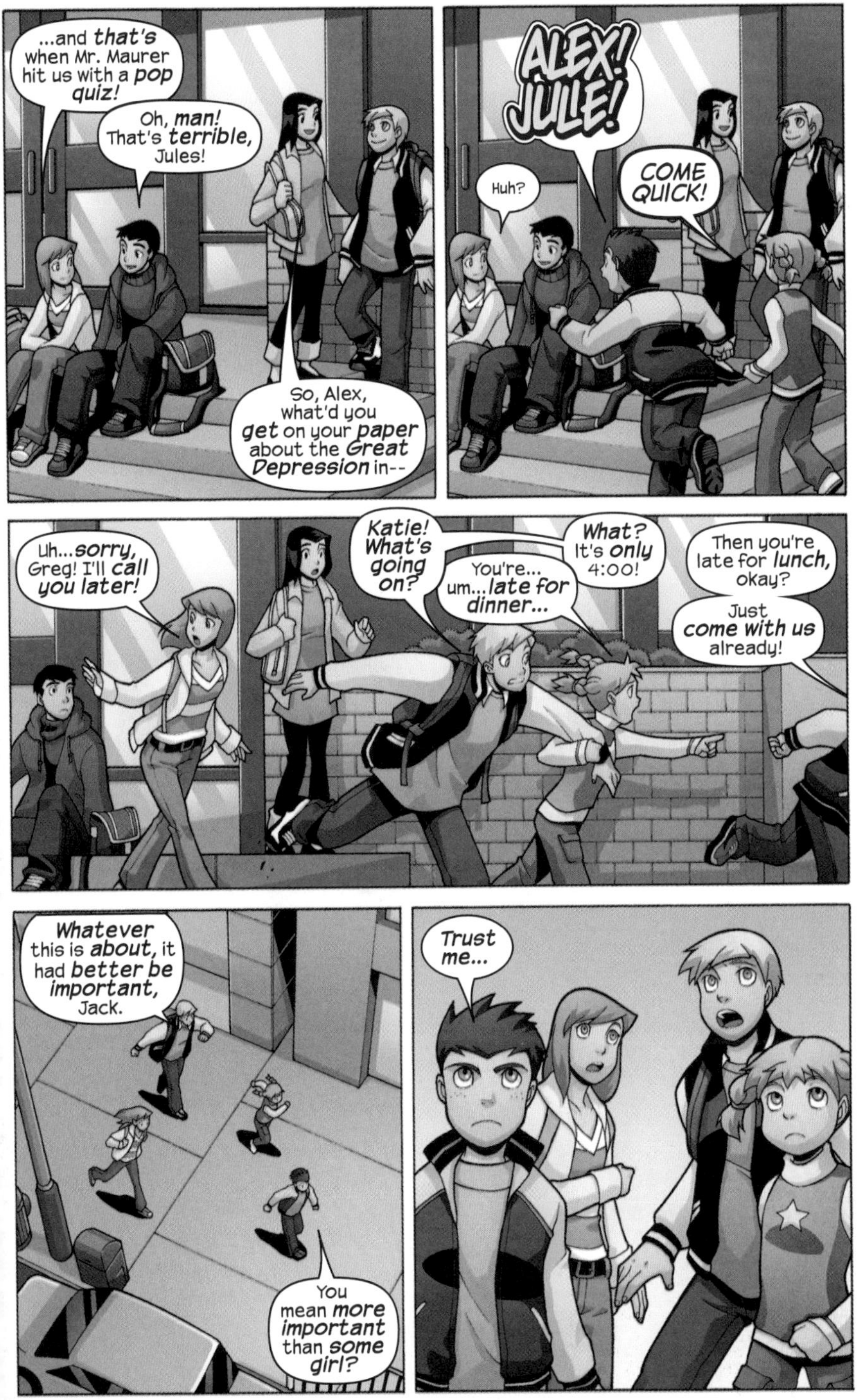
...and that's when Mr. Maurer hit us with a pop quiz!
Oh, man! That's terrible, Jules!
So, Alex, what'd you get on your paper about the Great Depression in--
ALEX! JULIE!
Huh?
COME QUICK!
Uh...sorry, Greg! I'll call you later!
Katie! What's going on?
You're... um...late for dinner...
What? It's only 4:00!
Then you're late for lunch, okay?
Just come with us already!
Whatever this is about, it had better be important, Jack.
You mean more important than some girl?
Trust me...

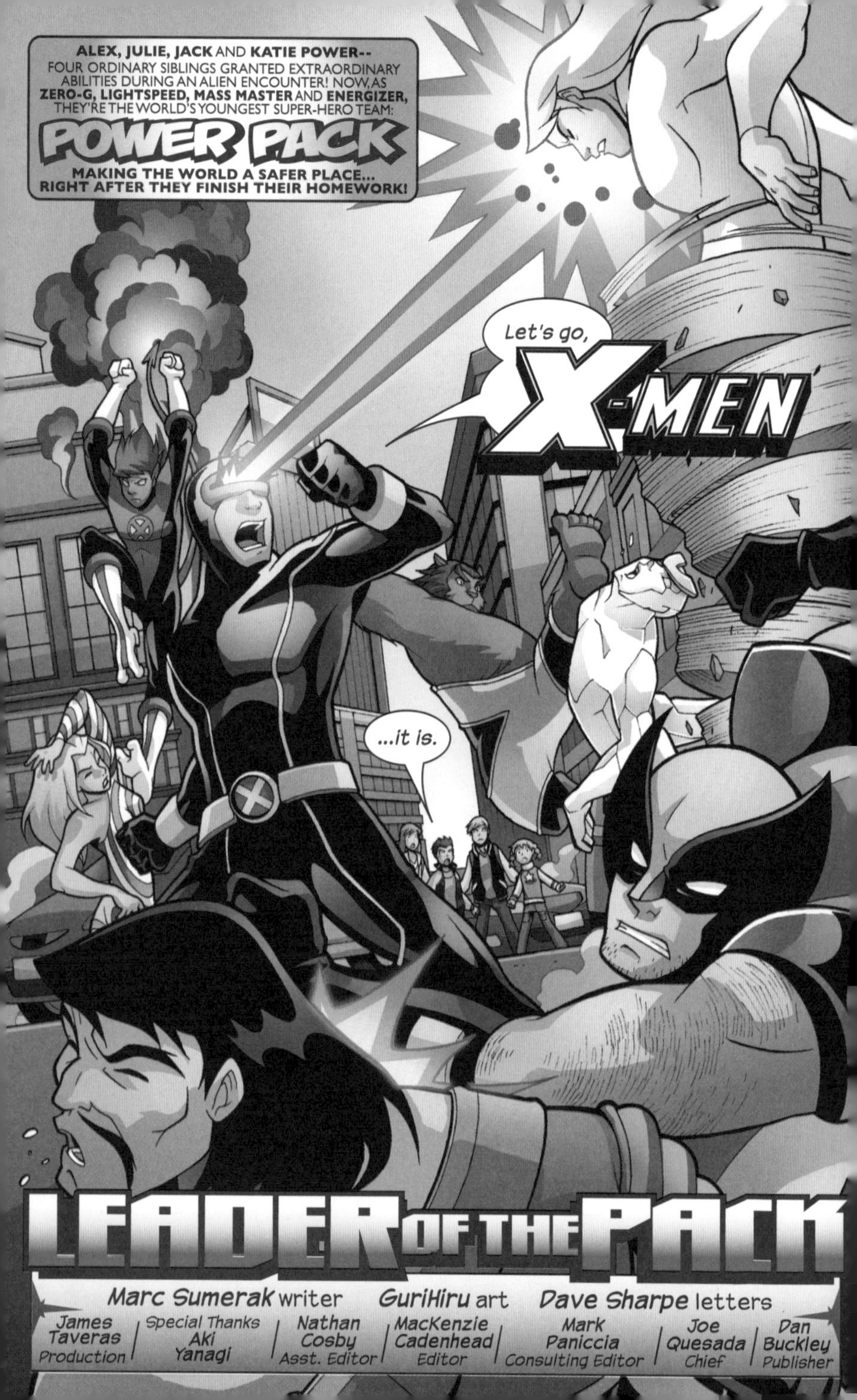

ALEX, JULIE, JACK AND KATIE POWER-- FOUR ORDINARY SIBLINGS GRANTED EXTRAORDINARY ABILITIES DURING AN ALIEN ENCOUNTER! NOW, AS ZERO-G, LIGHTSPEED, MASS MASTER AND ENERGIZER, THEY'RE THE WORLD'S YOUNGEST SUPER-HERO TEAM:
POWER PACK
MAKING THE WORLD A SAFER PLACE... RIGHT AFTER THEY FINISH THEIR HOMEWORK!
Let's go, X-MEN
...it is.
LEADER OF THE PACK
Marc Sumerak writer GuriHiru art Dave Sharpe letters
James Taveras Production
Special Thanks Aki Yanagi
Nathan Cosby Asst. Editor
MacKenzie Cadenhead Editor
Mark Paniccia Consulting Editor
Joe Quesada Chief
Dan Buckley Publisher

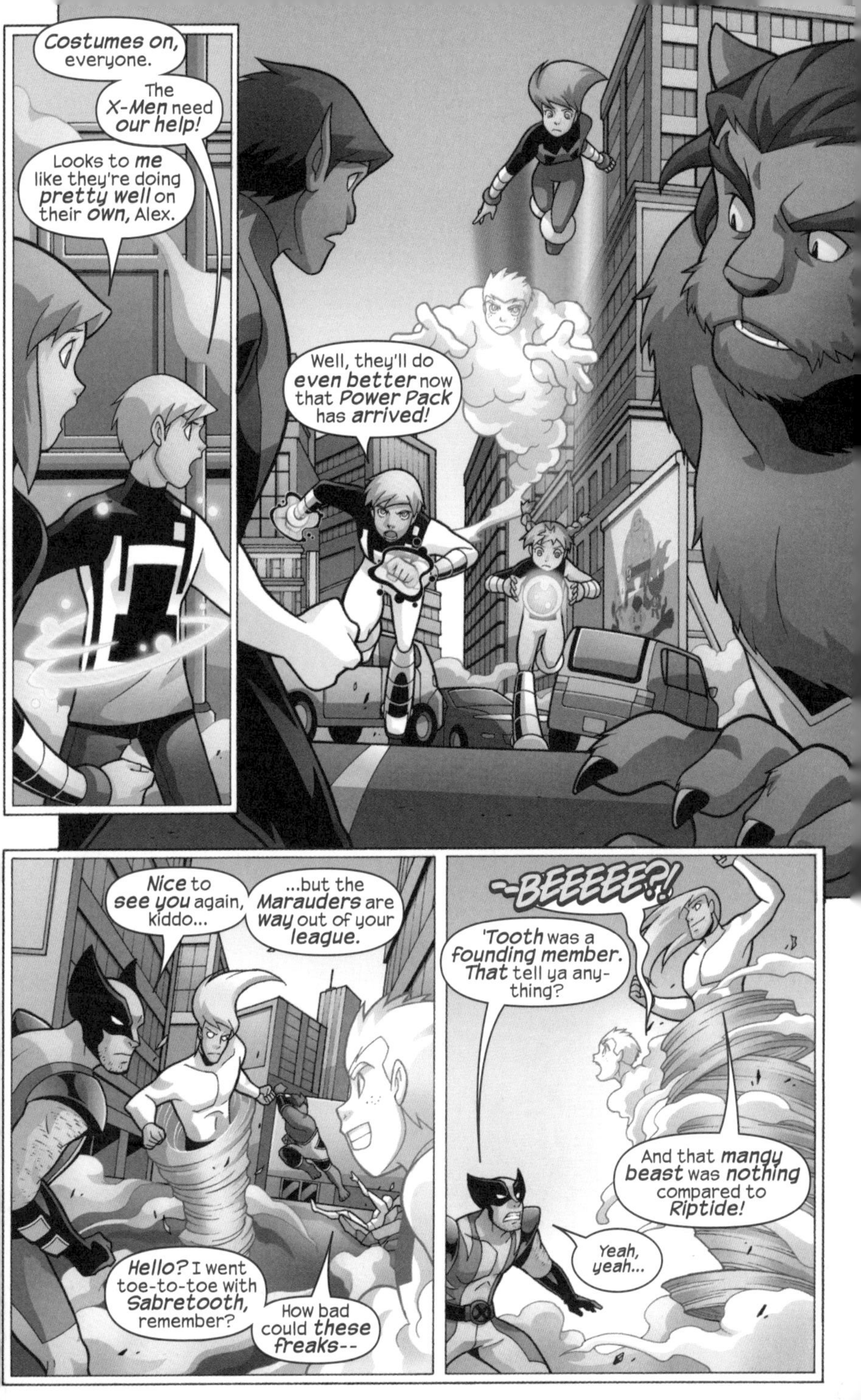
Costumes on, everyone.
The X-Men need our help!
Looks to me like they're doing pretty well on their own, Alex.
Well, they'll do even better now that Power Pack has arrived!
Nice to see you again, kiddo...
...but the Marauders are way out of your league.
Hello? I went toe-to-toe with Sabretooth, remember?
How bad could these freaks--
--BEEEEE?!
'Tooth was a founding member. That tell ya any-thing?
And that mangy beast was nothing compared to Riptide!
Yeah, yeah...

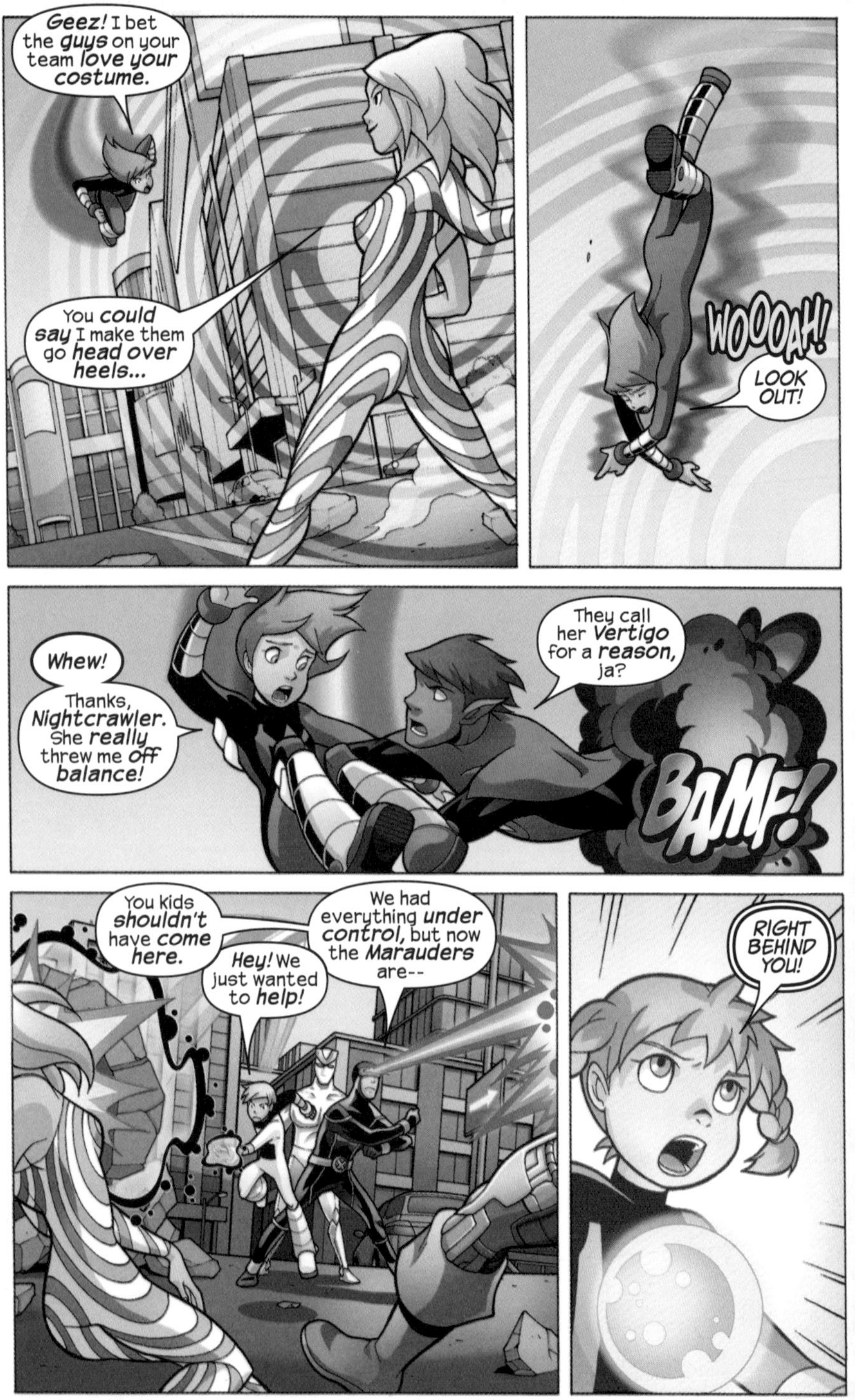
Geez! I bet the guys on your team love your costume.
You could say I make them go head over heels...
WOOOAH!
LOOK OUT!
Whew!
Thanks, Nightcrawler. She really threw me off balance!
They call her Vertigo for a reason, ja?
BAMF!
You kids shouldn't have come here.
We had everything under control, but now the Marauders are--
Hey! We just wanted to help!
RIGHT BEHIND YOU!

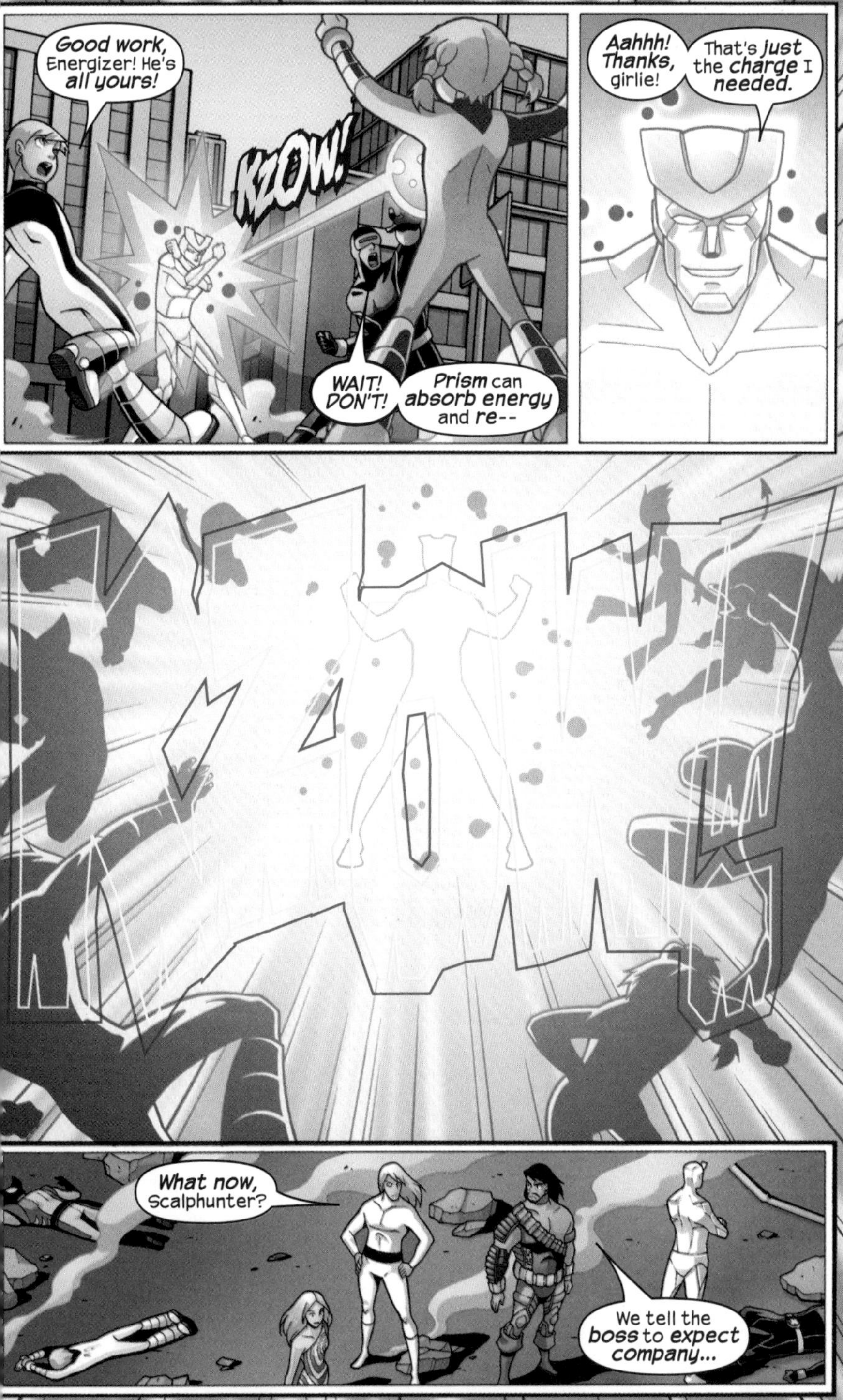
Good work, Energizer! He's all yours!
KZOW!
WAIT! DON'T!
Prism can absorb energy and re--
Aahhh! Thanks, girlie!
That's just the charge I needed.
What now, Scalphunter?
We tell the boss to expect company...

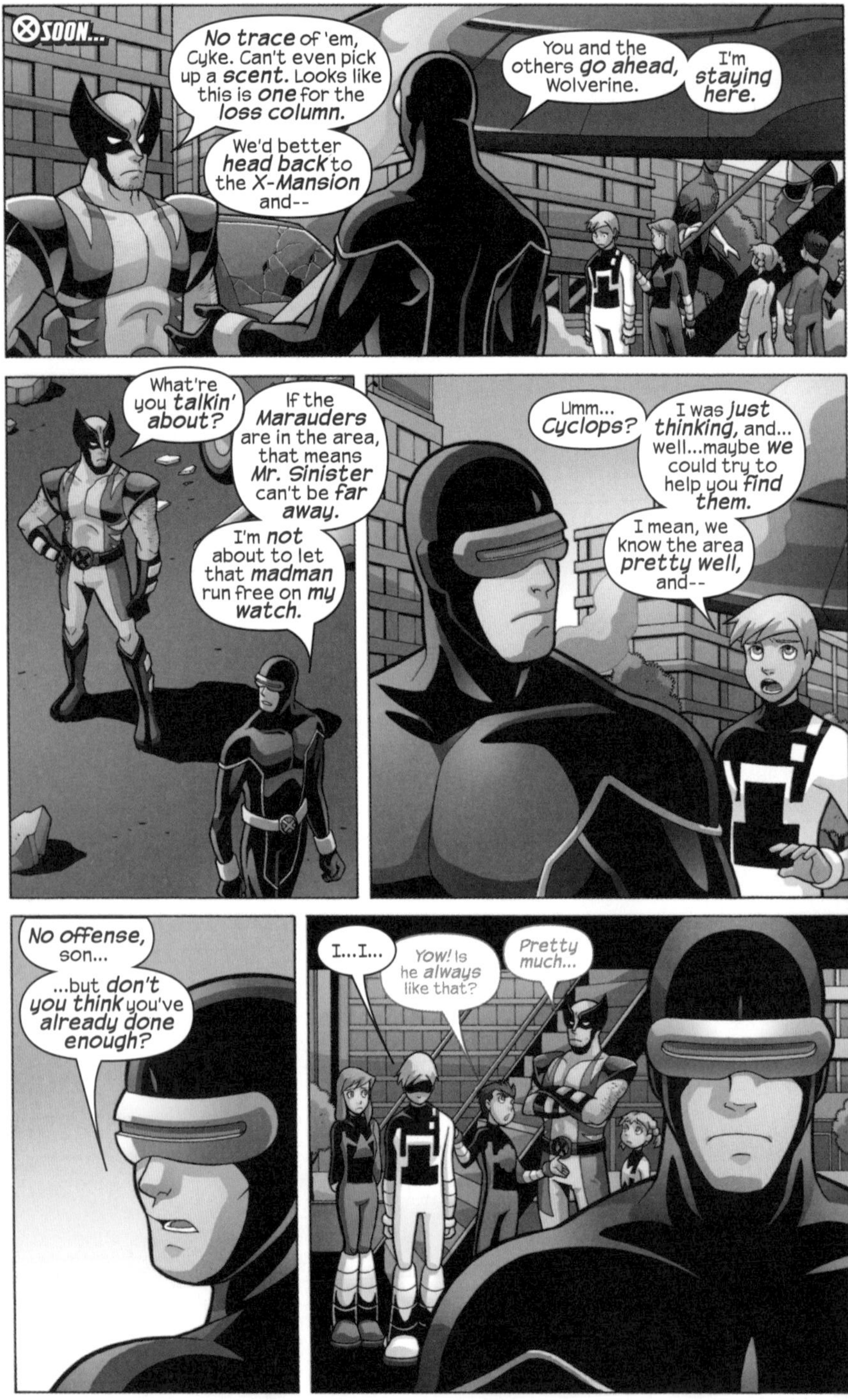

SOON...
No trace of 'em, Cyke. Can't even pick up a scent. Looks like this is one for the loss column.
We'd better head back to the X-Mansion and--
You and the others go ahead, Wolverine.
I'm staying here.
What're you talkin' about?
If the Marauders are in the area, that means Mr. Sinister can't be far away.
I'm not about to let that madman run free on my watch.
Umm... Cyclops?
I was just thinking, and... well...maybe we could try to help you find them.
I mean, we know the area pretty well, and--
No offense, son...
...but don't you think you've already done enough?
I...I...
Yow! Is he always like that?
Pretty much...

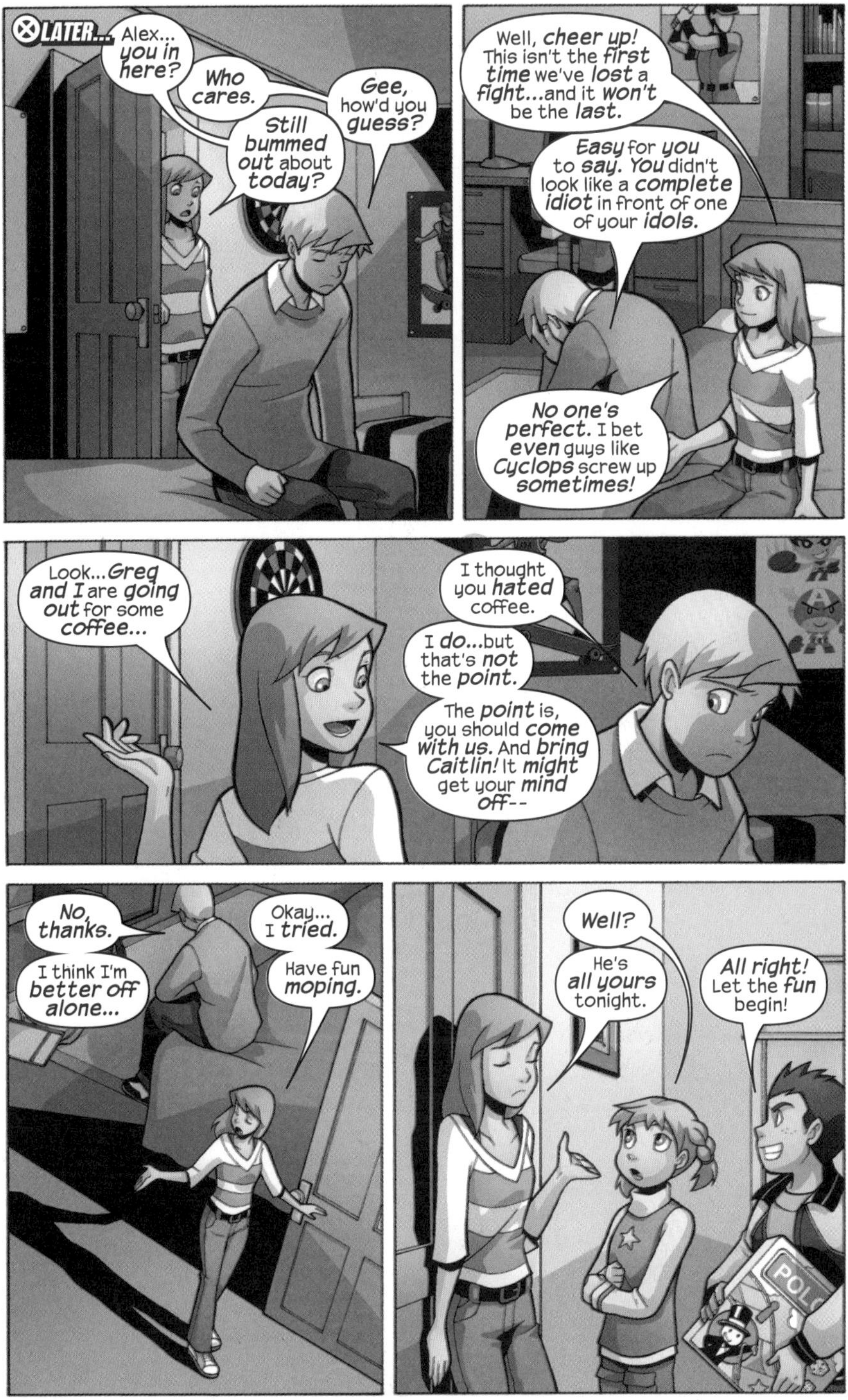
LATER...
Alex... you in here?
Who cares.
Still bummed out about today?
Gee, how'd you guess?
Well, cheer up! This isn't the first time we've lost a fight...and it won't be the last.
Easy for you to say. You didn't look like a complete idiot in front of one of your idols.
No one's perfect. I bet even guys like Cyclops screw up sometimes!
Look...Greg and I are going out for some coffee...
I thought you hated coffee.
I do...but that's not the point.
The point is, you should come with us. And bring Caitlin! It might get your mind off--
No, thanks.
I think I'm better off alone...
Okay... I tried.
Have fun moping.
Well?
He's all yours tonight.
All right! Let the fun begin!

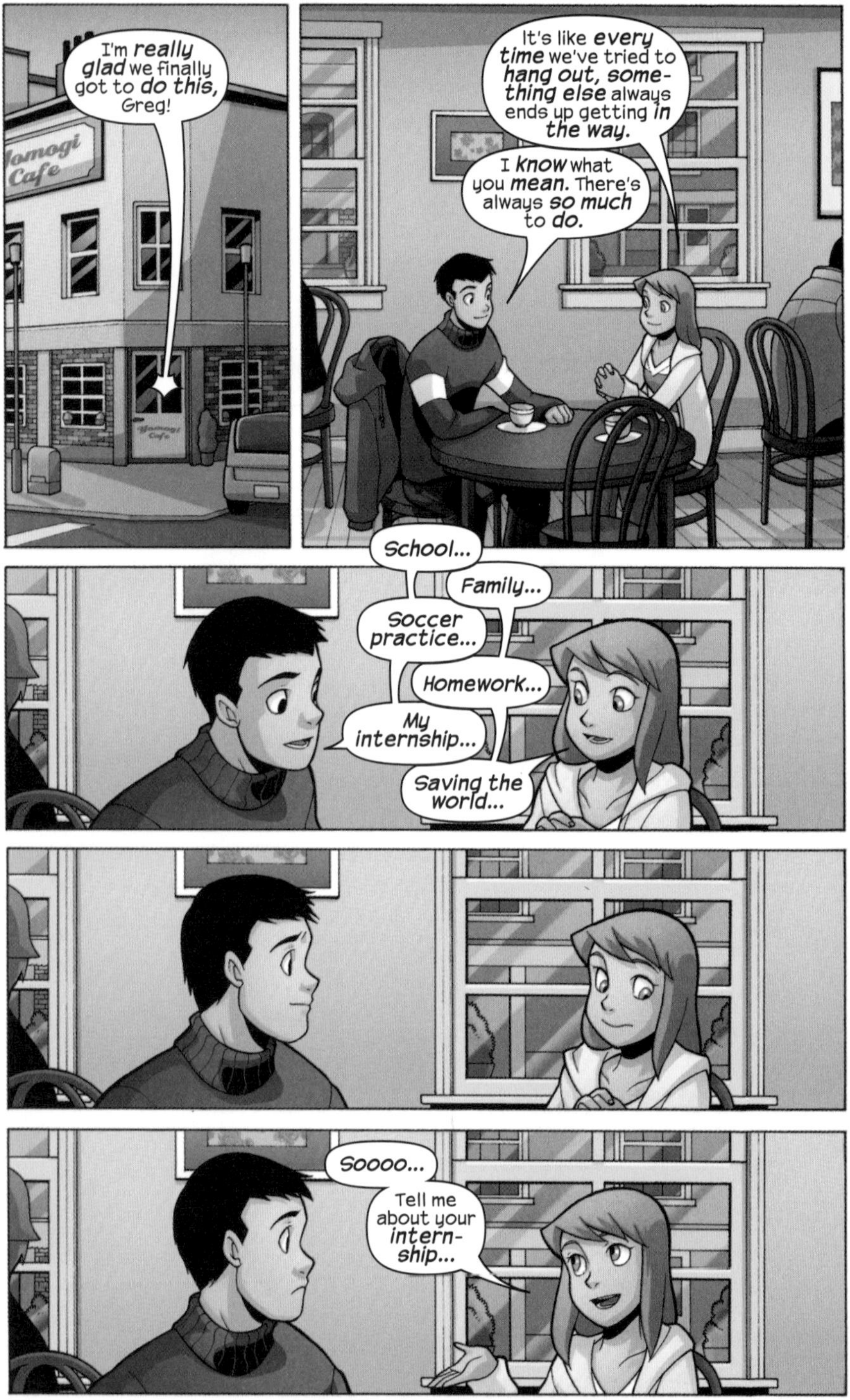
Yomogi Cafe
I'm really glad we finally got to do this, Greg!
It's like every time we've tried to hang out, something else always ends up getting in the way.
I know what you mean. There's always so much to do.
School...
Family...
Soccer practice...
Homework...
My internship...
Saving the world...
Soooo...
Tell me about your internship...

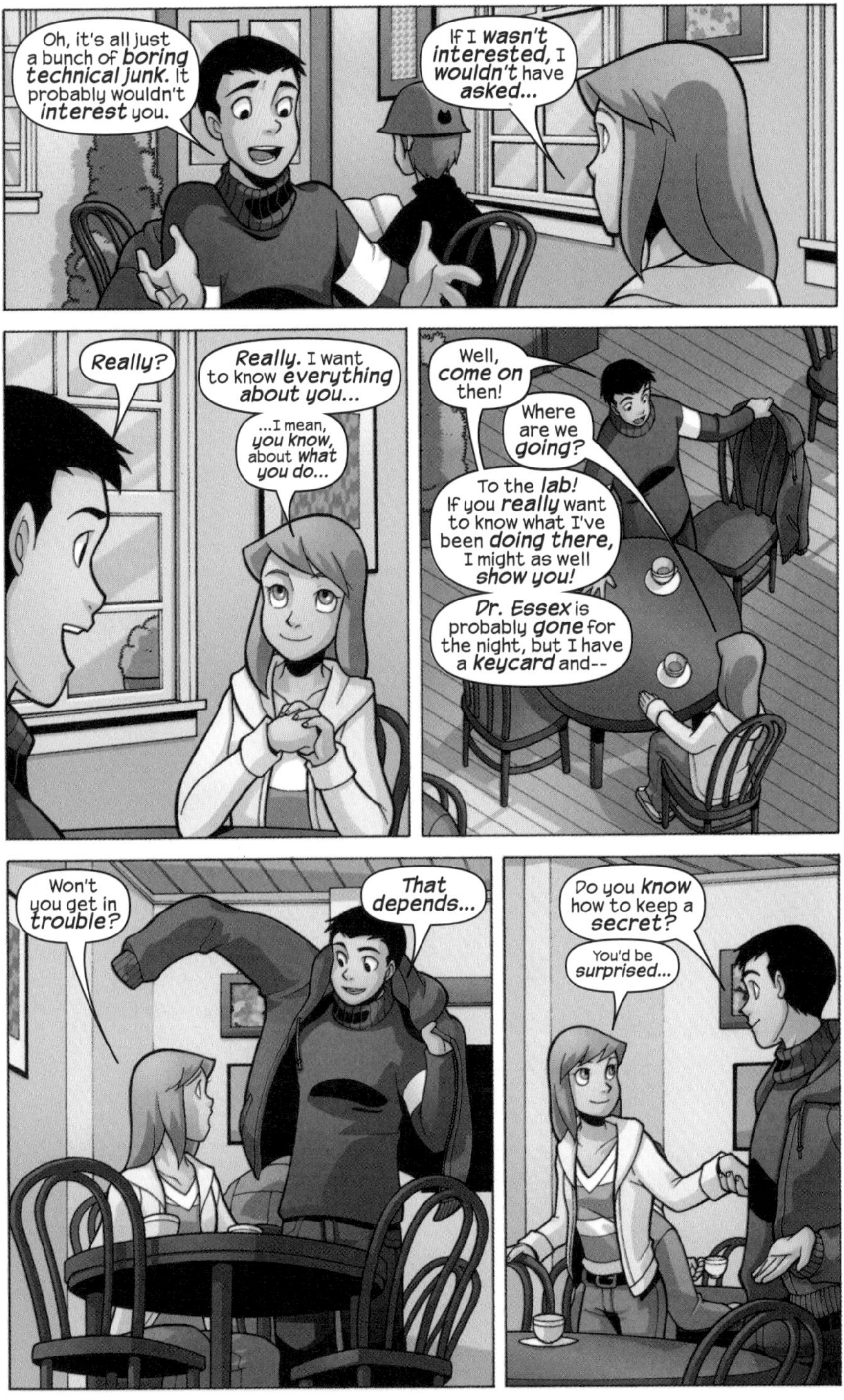
Oh, it's all just a bunch of boring technical junk. It probably wouldn't interest you.
If I wasn't interested, I wouldn't have asked...
Really?
Really. I want to know everything about you...
...I mean, you know, about what you do...
Well, come on then!
Where are we going?
To the lab! If you really want to know what I've been doing there, I might as well show you!
Dr. Essex is probably gone for the night, but I have a keycard and--
Won't you get in trouble?
That depends...
Do you know how to keep a secret?
You'd be surprised...

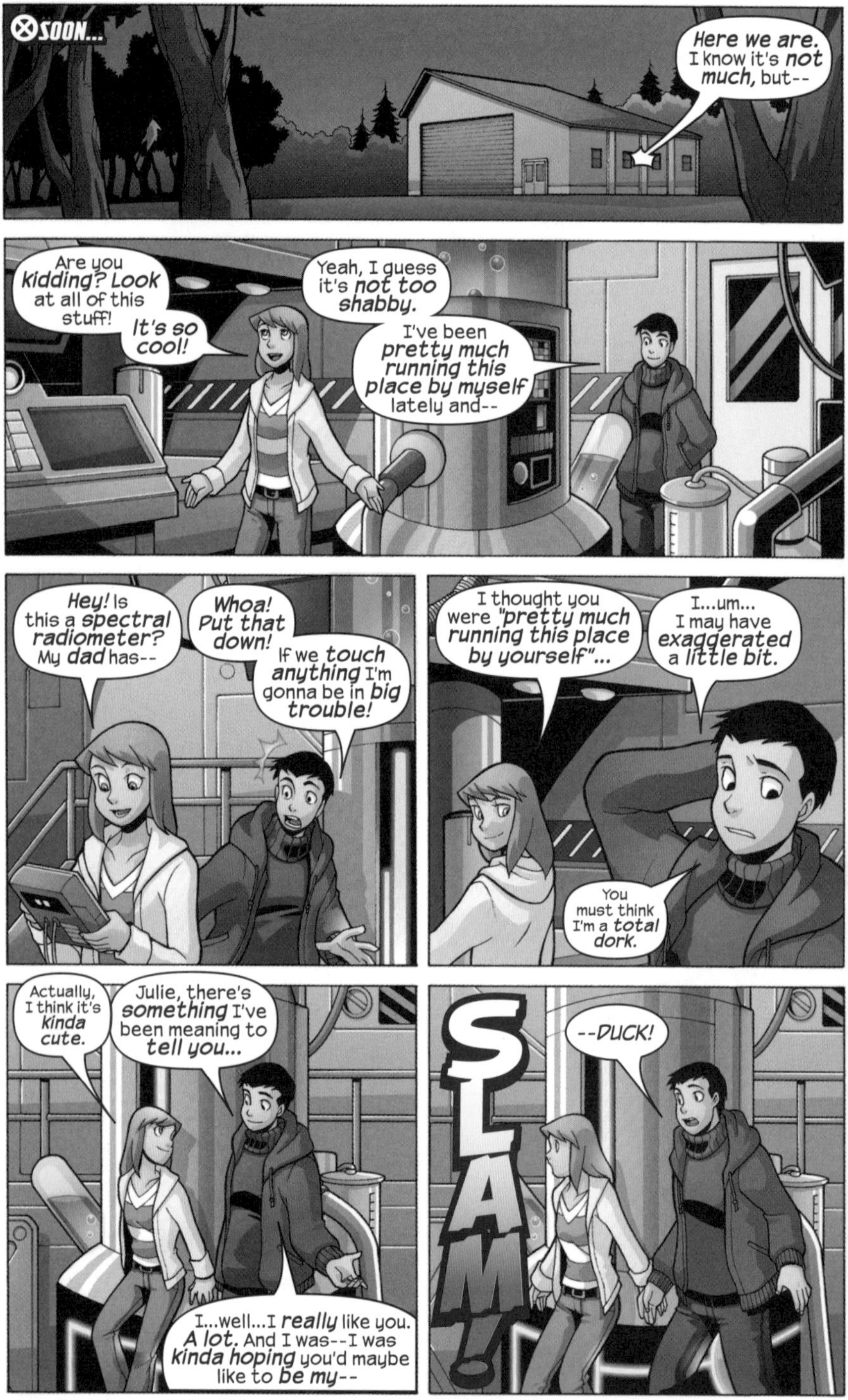
SOON...
Here we are. I know it's not much, but--
Are you kidding? Look at all of this stuff!
It's so cool!
Yeah, I guess it's not too shabby.
I've been pretty much running this place by myself lately and--
Hey! Is this a spectral radiometer? My dad has--
Whoa! Put that down!
If we touch anything I'm gonna be in big trouble!
I thought you were "pretty much running this place by yourself"...
I...um... I may have exaggerated a little bit.
You must think I'm a total dork.
Actually, I think it's kinda cute.
Julie, there's something I've been meaning to tell you...
I...well...I really like you. A lot. And I was--I was kinda hoping you'd maybe like to be my--
SLAM!
--DUCK!

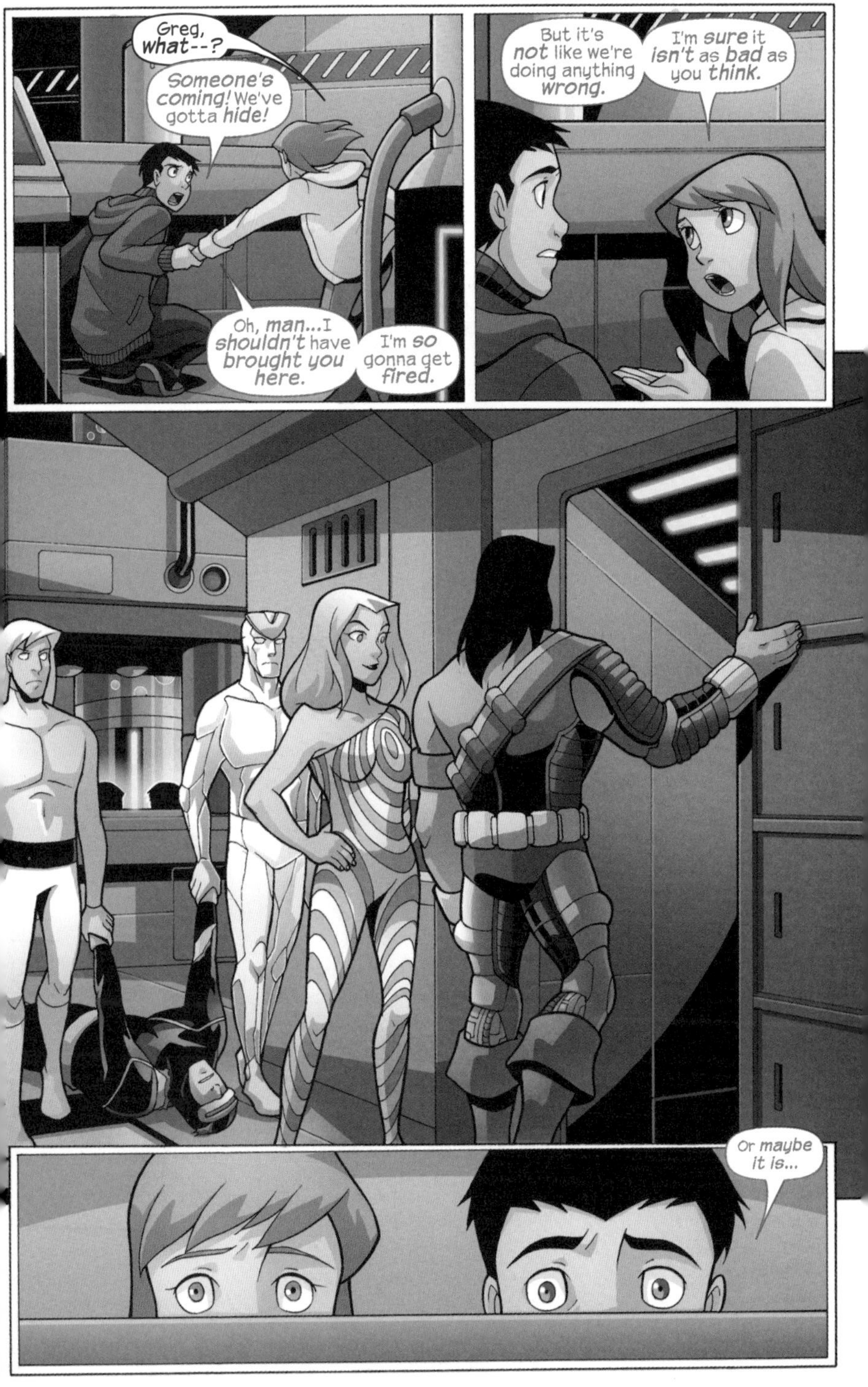
Greg, what--?
Someone's coming! We've gotta hide!
Oh, man...I shouldn't have brought you here.
I'm so gonna get fired.
But it's not like we're doing anything wrong.
I'm sure it isn't as bad as you think.
Or maybe it is...

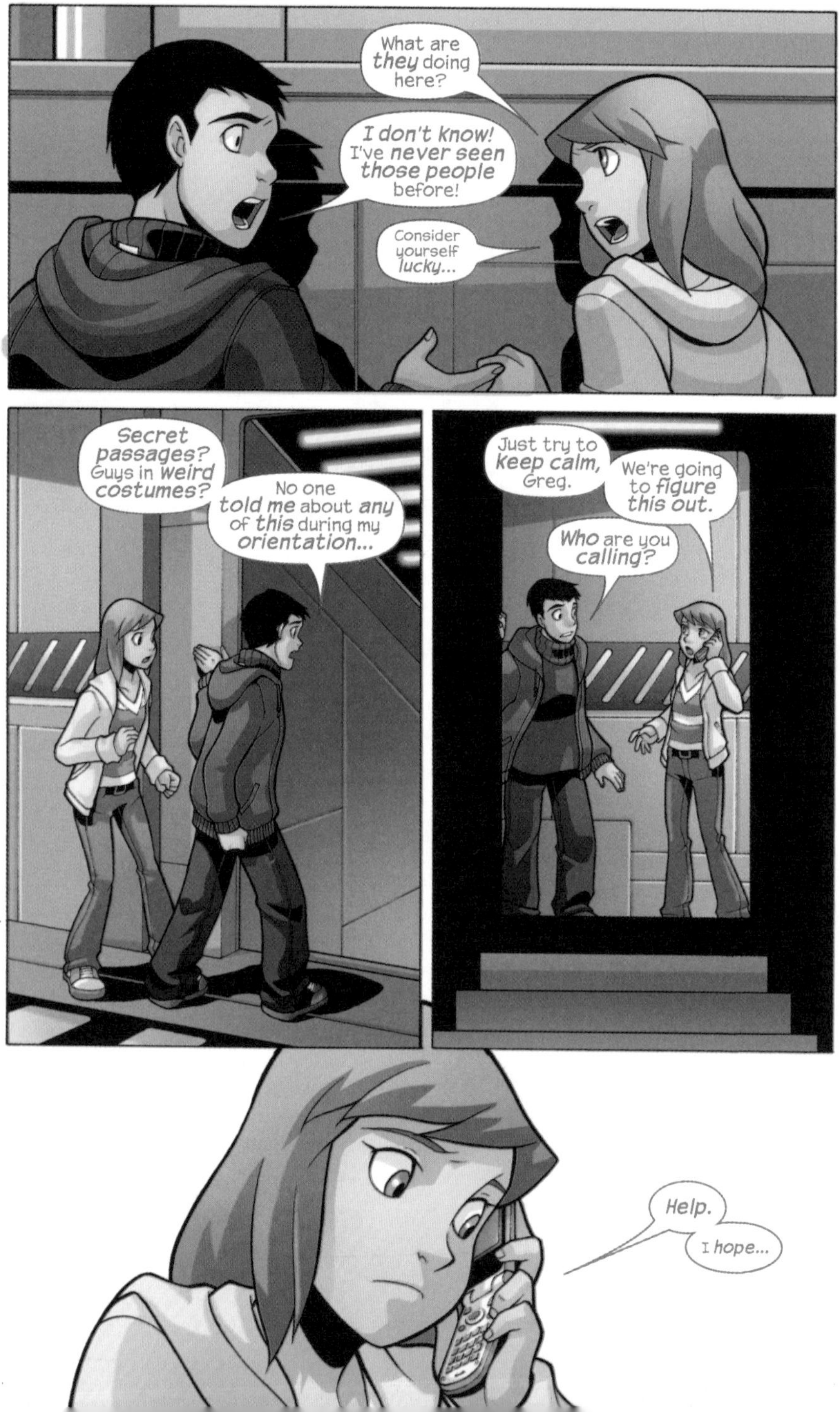
What are they doing here?
I don't know! I've never seen those people before!
Consider yourself lucky...
Secret passages? Guys in weird costumes?
No one told me about any of this during my orientation...
Just try to keep calm, Greg.
We're going to figure this out.
Who are you calling?
Help.
I hope...

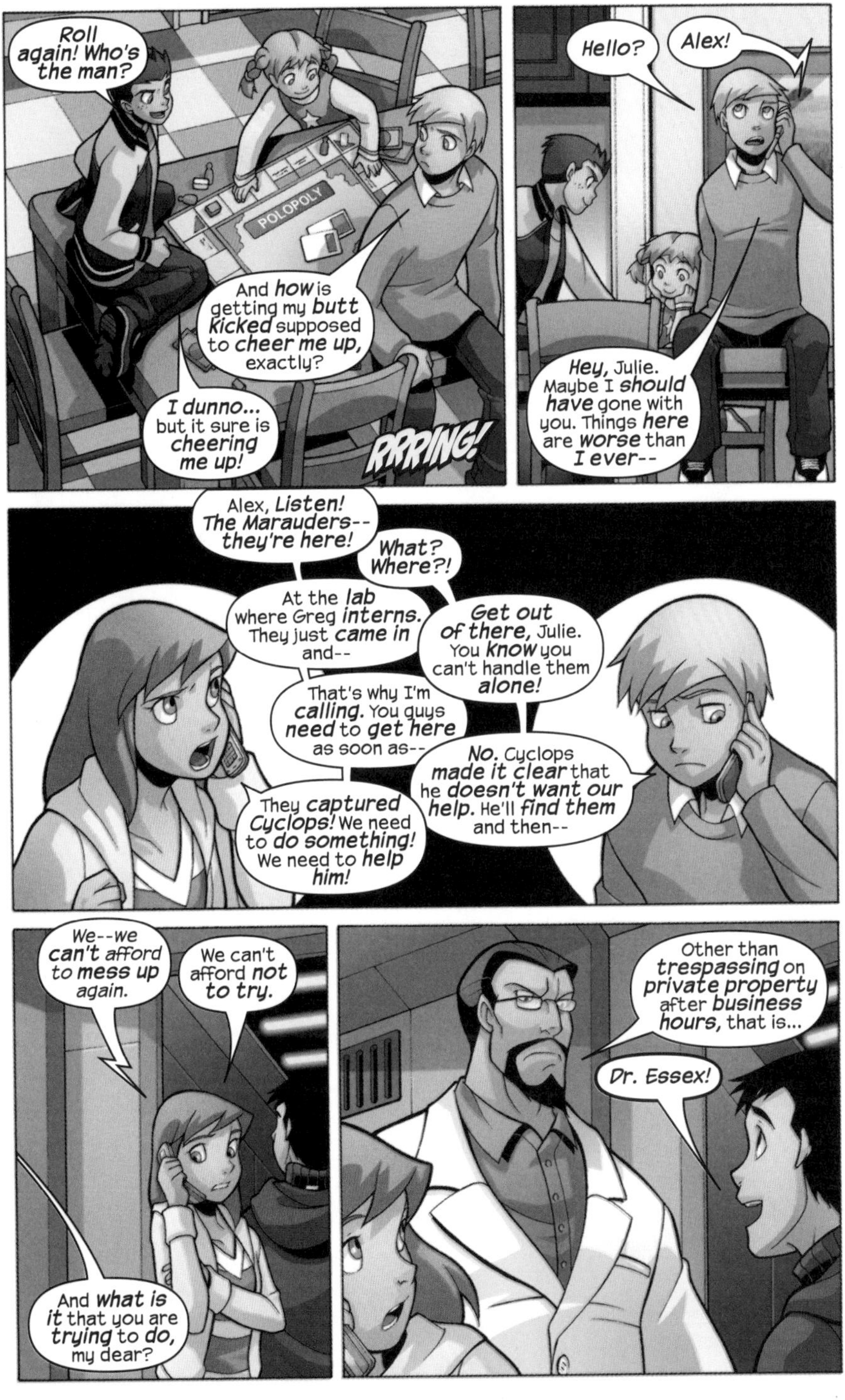
Roll again! Who's the man?
And how is getting my butt kicked supposed to cheer me up, exactly?
I dunno... but it sure is cheering me up!
RRRING!
POLOPOLY
Hello?
Alex!
Hey, Julie. Maybe I should have gone with you. Things here are worse than I ever--
Alex, Listen! The Marauders-- they're here!
What? Where?!
At the lab where Greg interns. They just came in and--
Get out of there, Julie. You know you can't handle them alone!
That's why I'm calling. You guys need to get here as soon as--
No. Cyclops made it clear that he doesn't want our help. He'll find them and then--
They captured Cyclops! We need to do something! We need to help him!
We--we can't afford to mess up again.
We can't afford not to try.
And what is it that you are trying to do, my dear?
Other than trespassing on private property after business hours, that is...
Dr. Essex!

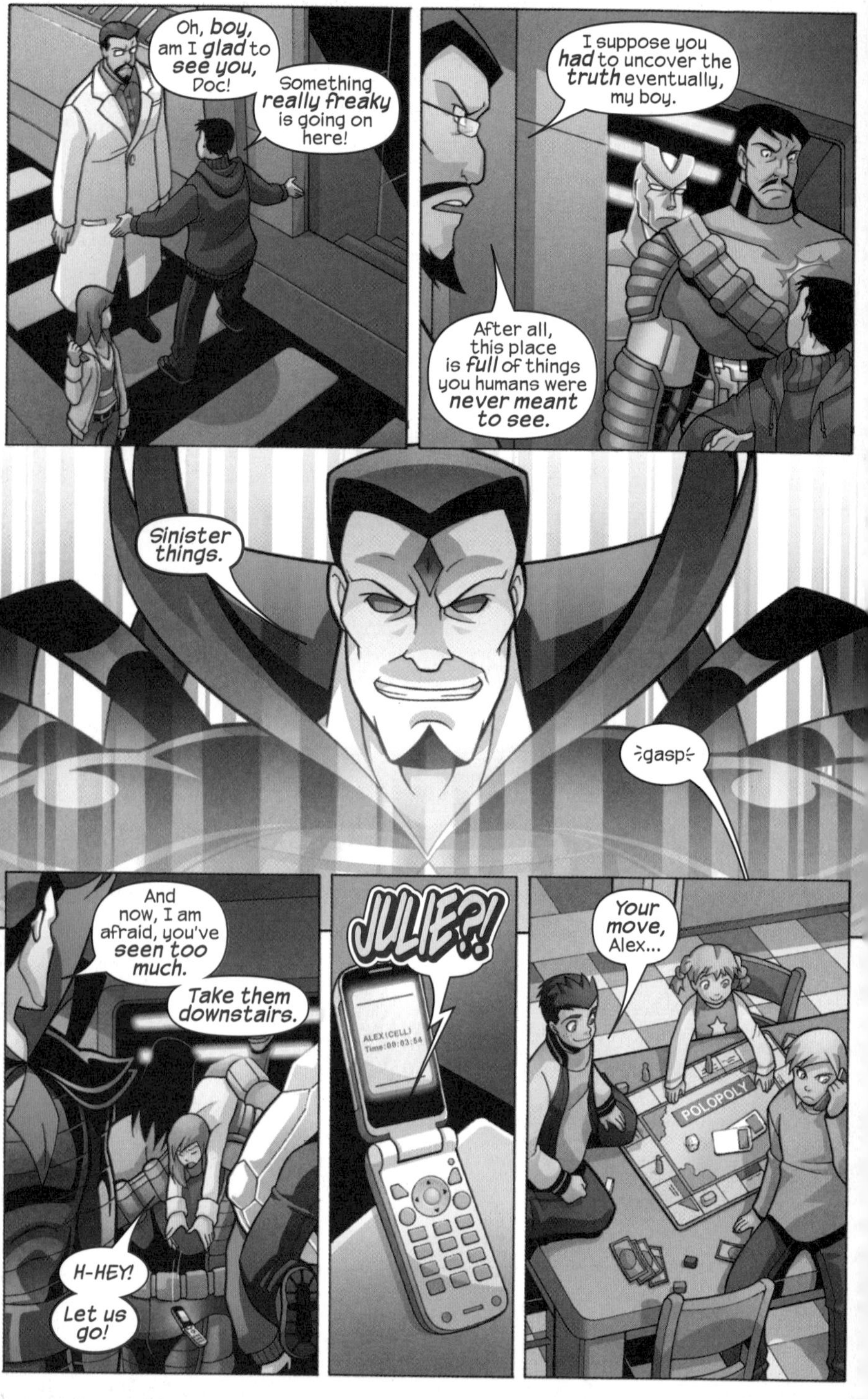
Oh, boy, am I glad to see you, Doc!
Something really freaky is going on here!
I suppose you had to uncover the truth eventually, my boy.
After all, this place is full of things you humans were never meant to see.
Sinister things.
gasp
And now, I am afraid, you've seen too much.
Take them downstairs.
H-HEY!
Let us go!
JULIE?!
ALEX (CELL)
Time:00:03:54
Your move, Alex...
POLOPOLY

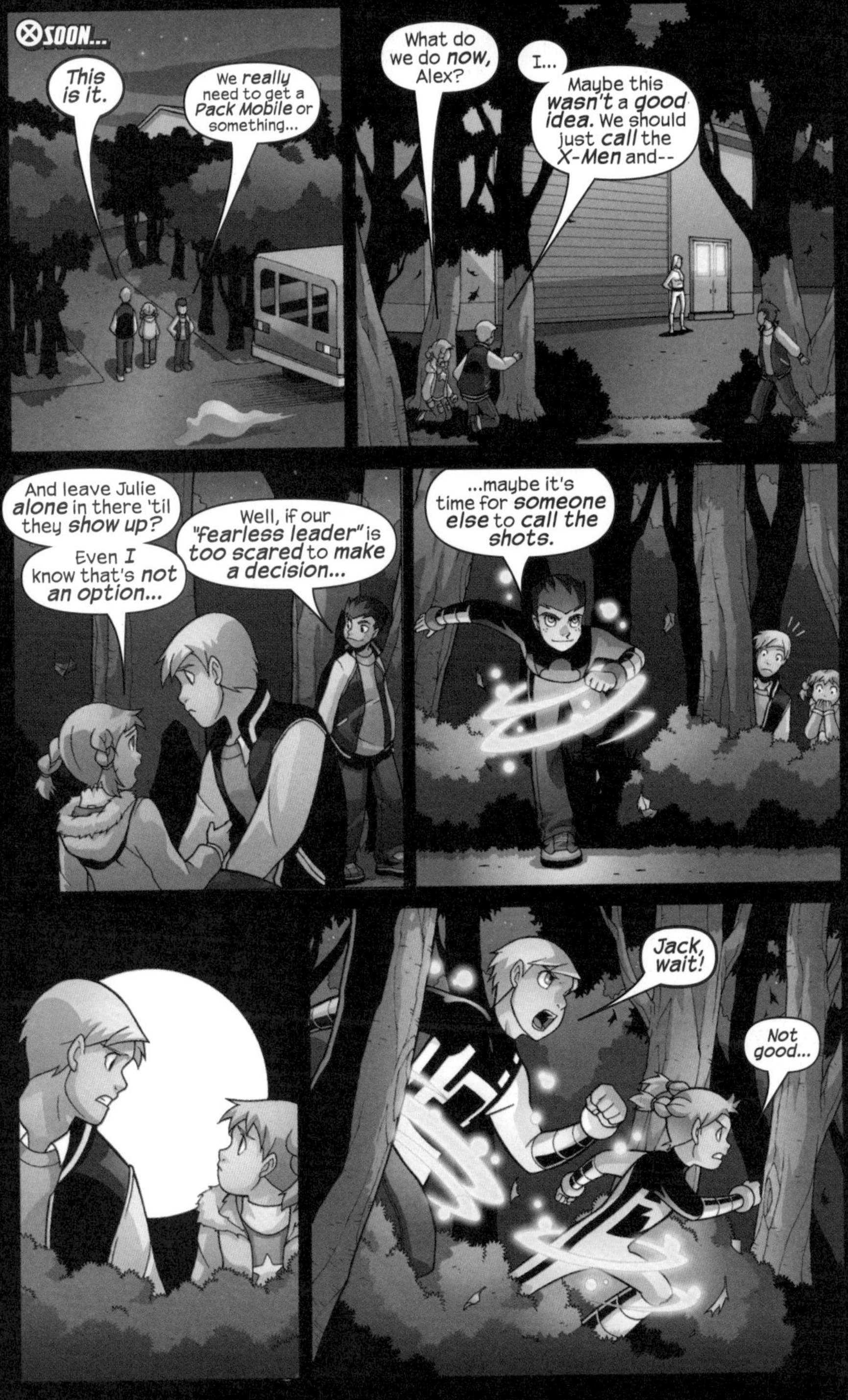
SOON...
This is it.
We really need to get a Pack Mobile or something...
What do we do now, Alex?
I...
Maybe this wasn't a good idea. We should just call the X-Men and--
And leave Julie alone in there 'til they show up?
Even I know that's not an option...
Well, if our "fearless leader" is too scared to make a decision...
...maybe it's time for someone else to call the shots.
Jack, wait!
Not good...

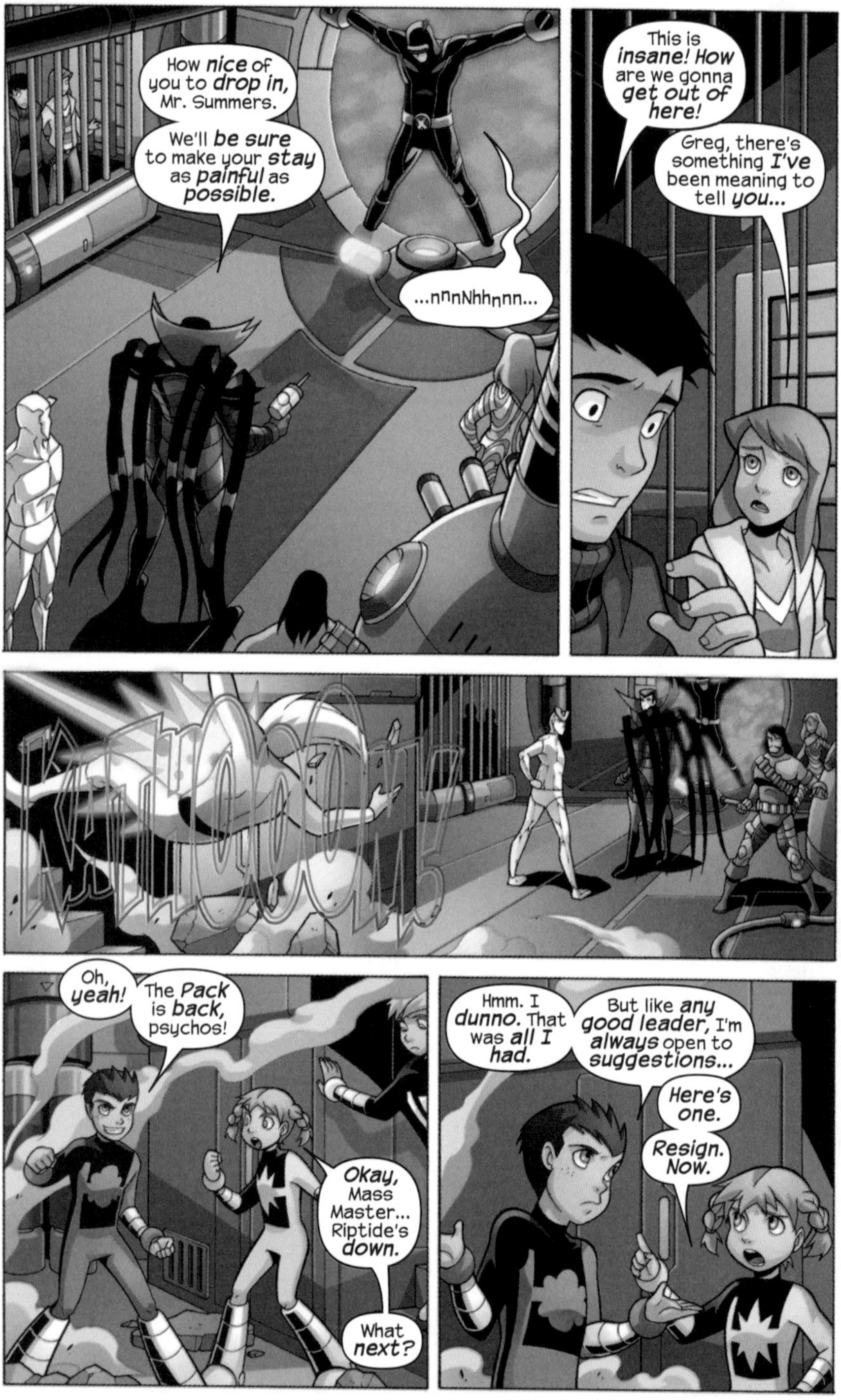

How nice of you to drop in, Mr. Summers.
We'll be sure to make your stay as painful as possible.
...nnnNhhnnn...
This is insane! How are we gonna get out of here!
Greg, there's something I've been meaning to tell you...
Oh, yeah!
The Pack is back, psychos!
Okay, Mass Master... Riptide's down.
What next?
Hmm. I dunno. That was all I had.
But like any good leader, I'm always open to suggestions...
Here's one.
Resign. Now.

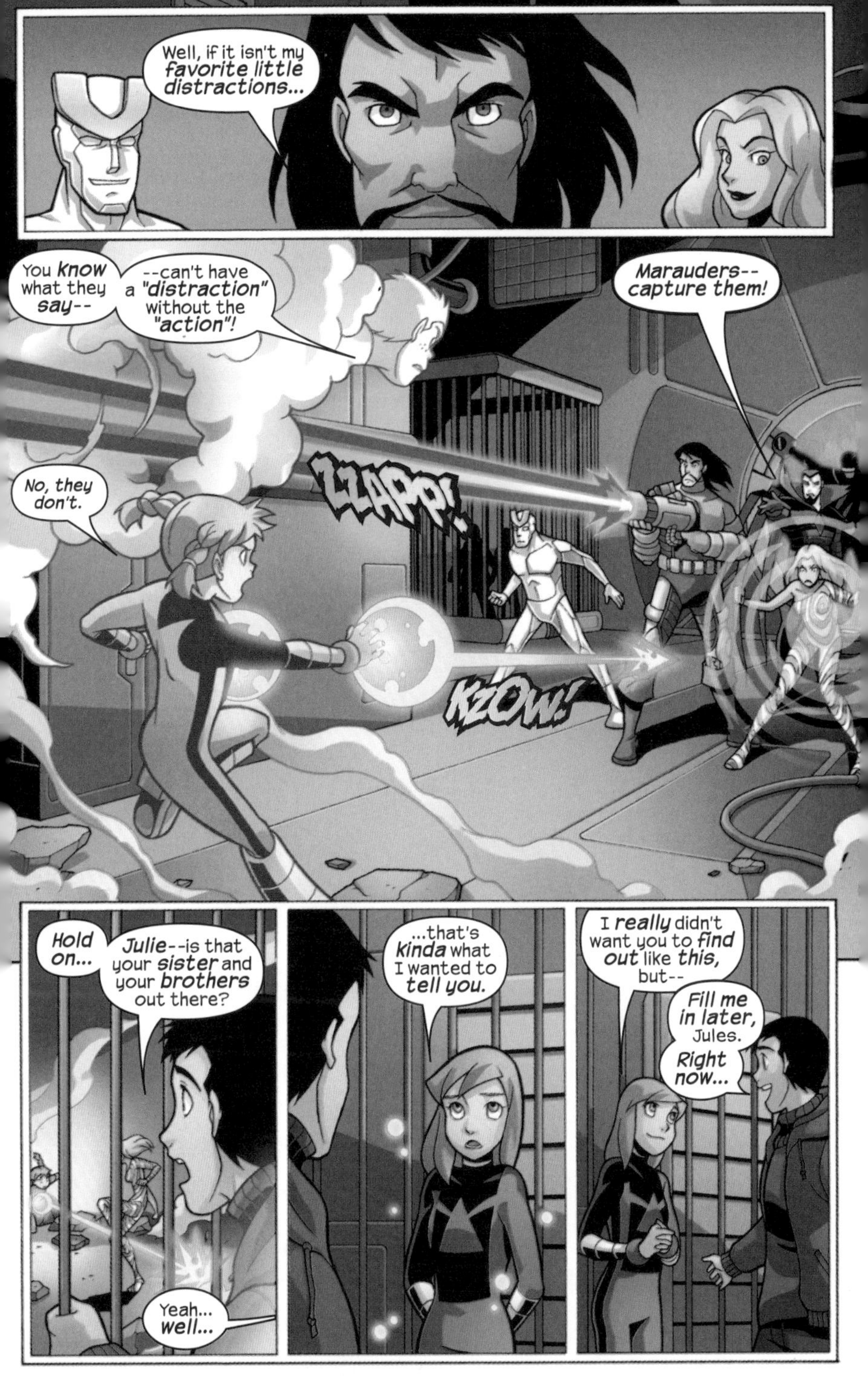
Well, if it isn't my favorite little distractions...
You know what they say--
--can't have a "distraction" without the "action"!
Marauders-- capture them!
No, they don't.
ZZAPP!
KZOW!
Hold on...
Julie--is that your sister and your brothers out there?
Yeah... well...
...that's kinda what I wanted to tell you.
I really didn't want you to find out like this, but--
Fill me in later, Jules.
Right now...

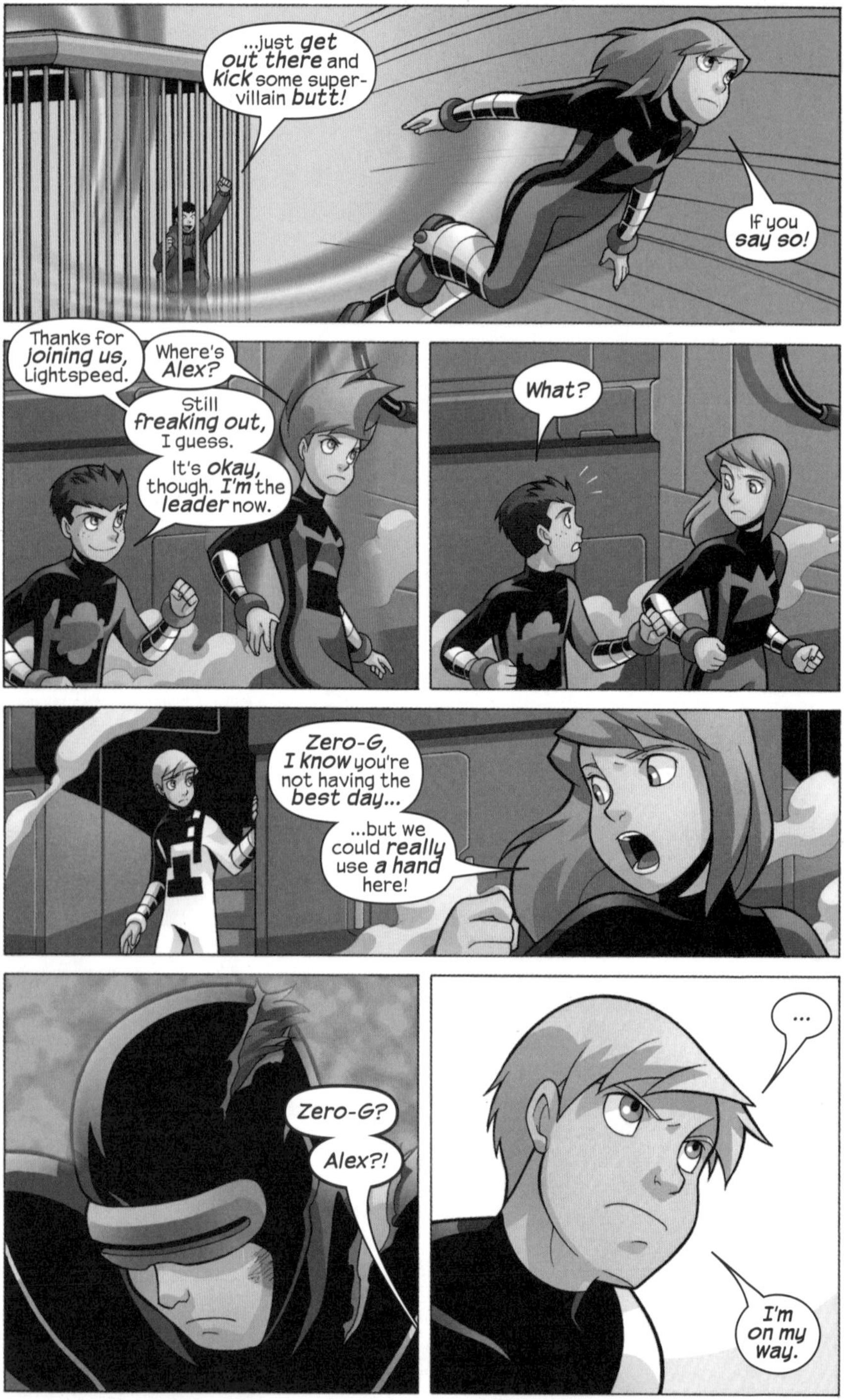
...just get out there and kick some super-villain butt!
If you say so!
Thanks for joining us, Lightspeed.
Where's Alex?
Still freaking out, I guess.
It's okay, though. I'm the leader now.
What?
Zero-G, I know you're not having the best day...
...but we could really use a hand here!
Zero-G?
Alex?!
...
I'm on my way.

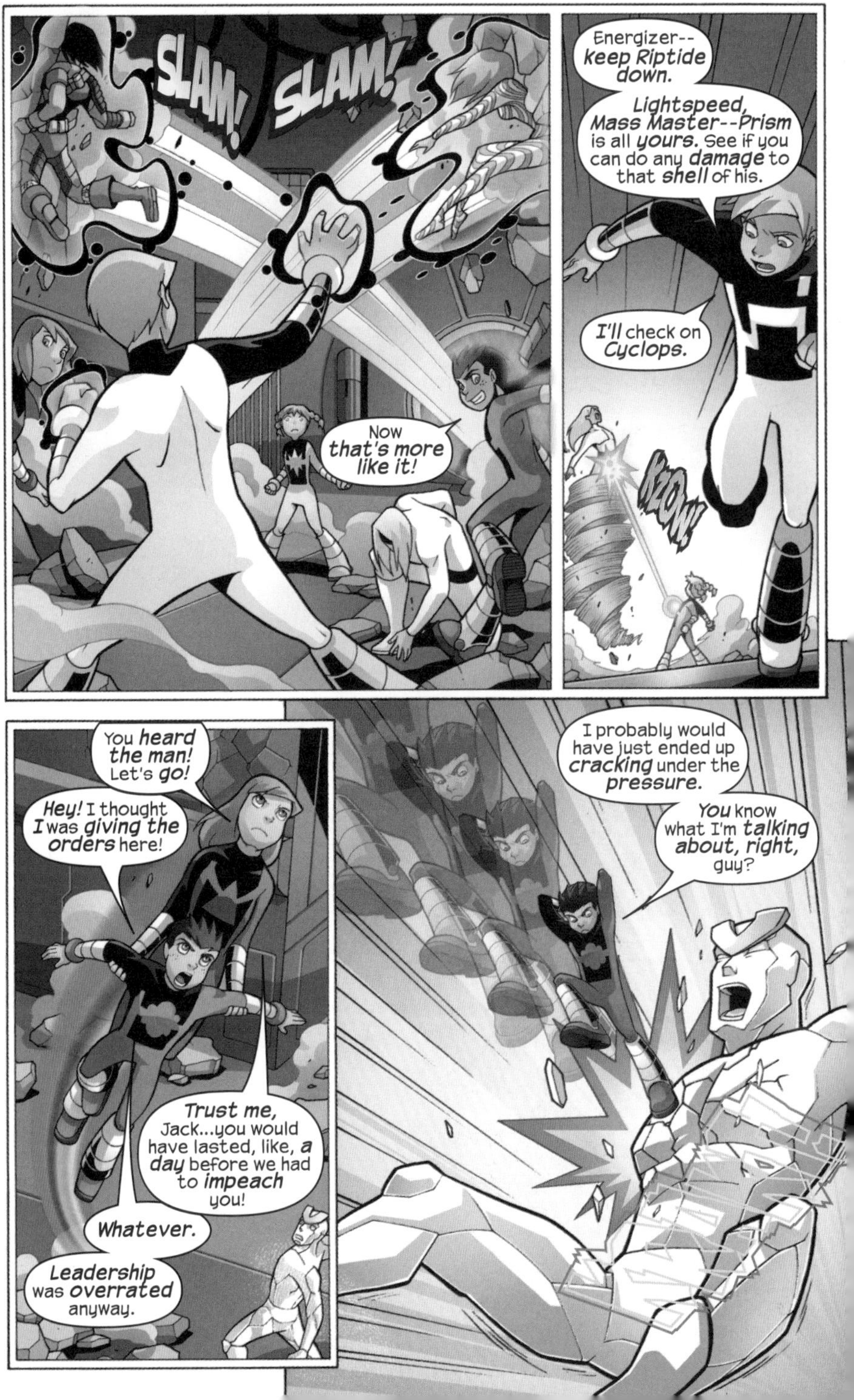
SLAM! SLAM!
Now that's more like it!
Energizer--keep Riptide down.
Lightspeed, Mass Master--Prism is all yours. See if you can do any damage to that shell of his.
I'll check on Cyclops.
KZOW!
You heard the man! Let's go!
Hey! I thought I was giving the orders here!
Trust me, Jack...you would have lasted, like, a day before we had to impeach you!
Whatever.
Leadership was overrated anyway.
I probably would have just ended up cracking under the pressure.
You know what I'm talking about, right, guy?

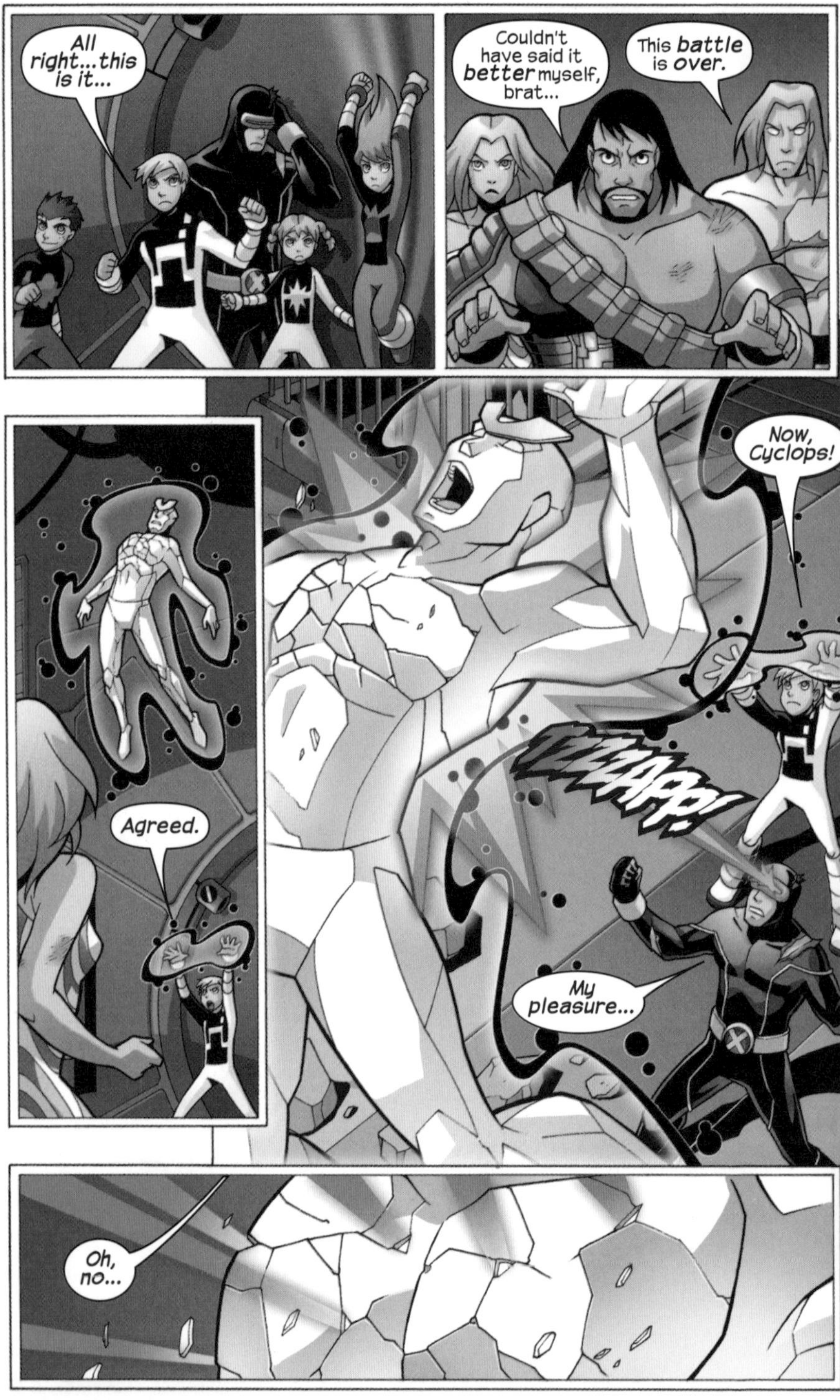
All right...this is it...
Couldn't have said it better myself, brat...
This battle is over.
Agreed.
Now, Cyclops!
ZZZAPP!
My pleasure...
Oh, no...

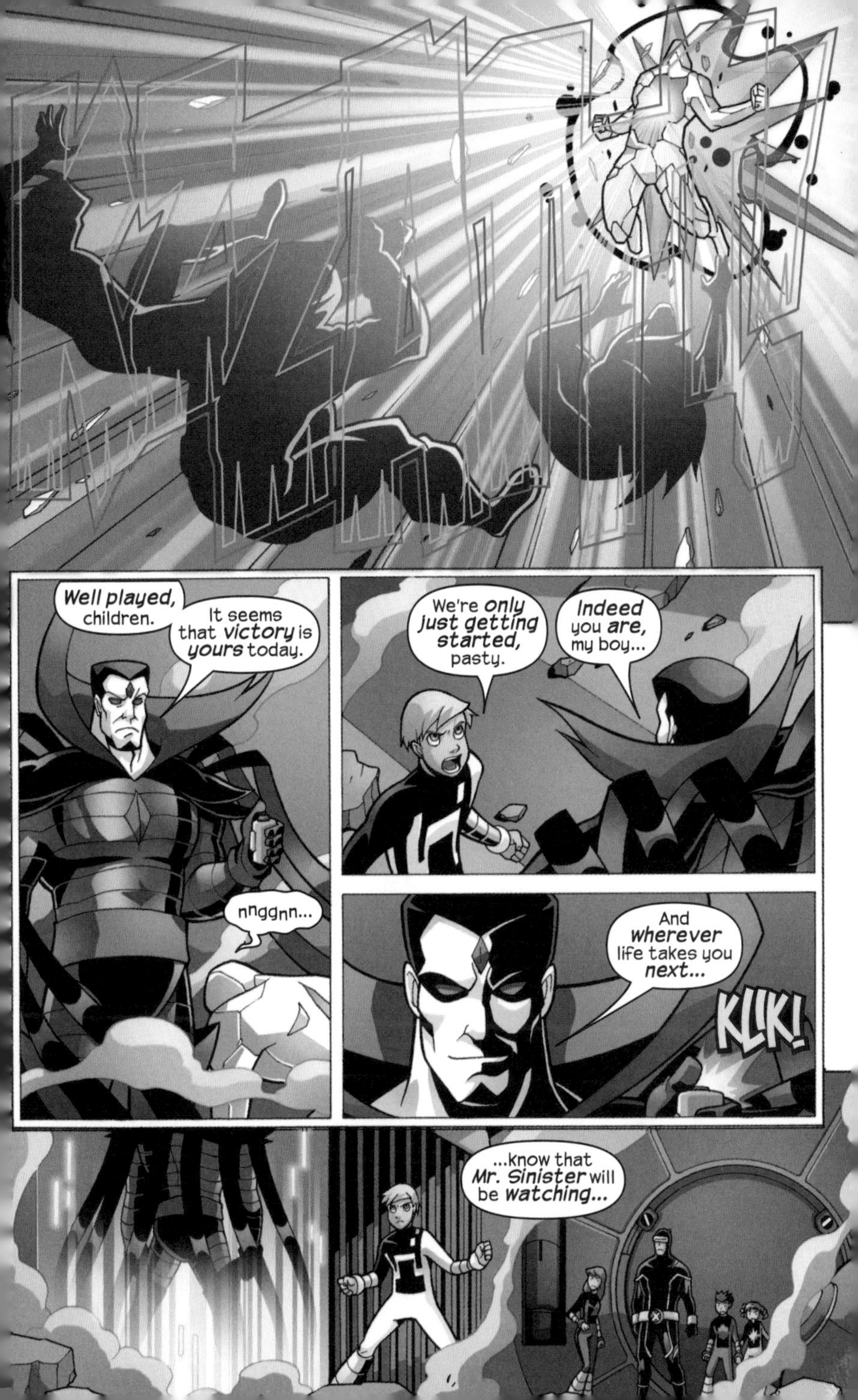
Well played, children.
It seems that victory is yours today.
nnggnn...
We're only just getting started, pasty.
Indeed you are, my boy...
And wherever life takes you next...
KLIK!
...know that Mr. Sinister will be watching...

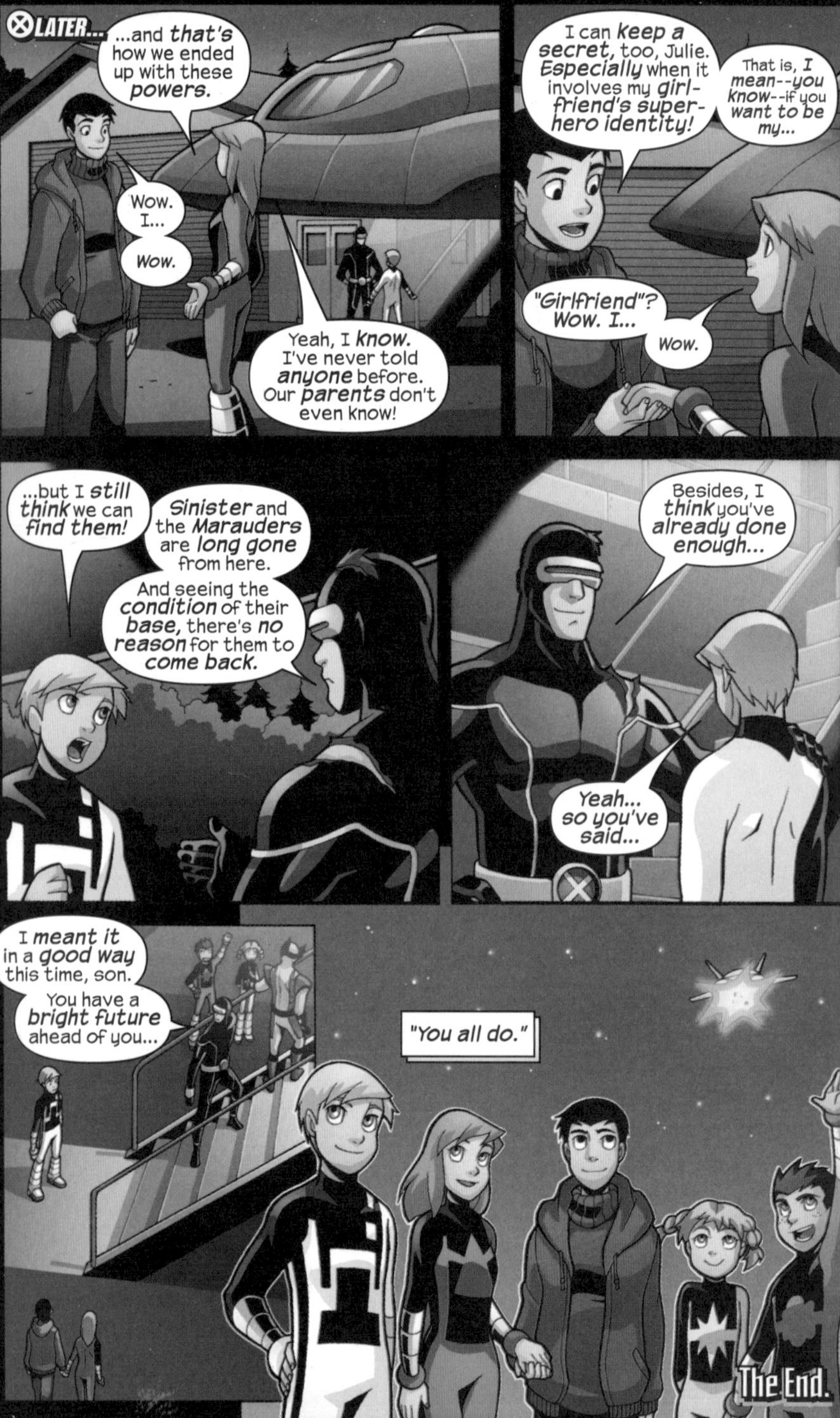
LATER...
...and that's how we ended up with these powers.
Wow. I...
Wow.
Yeah, I know. I've never told anyone before. Our parents don't even know!
I can keep a secret, too, Julie. Especially when it involves my girl-friend's super-hero identity!
That is, I mean--you know--if you want to be my...
"Girlfriend"? Wow. I...
Wow.
...but I still think we can find them!
Sinister and the Marauders are long gone from here.
And seeing the condition of their base, there's no reason for them to come back.
Besides, I think you've already done enough...
Yeah... so you've said...
I meant it in a good way this time, son.
You have a bright future ahead of you...
"You all do."
The End.